DOING JEWISH THEOLOGY

DOING JEWISH THEOLOGY

God, Torah & Israel in Modern Judaism

Rabbi Neil Gillman

JEWISH LIGHTS Publishing

Woodstock, Vermont

Doing Jewish Theology:
God, Torah & Israel in Modern Judaism

2010 Quality Paperback Edition, First Printing

For information regarding permission to reprint material from this book, please write or fax your request to Jewish Lights Publishing, Permissions Department, at the address / fax number listed below, or e-mail your request to permissions@jewishlights.com.

© 2008 by Neil Gillman

Page 274 is a continuation of this copyright page.

Library of Congress Cataloging-in-Publication Data
Gillman, Neil.
Doing Jewish theology : God, Torah & Israel in modern Judaism / Neil Gillman.
p. cm.
Includes bibliographical references and index.
ISBN-13: 978-1-58023-322-4 (hardcover)
ISBN-10: 1-58023-322-8 (hardcover)
 1. Judaism—Doctrines. I. Title.
 BM602.G55 2008
 296.3—dc22

         2008033822

ISBN-13: 978-1-58023-439-9 (quality pbk.)

10 9 8 7 6 5 4 3 2 1

Manufactured in the United States of America
Cover Design: Tim Holtz

Published by Jewish Lights Publishing
A Division of LongHill Partners, Inc.
Sunset Farm Offices, Route 4, P.O. Box 237
Woodstock, VT 05091
Tel: (802) 457-4000   Fax: (802) 457-4004
www.jewishlights.com

To
Livia Ruth Gillman Prince
and
Judah Gillman Kass

"It is the danger of every embodiment of the unconditional element, religious and secular, that it elevates something conditioned, a symbol, an institution, a movement as such to ultimacy.... (T)he whole work of theology can be summed up in the statement that it is the permanent guardian of the unconditional against the aspiration of its own religious and secular appearances."

—Paul Tillich

CONTENTS

Contents

INTRODUCTION

My Theological Journey

The process of selecting the material to be included in this book provided me with an opportunity to trace my theological journey from where I was some forty years ago to where I am today, and to anticipate the unfinished work that still lies ahead.

I entered The Jewish Theological Seminary of America in New York as a rabbinical student in 1954, simultaneously enrolling as a doctoral student in philosophy at Columbia University. I had had a limited background in Hebrew and Judaica, but I was a philosophy and French literature major at McGill University in Montreal. I was introduced to Jewish philosophy when I attended a lecture by Will Herberg at McGill Hillel. That lecture changed my life. I was then a young twenty-year-old, and this was the first time I had heard anything about Judaism that I found intellectually engaging. Jewish learning became my first priority. Three Seminary graduate rabbis in Montreal and a conversation with the then dean of Jewish philosophers, Harvard's Harry Austryn Wolfson, guided me to the Seminary. As Wolfson reminded me, whatever I planned to do in Jewish philosophy, I needed a basic Jewish education which I had never had, and the Seminary would provide me with that.

My Seminary years were at once exhilarating and frustrating: exhilarating for the sheer intellectual energy of the place and the richness of the material that I was encountering for the first time, and frustrating because of the disdain with which the school treated theology and philosophy. I have spent the better part of five decades trying to change that pattern without significant success.

Upon my ordination in 1960, Rabbi Louis Finkelstein, the seminary's chancellor, offered me the first in a series of administrative positions in the rabbinical school. I interviewed applicants, counseled students, assumed increasing responsibility for the administration of the school, and began to teach part-time. The gratification that I derived from my Seminary responsibilities undoubtedly contributed to a certain ambivalence about my doctoral work at Columbia. Ultimately however, I did complete the doctorate, left the Seminary administration behind, and began writing and teaching full-time.

My choice of a dissertation topic was more significant than I thought at the time. I had always wanted to write on religious epistemology. Did theological statements constitute valid knowledge claims, or were they covertly a form of poetry, expressing purely subjective feelings? Were they in principle capable of being true or false? That issue would haunt my thinking for decades.

I decided to write on the French Catholic existentialist Gabriel Marcel. First, having been raised in French Canada, French was my native language; second, his thought had been relatively unexplored in America and in English; and third, his approach was surprisingly Heschelian, though much more systematic and rigorous. Apart from the epistemological issues, he also wrote at length on the theological valence of hope and on our relationship to our bodies—two issues that, again to my surprise, became central to my agenda years later when I began to study Jewish views on the afterlife.

It was no accident that I chose to do my doctoral studies on the work of an existentialist philosopher. I had retained vivid memories of my first encounter with Will Herberg and had continued to communicate with him while in rabbinical school. First, his style—blunt, passionate, engaged—was hardly indicative of a detached professor of philosophy. What I heard was a more popular version of Buberian existentialism than I had studied in my philosophy courses at McGill, but it reflected a Jewish dimension entirely new to me. I learned other things from that lecture: first, there was a discipline called Jewish philosophy; second, Jewish philosophy had always nursed from philosophical currents in the Western world at large; and third, in its contemporary mode, this material spoke to personal issues that were apparently lurking in my subconscious.

So I entered the Seminary with a bifurcated personal theology: theological existentialism together with a halakhic traditionalism common to newly engaged Jews. The traditionalism was challenged almost from the outset by my Seminary studies. It became clear to me that few of my teachers and fellow students believed that God had spoken at Sinai or that the Exodus and revelation at Sinai were historical events. Much of biblical religion, I learned, was borrowed—however transformed in the process—from the surrounding cultures. Biblical criticism, both "lower" (text criticism) and "higher" (source criticism), was the reigning methodology. I found the conclusions of this inquiry intellectually convincing, but what it did to my theology, preeminently to my sense of the authority behind my observance, was another matter.

That encounter had a lasting impact on my theological evolution. From that moment, I sensed that the core theological issue was revelation. Either Torah was the explicit word of God or it was not. If not, then the words of Torah were human words, whatever role God played in the revelatory encounter. The remaining alternatives seemed to be slippery. If Torah was substantively a human document, then, first, it was the human community from the outset that served as the authority on matters of belief and practice; second, it became clear why biblical religion, as well as all later iterations of Judaism, would be shaped by the prevailing foreign cultures; and third, Judaism had always been and would continue to be whatever Jews said it was. This set of conclusions was echoed by the rest of my Seminary educators. Most of my teachers were historians, and their overriding message was that Judaism had a history—that everything Jewish had changed all the time, and, we assumed, would continue to change.

Now, every time I teach Jewish theology, I begin with the issue of revelation. I remain convinced that how we deal with this determines how we handle the issue of authority in belief and practice. How we understand authority determines how we deal with the claims of the tradition on us; how we deal with those claims determines how we shape our own Judaism. That conclusion opens the gate to a reconsideration of all of Judaism's theology, in particular how we understand God, for God is at the heart of Torah. With nontraditional understandings of revelation in place, where then did our ancestors learn of God? What is the standing of the varied and changing images of God that appear in our classical texts? What is the status of what theologians call "God-talk"?

Not all of these conclusions were obvious to me at the outset, and it took many years before they formed a coherent personal theology. But the germ was there. My theological journey can be understood as working through the implications of this original epiphany. If there has been a major focus to all of my teaching, it has been to affirm that a coherent theology is indispensable as the basis for a Jewish religious identity, and as part of that theology, to articulate a view of revelation that can support how one understands the authority of Jewish law.

My journey paralleled that of one of my teachers, Mordecai Kaplan. I studied with Kaplan for the first time in my second year without any prior sense of what he was going to teach me. Kaplan was then in his last years at the Seminary—he had joined the faculty in 1909 and was to retire in 1962—and his glory days as the icon of the faculty were behind him. The rising star in the faculty firmament was Abraham Joshua Heschel, whose neo-Hasidic traditionalism seemed much more responsive to my

post-Holocaust sensibility. I was a newly crafted, newly observant religious existentialist. I came to the Seminary to study with
Heschel; I was quite unprepared for Kaplan.

I studied with Kaplan for two academic years and fought
him throughout. It took about a decade for me to realize that
Kaplan was the only one of my teachers who could resolve all of
the conflicts created by the Seminary approach to Jewish studies.
Kaplan pulled together theology, ideology, and program. It was
not until I began to teach and felt the need to formulate a coherent theology of my own that I rediscovered Kaplan. Kaplan may
have taught me methodology, yet it was Heschel who taught me
what it means to live the life of a religious Jew. I continue to
have significant issues with the thinking of both of my teachers,
but I also remain indebted to them.

The other thinker who shaped my thinking was Paul
Tillich. Tillich's *Dynamics of Faith*, which I read for my work at
Columbia, gave me the vocabulary for capturing the power of
Jewish theological claims once I no longer could believe that
they represented the explicit word of a supernatural God. The
terms *symbol* and *myth* (in the academic sense of the latter)
became omnipresent in my teaching and writing, however much
criticism they inspired.

My identification with the thinking of Kaplan and Tillich
represented my gradual shift toward religious naturalism. That
shift represented my growing awareness that if religions are the
creation of a human community, then to grasp why any religion
emerged the way it did demanded an understanding of why
people are the way they are. That inquiry was properly the
domain of the social sciences. Anthropologist Clifford Geertz's
seminal essay "Religion as a Cultural System" then pulled
together all of the various strands of what had been a disjointed
study. It helped me understand just how a religion, in all of its
complexity, functions. I refer to it throughout my work. Geertz
taught me that religion is much more than theology.

More recently, as an outgrowth of my work on religious
epistemology, I have begun to read in neuroscience. Knowledge

is the work of the brain, and it has become a source of radical amazement (to quote Heschel) to me how biological processes in my brain can lead to a concept of God. More than a decade ago, at the invitation of the late Dr. Mortimer Ostow, a prominent psychiatrist and psychoanalyst, I began meeting with a group of psychoanalysts and Seminary colleagues to explore the psychological effects of prayer. This workshop, which began with a close reading of psalms and the liturgy, has now focused on the psychodynamics of faith development. There is a growing literature in the new field of neurotheology that awaits me.

A few words about this book. Considerations of space compelled me to select less than half of the material that, under ideal circumstances, I would have wanted to include. I selected weightier material over slighter content, and more recent publications over earlier ones. I have also aimed to cover the broader range of theological issues covered in my teaching.

I have tried to preserve the individual versions of this material as originally published. In line with my current practice, however, I have edited them to avoid using masculine pronouns for God, or the assumption that every rabbi and every Jew was a "he." Occasionally, I altered a formulation that I now found to be unacceptably awkward. In the endnotes, I updated bibliographical data to reflect more recent editions of certain books.

I must express my profound indebtedness to my students who have helped me prepare this volume for publication. Daniel Ain, now Rabbi Daniel Ain, has been my primary research assistant for more than three years. He worked closely with me from the outset. I am thrilled that he will be moving on to a career in the rabbinate, and I wish him much fulfillment. More recent conversations with Noah Farkas, now Rabbi Noah Farkas, helped clarify my theological agenda. Amiel Hersh was responsible for obtaining permission to republish this material from copyright holders. Nava Kogen worked on converting the original, previously publish articles into a tech-friendly format. Philip Weintraub reviewed the last revisions of the manuscript and compiled the glossary. Nicole Guzik has undertaken the unenviable task of putting the books and articles in my office into some usable order. I thank them all.

I have never believed that scholarly research can be detached from classroom teaching. In one form or another, the substance of this book has been shared with my students in Seminary classrooms and in congregations around the country. More recently, Rabbi Leon Morris, executive director of the Skirball Center for Adult Jewish Learning at Congregation Emanu-El in New York City, has afforded me new opportunities to teach serious adult Jewish learners. All of my students in all of these settings have a share in this work and I thank them for that.

This is the fifth of my books to be published by Stuart M. Matlins and his staff at Jewish Lights Publishing. As before, I can only testify to both the graciousness and the sheer competence of everyone in Woodstock, Vermont. Emily Wichland, again, worked closely with me on every detail from the original proposal to the final product, often on a day-to-day basis. Would that every author might enjoy such cooperation!

My wife Sarah, my daughters Abby and Debby, my sons-in-law Michael and Danny, and my grandchildren Jacob, Ellen, Livia, and Judah are an unceasing source of joy and support in all I do.

The publication of this book anticipates my imminent retirement from the Seminary after more than five decades of association with the school, its administration, and my colleagues on the faculty—a community of men and women whose human qualities are fully the equal of their scholarly achievements. I will continue to teach in other settings, but I anticipate more time to read, reflect, study, and write.

I conclude by echoing the words of the morning liturgy, the very words that my teacher Mordecai Kaplan used to open every one of his classes: May God, who has enabled me to reach this day, grant me the discernment and the understanding to heed, study, teach, and fulfill all the words of God's Torah with love.

PART ONE

GOD

CHAPTER 1

I BELIEVE

I believe, first, that the function of religion is to discern and describe the sense of an ultimate order that pervades the universe and human experience. With that sense of an ordered world intact, we human beings also have a place, we belong, we feel ultimately "at home"; without it, we are in exile, "homeless" and our lives are without meaning. The whole purpose of religion, its liturgies, rituals, and institutions, is to highlight, preserve, and concretize this sense of cosmos, and to recapture it in the face of the chaos that hovers perpetually around the fringes of our lives as we live them within history.

THE NATURE OF GOD

I believe that all human characterizations of God are metaphors borrowed from familiar human experience. Precisely because God transcends all human conceptualization, we can only think of God through metaphors. Our ancestors discovered God in their experience of nature and history. Those experiences, as understood, interpreted, and then recorded in Torah and the rest of our classical literature, serve as the spectacles through which we recapture the experience of God for ourselves. They teach us what to look for, how to see, and how to interpret what we see. We discover God, but we invent the metaphors that capture the variegated qualities of our experiences of God. They bring God into our lives and then in turn, help us discover God anew.

Our tradition provides us with a rich kaleidoscopic system of metaphors for God. We appropriate some of these, reject others, and add some of our own that reflect our personal experience of God. I accept most of those traditional metaphors—for example, that God is unique, personal, ultimate yet remarkably vulnerable to human claims, that God creates, reveals, and redeems, and that God is the ultimate source and principle of this ordered world—precisely as metaphors.

Knitted together, these metaphors form the complex Torah myth. This myth provides the structure of meaning that explains why things, including all of nature and history together with the realities of the human experience in all its complexity, are the way they are for us as Jews.

COVENANT

I believe that the covenant is the linchpin of the Jewish myth, the primary metaphor for Jewish self-understanding. But the covenant is itself the implication of a far more subtle characterization of God, what Heschel tried to capture in his use of the term "God's pathos." God entered into a covenant with the Jewish people because ultimately God cares desperately about creation, about people, and about our social structures. A caring God enters into relationships with communities. The fact that our ancestors used this metaphor for their relationship with God is further testimony to their concern with structure, for it is precisely their sense of covenantedness that led to their further understanding of law as the primary form of Jewish religious expression.

AUTHORITY

I believe that the ultimate locus of authority for what we believe and how we practice as Jews is in ourselves. That is the irreversible gift of modernity. I also believe that we can and must voluntarily surrender some of that authority, primarily to our communities, for without community we would be totally bereft (without a *minyan*, I cannot genuinely worship as a Jew), and ultimately to God as we experience God in commanding relationship with us. But we reserve the right to determine how, and in what areas, and to what extent we surrender that authority. In the last analysis, we obligate ourselves.

DIASPORA

I believe that one of the necessary implications of the notion of the monotheistic God is that God is accessible to any human being, from any point on earth. The Bible presents various models about how sacred space is created, but one of those models, central to all of later Jewish history, is that it is the Jewish community that sanctifies space simply by determining that it is from this point on earth that we will address God. There is then no overriding *religious* (though there may be a political or social) objection to the claim that we can live fully religious lives as Jews wherever we find ourselves. This is not meant to undermine the claim that our historic *national* ties can *best* be fulfilled in a land that is ours. But it also recognizes that the diaspora community, from antiquity to our own day, has contributed richly to the resolution of manifold religious and spiritual issues for Jews throughout the world.

DEATH AND THE END OF DAYS

I believe that an inherent part of the way we structure time as Jews must include a vision of the end of days. Creation and eschatology form the parentheses for the Jewish understanding of time. They characterize the beginning of time and its end, and without a beginning and end, there would be no middle. We would then not know where we stand in the canvas of time, just as a portrait without a frame would lack coherence and integrity. But Jewish eschatology must be understood as part of our mythic structure. As such, it says more about how we are to deal with our lives in the here and now than of what will happen at the end of days. It says that we must understand that the tensions and outbursts of chaos that we experience in the here and now are an inevitable part of our human experience within history, and that they will be banished in an age that will be the total embodiment of cosmos.

I believe that classical Jewish eschatology invariably structures its vision of the cosmos to come at the end as a recapitulation of the cosmos that was at the beginning. For that reason, the emergence of the doctrine of resurrection was an inevitable outcome of the view that death was not part of God's original plan for creation. If death is chaos, then the ultimate embodiment of cosmos will be marked by the death of death, which is the message of the "Had Gadya" hymn with which we conclude our Passover seder, the festive meal that celebrates our earlier redemption.

That at the end, God slaughters the angel of death is, as my teacher Professor Shalom Spiegel used to teach, the culminating victory of the monotheistic idea. If God is truly God, then my death can have no lasting victory over God's power, for God alone enjoys ultimacy. The belief that in time, God will resurrect the dead is also a remarkable testimony to the significance to God of the only lives we have or know, which is as beings incarnate through our bodies in space and time.

Chapter 2

ON KNOWING GOD

My burning theological and philosophical issue is religious epistemology—that is, the nature and origins of our knowledge of God.
For more than thirty years now, I have been struggling with how,
in principle, human beings can gain an awareness or knowledge of
God. I recall an extended discussion with one of my teachers at
Columbia when the issue was posed in a crude but striking way:
Are our theological claims knowledge claims—that is, capable of
falsification and verification, of being true or false? Are they factual
claims? Do they tell us about something that is "out there,"
beyond us, beyond our perceiving apparatus? Or are they poetry—
that is, purely subjective expressions of personal feelings or wish
projections? Or is there some alternative in between these two
polar positions? I in no way demean the value of poetry, but I have
stubbornly resisted the notion that theology is (only) poetry.

The issue became the subject of my doctoral dissertation
on the thought of the early twentieth-century French Catholic
existentialist Gabriel Marcel, and I have returned to it again and
again in my writing and teaching.

I begin with the methodological assumption that no
human being can have a totally objective and literally accurate fix

on God. We have no photographs of God. That is what makes God, God. To claim that human beings can comprehend God's essential nature is to slip into idolatry, the cardinal Jewish sin. Maimonides said that centuries ago. What kind of God could possibly be comprehended by the human mind and human language? Only some idol. One alternative to idolatry is worshipful silence, which would lead to sterile agnosticism. The other, preferable option is the claim that all statements about God are metaphorical or mythical, where a myth is understood as a set of metaphors systematized and extended into a coherent structure of meaning.

To the challenge: do we then invent God? I respond: no, we discover God and invent the metaphors and the myths. Which comes first is not clear. Sometimes, metaphors are revelatory; they enable us to see and identify what we might otherwise ignore. But our metaphors originate in experiences that I claim are veridical. The experiences and the metaphors feed into each other; experiences suggest metaphors that are then refined by later experiences; these refined metaphors, in turn, illuminate new experiences, and the process continues.

But how do I substantiate the claim that the experiences are veridical, that they reveal objective realities? What does it mean to experience God? It would seem that we do not see or experience God as we see or experience an apple (though apparently Moses and the elders in Exodus 24:9, and Isaiah, all did— though we don't really know what precisely they saw; of course, our ancestors frequently heard God's voice, but that raises a host of other questions that we will not address here). But is the difference between seeing God and seeing an apple an intrinsic difference? That is, do we require a dual epistemology, one for knowing natural objects and another for knowing God? Or is there one basic way for humans to experience anything, and hence to acquire knowledge of everything?

I claim that a single epistemology is sufficient. To substantiate that claim, I begin by suggesting three possible analogies for the epistemological process involved in knowing God: seeing a basketball team's passing game, seeing an ego, and seeing a quark.

In each of these instances, what we see is patterned activity. In the first, seeing a passing game is different from seeing a star basketball player. We clearly see the player as we see an apple; we know what he looks like or we identify him by the name and number on his shirt. But seeing the passing game involves seeing an in-between activity, a patterned relationship in which the ball is moved back and forth between five players. A passing game is never static, never immobile; it is intrinsically dynamic. This pattern exists over a limited spatial and temporal frame: the basketball court and forty-eight minutes. But it is perfectly clear that we do see a passing game and pass judgments on its quality: sharp, ragged, sloppy, and so on (all, it should be noted, metaphors). Further, though I know nothing about passing games, the coach does, and he can bring a wealth of experience to bear on what he sees and judge it. In other words, there is an interactional quality to this experience; both of us see the same objective game, but, in a way, we also see different games, or we see the one game differently, depending on what we bring to the experience out of ourselves. But there is a passing game out there; it is not an invention of basketball coaches and players.

Similarly, to see an ego is not to see an apple. An ego is not an entity that we can see if we dig deep enough into a human being. (Likewise, the question "where is the psyche?" is silly; the psyche is not in a place.) To see someone's ego is to see one specific, complex, pattern of human behavior, that dimension of the person's behavior which reveals stability and balance. Here too the frame is limited, to the individual human being and his or her life experience. Again, the experience is interactional: the psychologist and I see the same behavior, but the former brings a wealth of professional training and experience—doctoral studies in clinical psychology and years of observing human behavior—that enables him or her to see what I can't see.

To the question "Did Freud (or whoever first talked about egos) discover the ego or invent it?" the answer is clearly

"Both." Freud discovered the pattern, at least partially because he was looking for it and knew what to look for. But then he identified it, gave it a name, and fitted it into his broader psychodynamic theory (or myth). Freud discovered the ego because it was out there to be discovered. The ego itself, in distinction to its name, is not a fiction, not a pure invention out of the blue.

Another way of saying this is that though the psychologist and I see the same behavior, the psychologist interprets what he or she sees in a way that I can't. "We see with our brains, not with our eyes," my ophthalmologist claims. All seeing is interactional, and we invariably bring interpretive structures to our seeing. Of course, a psychologist whose interpretive structure (that is, his or her psychodynamic theory) does not include the myth of the ego will not see an ego. Again, we use metaphors to characterize the ego that we see: strong, weak, shaky, flimsy, solid, and so forth.

To elaborate: to see an ego is to see a pattern that is, in a sense, invisible. What we do objectively see is the way the child plays with blocks and interacts with teachers. But the psychologist "sees through" the overt behavior and then "sees" a solid or flimsy ego. Where is the ego? It is "in" the child, or "in" the behavior, or, more precisely, "in" the activity that the child performs.

Finally, let's talk about seeing a quark. Again, seeing a quark is not like seeing an apple.[1] But a trained nuclear physicist brings her interpretive structure (theory or myth) to look at the computer printout of the activity that took place in her supercollider and then claims to see a quark. I look at the same printout and see a chaotic mass of numbers; she sees a quark. Or, she interprets what she sees as a quark, or she "sees through" the printout to the "invisible" quark. Again, the experience is interactional: without the theoretical structure, the physicist would be like me, seeing nothing of significance. Again, the frame is rather limited—but the parallel holds. Does the physicist invent the quark or discover it? Again the answer is both: she discovers the pattern, but because her theory provides her with a name and a way to identify it when it is there, she can then see the quark. But the quark-pattern is out there to be discovered; it is not a fictitious creation of the physicist.

Seeing God is like seeing any of these, probably most like seeing an ego, in the sense that God is a pattern of activity that is "in" history and nature, as an ego is "in" the person. Here, the frame of reference is immense, the broadest possible canvas: all of nature, history, and human experience. Again the experience is interactional: the believer brings his interpretive structure (the Torah's religious myth) to his seeing, and sees the pattern that we call God. Do we discover God or do we invent God? Both. We discover the patterns and then identify them, name them, and the names are our inventions, just as we invent the names "ego" and "quark." We can do this because the patterns are out there to be discovered.

What are these God-patterns? They constitute what I call the core of the classic, metaphorical system for God in Judaism: a sense of the integrity of all things (God is *ehad*, one); a sense of a transcendent reality that governs all of history and nature; a sense that this reality is personal—that is, relates in a personal way with all of reality; and finally, what Heschel, in his book, *The Prophets*, called "the divine pathos," a sense that this transcendent reality cares about creation and about me.

An excellent biblical description of the process involved in becoming aware of God's presence is Exodus 14:30–31. Here, what the Israelites literally saw were dead Egyptians, but the interpretive structure of the text—the myth, or the perspective of the editor—leads the text to suggest that what they actually "saw" was God's mighty hand. This reading is the basis for the first clause of the passage, the claim that God redeemed the Israelites from Egypt. That claim is actually the conclusion of the passage, though it comes first in the text. Or, more precisely, it reflects the spectacles—the myth—that determined how the editor of the text read the experience at the sea. The same process applies to the canonical interpretations of the Maccabean victory (as recorded in the Chanukah liturgy), or to Joseph's claim that God's hidden hand was directing the entire history of our ancestors' experience in Egypt (Gen. 50:20), or to the thinking that led the canonizers to include the Book of Esther in the biblical canon (B. Megilla 7a); it leads us to say that it was God who brought about the creation of the modern State of Israel. None of these is objective history; all of it is interpretive history or historiography.

The only way of denying that there is an "out there" or objective dimension to the experience of egos, quarks, and God is by not wanting to see those realities, by not having the ability to see them, by denying the interpretive structure that the beholder uses, or by selecting some other interpretive structure (such as the secular Israeli myth). But we cannot do without some structuring myth; without it, our experience is chaotic, literally meaningless. No one can claim that we invent egos and quarks, unless, again, we don't believe that such realities are there in the first place or that they are worth noting. What we do is identify certain patterns and then give them a name. Or we have the name, and then identify the patterns as, in fact, present in our experience.

Another way of characterizing the process is to use the analogy of the childhood game of connect the dots. We connect the dots by number and we see, say, a bunny rabbit. But what if the dots are without numbers, or if many different numbers are assigned to each dot? There are then multiple ways of connecting the dots. But the various patterns that we uncover in connecting the dots are not invented. They are out there to be discovered.

To use still another language, seeing is not believing. We see what we already believe we will see, or what we expect, or hope, or wish to see, or what we are trained to see.

How different is seeing an ego, quark, or God from seeing an apple? Not intrinsically different. We don't really see an apple; we see a colored patch, and our interpretive structure (our brain) identifies what we see as an apple. The apple may be more exposed to light than an ego, it may require a much less elaborate interpretive structure, much less education than psychology and physics, but the process is the same. If we were raised in a culture that didn't know of apples, we would see the patch but we would be incapable of identifying what we see. I realize this each time I see some strange tropical fruit in my grocery store. I see something, but I don't know how to identify what I see; the problem is not perceptual but interpretive or epistemological— not with my eyes but with my mind. If we can see an apple, then we can see egos and quarks and God. If we don't really see apples, then, again, we don't really see egos, quarks, and God. In other words, seeing is intrinsically complicated, and there is a subjective input to all seeing, even to seeing an apple.

Are these seeings falsifiable and verifiable? In principle, yes, by the process that John Wisdom, in his seminal paper, "Gods,"[2] called connecting and disconnecting; that is, by tracing the various patterns that different people see, emphasizing the connections we look for and dismissing the ones that don't cohere with our pattern, and then comparing and sharing them in a social experience. They can be falsifiable because it is, in principle, possible to submit evidence that would lead me to reject any one pattern and the claims it leads me to assert. That is what juries do in complex cases. They share the patterns traced by the prosecution and the defense, reach an agreement on which is the more convincing pattern, and then they acquit or convict. Sometimes, they are hung, unable to reach a verdict, and then the case is argued again. We find an example in the 1995 highly publicized criminal trial of former American football star O. J. Simpson, who was accused and acquitted of murdering his wife and her friend, and the following civil trial in 1997, when the jury found Simpson liable for wrongful death. The two O. J. Simpson juries disagreed on the burden of the evidentiary patterns they were exposed to, partly because the patterns in the two cases differed somewhat, but also because the two juries brought differing interpretive structures to their seeing of the various patterns.

In the case of God, the process of falsification and verification has taken place over centuries in the social context of

Israelite, and later, Jewish history; the patterns are infinitely complex because the canvas is immense, nothing less than all of history, nature, and human experience. There are also many differing patterns. The whole task of Jewish religious education is to train a new generation of Jews to trace and accept the interpretive structure that Jews have used to see the world. That is more complicated than even atomic physics and psychology. True, the process is not as tight as in elementary science, but it is thoroughly appropriate to the subtlety and elusiveness of the data.

Jewish thought is replete with instances of a kind of falsification where later generations repudiate the theological claims of their predecessors. The Book of Job, for example, subverts the classic Torah notion that suffering is inevitably God's punishment for sin; at the very end of the book (42:7–8), God does the subversion, informing Job that the consolers who told him that his suffering was punishment "have not spoken the truth about Me" (though the earlier notion has retained its hold in certain parts of the community, as witness some right-wing responses to the Holocaust). But Jonah 4:2 totally reverses the notion in Exodus 34:6–7 that God must inevitably mete out retribution for sin, because now repentance is in the picture. Here the new notion is canonized in our *Selihot* liturgy on Yom Kippur, and the original Exodus notion is universally recognized as archaic and no longer operative. In each of these cases, the author's personal experience confronted the received tradition, and the personal experience won out. The process as a whole is roughly similar to Thomas S. Kuhn's description of how scientific paradigms are overthrown in his *The Structure of Scientific Revolutions*.[3]

If seeing God is falsifiable and verifiable in the way I have described, then our theological claims are factual. They deal with an "out there." They are not merely poetry. They are also capable of being true or false, using what I call a "soft" correspondence theory of truth. The claims are true because they correspond in a rough kind of way with what generations of Jews have perceived in the world out there, all the time acknowledging the complexity of the data against which our claims are measured.

The tension, then, is between the subjectivism and objectivism of religious claims. My conviction is that we can never escape our humanness, the subjective interpretive structures that we bring to all of our experience. Without these structures, we would experience nothing of significance. True, we have no sense of what objective reality looks like, independent of our interpretive structures. But I am also convinced that this inherent subjectivism does not doom all of our theological claims to being pure human inventions, all fictions. What I have tried to indicate through the analogies suggested above is that we have familiar ways of gaining knowledge of realities that are elusive, beyond the range of normal human perception, but remain real, objectively the case, and hence factually valid.

Chapter 3

THE DYNAMICS OF PROPHECY
IN THE WRITINGS OF
ABRAHAM JOSHUA HESCHEL

It was my privilege to study with Abraham Joshua Heschel at The Jewish Theological Seminary of America from 1954 to 1960. I was subsequently his colleague on the faculty of that school until his death in 1972, and I have spent more than four decades studying and teaching his thought. I have long been convinced that his early writings on prophecy, together with the Hasidic environment into which he was born, served as the major springboards for his mature theology. I have long wished for an opportunity to explore that relationship in a more rigorous manner.

This chapter addresses three issues. I begin by locating Heschel's writings on prophecy in the context of his life's work. Second, I focus more narrowly on the theological core of his thought, namely the concept of God that, Heschel believed, served at the heart of the prophet's self-awareness. Finally, I speculate on how Heschel might have dealt with some of the epistemological issues raised by the phenomenon of prophecy.

HESCHEL'S THREE WORLDS

Abraham Joshua Heschel was arguably the most insightful Jewish theologian of the twentieth century. He was born in Warsaw in 1907 and died in New York in late December 1972 at the age of sixty-five. His career can be divided into three separate phases, each of which can be identified with the three countries in which he spent his life: first, his early years in Warsaw from his birth until 1928, when he left his home as a young man of twenty-one to study first in Vilnius and later in Berlin; second, his stay in Germany from 1929 to 1938, when he was expelled by the Nazi regime and returned to Poland until 1940, when, literally weeks before the Nazi invasion, he left for America; and finally, the years of his maturity, teaching first at Hebrew Union College in Cincinnati until 1946, and then at the Seminary in New York from 1946 until his death in 1972.[1]

Each of these three worlds—Warsaw, Berlin, and America—left a decisive imprint on his character and his thought. The hothouse world of Eastern European Hasidism shaped the mystical core of his theology. It can be claimed that Heschel began as a Hasid and remained a Hasid throughout his life. It was also in Warsaw that he gained his incredible mastery of the entire corpus of traditional Jewish biblical and rabbinic learning together with medieval Jewish philosophy, kabbalah (the classical Jewish mystical tradition), and finally Hasidism, the latest incarnation of the Jewish mystical tradition. He simply knew it all. In Berlin, he was exposed to the world of Western scholarship; to philosophy, science, and the academic study of religion; and to what was arguably the most cosmopolitan Jewish community in Europe at that time. Finally, these two worlds fused with the America of the postwar years, where he published an extensive series of scholarly and popular books in just about every area of Jewish thought in English, Hebrew, and Yiddish; and at the same time, he became the leading Jewish liberal activist on a wide range of social and political issues, preeminently the issues of race, Jewish-Christian relations, and the opposition to the Vietnam War.

It was during the second of these three periods, in Germany in the years 1930–1932, that Heschel first devoted himself to the subject of prophecy. His doctoral dissertation at the University of Berlin was eventually published by the Polish Academy of Arts and Sciences in Kracòw in 1936 as *Die Prophetie*, and later in America in an expanded English translation, in 1962, as *The Prophets*.

These dates are significant. In 1930, Heschel was a twenty-three-year-old doctoral student. His study of prophecy is his first extended scholarly work, and, apart from a popular biography of Maimonides that was published in 1936, it became his first published scholarly book, though his bibliography lists more than thirty monographs and a number of Yiddish poems that were published between 1922 and 1936.[2] As a doctoral dissertation, it was conceived of and written in the classic, Western academic format, with extensive footnotes referring the reader to the scholarly literature, Jewish and otherwise, on the topic. Even its later English version, *The Prophets*, is strikingly different than the books that Heschel published during that same period and that established his reputation in the Jewish and Christian theological communities. It is strikingly different in tone and style than *Man Is Not Alone* (1951) and *God in Search of Man* (1956), his two major theological statements, or *The Sabbath* (1951), still his most widely read book, all written in the poetic style for which he became renowned. *The Prophets*, in contrast, remains the most classically academic of his books.

But for all of its overtly scholarly format, *The Prophets* is a passionate book. It has a thesis, in the technical sense of that term, and this thesis is advanced with feeling and with power. It is also in its own way a highly personal book. It may have begun as an academic exercise, but Heschel's choice of that topic for his doctoral dissertation was far from accidental. In the television interview that Heschel granted just weeks before his death, he remarks that his decision to work on the expanded English version of the book, precisely in the 1960s, at the height of the uproar over the Vietnam War and in the midst of the racial crisis in America, was intended to be a calculated political and spiritual statement. He clearly felt that America needed to hear a prophetic voice, and he was determined to serve as that voice.

THE GOD OF THE PROPHETS

Heschel's study of prophecy is an attempt to penetrate the prophetic consciousness on its own terms. He systematically rejects all attempts to reduce the prophetic experience to simple humanism, self-delusion, or literary fiction. He insists that we take at face value the prophets' claims that they were speaking God's word. What he provides is a phenomenology of the prophetic mindset. But the work is also Heschel's first serious theological inquiry, and it touches upon just about every detail of his later theological writings. Heschel places God at the heart of the prophets' self-awareness and then asks: What does this experience tell us about the God of Israel, about the prophetic image of God? At a certain point in Israelite history, over a span of about three centuries, a group of men claimed to be speaking in the name of the God of Israel and delivered God's message to their community. How did they understand their role? And what kind of a God appoints prophets?

The term that Heschel settles upon to characterize the character of the God of the prophets is "the God of pathos." The four central chapters in the English version of the book—a total of about sixty pages—deal with his understanding of that term. At least three other chapters allude to it, and the book as a whole concludes with an appendix titled "Note on the Meaning of Pathos," in which the author reviews the history of the various uses of that term from Aristotle and Cicero through Hegel and Northrop Frye, most of which, he notes, differ from the way in which he uses the term.[3] It is abundantly clear, then, that the term is central to Heschel and that he has a great stake in our proper understanding of what he means by it.

19

What does he mean by the divine pathos? This is his first attempt at a definition.

> To the prophet ... God does not reveal Himself in an abstract absoluteness, but in a personal and intimate relation to the world. He does not simply command and expect obedience; He is also moved and affected by what happens in the world, and reacts accordingly. Events and human actions arouse in Him joy or sorrow, pleasure or wrath. He is not conceived as judging the world in detachment. He reacts in an intimate and subjective manner, and thus determines the value of events.... (M)an's deeds may move Him, affect Him, grieve Him ... gladden and please Him. This notion that God can be intimately affected, that He possesses not merely intelligence and will, but also pathos ... defines the prophetic consciousness of God.[4]

Using a metaphor from music, Heschel claims that pathos is "the ground tone" of all of God's relationships to the world, the attitude or stance that underlies all other divine attitudes.[5] To use a more popular term, underlying the prophetic consciousness and inspiring all prophetic activity is the assumption that God cares, personally and passionately, about the Jewish people, about humanity, about human civilizations and history, indeed about all of God's creation.

Heschel is very much aware of the scandalous nature of this image of God, particularly for the philosophical and conventional religious mindset. He is amply aware of the distinction between the God of the philosophers and the God of Abraham, Isaac, and Jacob, and of the distinction between the "living" God and the "idea" of God. This awareness impels him to initiate a sustained inquiry into the history of how God has been imaged in the literature of philosophy and religion. The scholarly core of his book, it remains the most sustained scholarly inquiry in all of Heschel's writings and it exhibits the incredible range of Heschel's philosophical learning. His purpose is to recover what he understands to be the "biblical God," to claim that this image has to be taken seriously, and to make clear that this biblical image of God should enjoy the same serious consideration as the God of the philosophers. In effect, Heschel sends us back to the Bible and urges us to read the Bible on its own terms, not colored by our exposure to philosophical speculation. Why, he asks rhetorically, should we assume that the God of the prophets is inherently less sophisticated, less worthy of intellectual approbation, than the God of the philosophers?

Allow me to outline briefly the main arguments in this sustained inquiry. In trying to isolate these points, I encountered once again my enduring frustration in trying to teach Heschel to others. Even in this, his most scholarly book, Heschel does not write in a classic academic style. He does not pursue a vectoral argument, going from point 1 to point 2, then to points 3 and 4, and onward. He does not write in a straight line, where the argument builds from assumptions to conclusions. Instead, he writes in a spiral form; a central point is made early on, and then dropped, reoccurs and then is dropped again, only to reappear in a new form, enriched by what has come in between. I advise my students who are reading Heschel for the first time: If you don't understand a point, never drop out but just move on; it will return again and again. Eventually, you will catch on!

First, pathos is a relational term; it is a statement, not about God in God's essence, but about God's relation to humanity. It therefore locates the human person within the range of God's concern. It also brings history into the heart of God's concerns. The prophetic God is involved in human history. Instead of viewing God as the object of human inquiry, as it is in the philosophical enterprise, Heschel claims that in prophecy, humanity becomes worthy of serving as the object of God's perception. The roles are reversed.

Second, *pathos* is a dynamic term, in contrast, for example, to *covenant*, which he claims is a static term. If covenant defines God's relation with humanity, there are only two possibilities:

either the covenant is upheld or it is dissolved. In contrast, pathos allows for a dynamic multiplicity of relationships, precisely the multiplicity of relations captured in the biblical narrative where God appears as in turn hopeful about humanity, then frustrated, then yearning, pleased, angry, resigned, and then hopeful again, only to become frustrated once more.

Third, pathos separates the biblical God from the philosophical God as portrayed, for example in Aristotle. For Aristotle, God is the unmoved mover, "pure form, eternal, wholly actual, immutable, immovable, self-sufficient, and wholly separated from all else."[6] In contrast, Heschel will argue, the biblical God is "the most moved mover." "An apathetic and ascetic God would have struck biblical man with a sense, not of dignity and grandeur, but rather of poverty and emptiness."[7] The biblical God is needy, lonely, vulnerable. The God of the prophets can be hurt, for once we care about someone, we have left ourselves open to being hurt by that person.

Fourth, the world ruled by the biblical God contrasts sharply with the notion of a world ruled by fate, by some supreme force to which even the gods are subject: a blind, primeval, determining power that ultimately governs all that happens on earth and upon which even the gods are dependent, as in all forms of pagan religion. In biblical religion, in contrast, nothing is predetermined. As God is free, so are we, and we have the power to compel God to change every divine decree. The plans of the biblical God can change, as people change. The biblical God creates the possibility of repentance and return. The fate of the world, the fate of history rests on human decisions. In the meantime, God waits.

Fifth, and finally, the notion of pathos affirms the legitimacy of the emotions. Heschel undertakes an extended inquiry into the way in which philosophy has understood the place of emotion in human life and in God. With manifold references to the scholarly literature, he discusses the philosophical understanding of emotion as an expression of passivity and as undignified, the elevation of reason over feelings, the affirmation of apathy as more elevated than emotion, the history of mind-body dualism in philosophical literature, and the place of emotion in the Bible and its anthropological implications. He concludes with this passage, which, I confess, I continue to find one of the most powerful in all of his writings:

> Is it more compatible with our notion of the grandeur of God to claim that He is emotionally blind to the misery of man than profoundly moved? In order to conceive of God not as an onlooker but as a participant, to conceive of man not as an idea in the mind of God but as a concern, the category of divine pathos is an indispensable implication. To the biblical mind, the conception of God as detached and unemotional is totally alien.[8]

In legitimizing God's emotional life, Heschel at the same time legitimizes human emotions. If God can get angry, so can we.

God's anger poses a particular problem to many readers of the prophets, and Heschel devotes two entire chapters (16 and 17) to this issue. He understands that our embarrassment at God's anger stems from our discomfort with our own anger. Again, he traces the long cultural history of anger; and again, he tries to understand the precise form in which anger appears within God's pathos. For anger, he proposes to substitute the term "righteous indignation,"[9] which he opposes to indifference. He notes how thin is the line between anger and love, that in fact anger is often an expression of love. The God of the prophets "is not indifferent to evil."[10] But God's anger is contingent, reactive, conditional, and always momentary—in contrast to God's love, which is abiding.

HESCHEL'S SOURCES

Another of my enduring frustrations in studying Heschel's writings is his reluctance to acknowledge the thinkers or the books that influenced his own thought. In trying to trace the influences that led him to formulate the notion of divine pathos, I am indulging in a measure of speculation.

My sense is that there are three such influences, two of them from his earliest years and the third, from his maturity. The first of these lies in Lurianic mysticism, which shaped the Hasidic world into which Heschel was born. Lurianic kabbalah is a rich and complex body of mystical speculation that I can only begin to capture in these brief remarks.

Isaac Luria was a seminal thinker who lived in Safed, Palestine, in the sixteenth century and who promulgated a myth of cosmology and redemption that transformed and transfixed the Jewish world for generations. One of the cornerstones of Lurianic cosmology is a myth of creation by emanation. Here, Luria departs radically from the apparent plain sense of the biblical notion of creation. In Genesis, God is described as creating a world that is separate and apart from God. Eventually, in the postbiblical tradition, this led to the notion that God created the world *ex nihilo*, literally "out of nothing," though this is not precisely the plain sense of Genesis 1. An exploration of this issue would, however, take us far afield.[11]

In place of the biblical account of creation, Luria taught that God created the world by emanation out of what may crudely be called God's own being, or even more crudely, out of what may be called "God-stuff." If that is the case, then God does not abide outside of, apart from, or independent of the created world. Instead, creation as a whole is imbued with the presence of God. This notion skirts one of the classical Jewish heresies, namely pantheism. But Luria avoids that heresy by nearly tumbling into another possible heresy, namely that of dualism. He suggests that one dimension of God, God as *Ein Sof*, Infinity—the transcendent or hidden God, the *deus absconditus*—persists independently of that dimension of God that is identified with the created world and is conventionally called the *Shekhinah*, the immanent God, that aspect of God as present in and throughout creation.[12]

This notion of God as immanent in creation transformed Jewish thought and became one of the core theological assumptions of Hasidism, which reigned among Eastern European Jewry from the eighteenth century almost to our own day. Heschel was born into this world; he traced his ancestry to the circle of Hasidic masters surrounding the founder of Hasidism, Rabbi Israel Ba'al Shem Tov (roughly 1700–1760).[13] Heschel's father was a Hasidic rabbi, and Heschel himself had been designated to inherit the leadership of his father's community until he decided to leave Warsaw to study in Berlin. He imbided Hasidism from the cradle. And the notion that God is everywhere to be perceived in the most intimate and immediate dimensions of reality is at the core of the notion of the divine pathos.

The second influence is much easier to trace. It lies simply in Heschel's study of Scripture, which he read from his infancy and which he encountered without any of the philosophical assumptions that guide the reading of those of us who begin with a Western education. Heschel encountered Western culture later in life. At the outset, he read the Bible on its own terms, and his encounter with the biblical image of God led him to the immediate conclusions that God was intimately involved with all of history and that God cared passionately about the world and about all of creation. Those conclusions required no great leap. They were simply obvious, present in every verse of the Bible. When we read these biblical passages, we have to overcome our philosophical assumptions. Heschel had nothing to overcome. He simply read what was there. What other conclusions could he possibly derive?

The third influence was his own gradual, emerging passion for social justice. That message too he found in prophetic literature, but he also discovered it in himself during his stay as a Jew in Germany in the 1930s, and it flowered in America in his encounter with American racism and with the Vietnam War, the latter of which he believed was nothing less than a holocaust perpetrated by America on innocent women and children. He used to ask in class, "What would Isaiah do if he lived in America in the 1960s? What would he say about racism? What would he say about this war in which America is systematically killing widows and orphans? What would he say about poverty? about oppression?" As it was inconceivable to the young Heschel that he himself could be indifferent to what was going on in the world about him, it was simply inconceivable to him that God would be indifferent to the course of twentieth-century history. But then what does this tell us about God?[14]

GOD'S PATHOS IN HESCHEL'S
MATURE THEOLOGY

I claimed at the outset that Heschel's notion of divine pathos eventually served as the cornerstone of his later, mature constructive theology. In teaching Heschel, I insist that my students begin their reading of the later Heschel by studying the chapters on pathos in *The Prophets*. For evidence of that influence, simply look at the titles of his two major books: first, *Man Is Not Alone* (1951); and then *God in Search of Man* (1955). Between these two, he published a collection of papers on prayer and symbolism that he titled *Man's Quest for God* (1954). His very use of these titles assumes a God who is in intimate relationship with humanity.

But it is not simply a matter of titles. The core of both of these studies is Heschel's description of the religious experience. He views it as transactional, as demanding both an active or aggressive revelatory role by God and an equally aggressive perceiving role by human beings. Heschel uses various terms to characterize these mutual roles—his terminology is never precise—but for the human role, he settles on "radical amazement," and for the divine role, he reverts to "pathos." By "radical amazement" he means, as the literal meaning of the term "radical" implies, a stance of "root" amazement, a stance that takes nothing in the world for granted, that views the world in perpetual wonder. In one of his formulations, he characterizes this stance as one of wonder over the fact that there are facts in the first place. It is a stance that views a grain of sand as a drama.

When we view the world through the eyes of radical amazement, what we perceive is a world infused with the presence of God, a God who stands not in detachment from the world, but who is present everywhere, who cries for attention—not only in history but even in nature as well—a God who pursues us, a God who is perpetually in search of human acknowledgment. This is partly the *Shekhinah* of Lurianic kabbalah, that dimension of God present throughout creation. But it is also the divine pathos of *The Prophets*, now extended and reconceptualized into a driving, aggressive, forceful power that demands recognition—though for the better part of our lives, that divine presence is obscured, hidden, by the overwhelming grayness that is so characteristic of the way we are educated to encounter the world. To use another Hasidic metaphor, we have to learn to see through the shells that encase God's presence in the natural world.

The God that permeates all of creation is the same God that appoints prophets. The biblical God has this quality of self-transcendence, which expresses itself both in the act of creation and in prophecy. If, as Heschel claims, "man is not alone," then neither is God alone. This God is in need of a world, in need of man, in need of recognition by humanity. This God is then also "in search of man," and the prophet is the most vivid expression of this divine need.

Much of the time this divine need is frustrated. But then there are those rare moments of illumination when "heaven and earth kiss," moments in which "there is a lifting of the veil at the horizon of the known, opening a vision of what is eternal in time."[15] These moments are presymbolic, preconceptual, and universal because they precede verbal, cerebral, and hence credal formulation. They are, simply put, intuitive to human nature as such. All of the institutions of religion are designed to create settings where these rare moments may occur and to treasure their memories through the grayness of the in-between.[16]

HESCHEL'S EPISTEMOLOGY

A few words, now, on the epistemological issues raised by this understanding of prophecy and the religious experience. One cannot read prophetic literature without wondering how the community was to know who was the true prophet, and who the false prophet. The biblical test is articulated in Deuteronomy 18:21–22: "If the prophet speaks in the name of God and the oracle does not come true, that oracle was not spoken by God; the prophet has uttered it presumptuously: do not stand in dread of him." That test is quite useless before the fact, but that is precisely when the question arises. Besides, we have at least one biblical prophet—Jonah—whose prophecy did not come true precisely because his prophecy was attended to; that is, he was Israel's only successful prophet. Nineveh repented and God relented. That Jonah was furious at God for making him look like a false prophet (Jonah 4:1–2) exposes the deuteronomic test as singularly futile.

Heschel does not deal with this epistemological issue in *The Prophets*, but he does deal with it in his later theological writings in his typically unsystematic way. His view can be summarized in his claim that God has to be understood as an "ontological presupposition."[17] By this he means that God can never emerge as the conclusion of an inquiry, but rather as its assumption, its presupposition. God's very being—what we sometimes call, crudely, "the existence of God"—has to be presupposed. If God is not present at the outset, God will never emerge at the end.

Let us put this another way. We never experience the outside world as it really is, objectively. We bring our own linguistic, educational, gender, and cultural backgrounds, even our biochemical makeup with us as we shape our experience of the world. To use some obvious examples, black Americans and white Americans literally see a different America, as do Israelis and Palestinians, who see a different Middle East. Which is the "real" America? Is there a "real" America? We never capture "reality" as it is. Rather, we construct reality.

My sense is that believers and nonbelievers "see," that is, construct, a different world out of the "out there." To use another metaphor, they use a different set of spectacles. When Heschel refers to God as an ontological presupposition, he says that the believer—and primarily the prophet, for our purposes here—begins with the prior conviction that there is a God in the world, that this God cares about the world, and that God has selected this prophet to speak to the world on God's behalf. The divine pathos, then, is one dimension of the spectacles with which the prophet constructs his reality. Or, to quote a Hasidic maxim, "Where is God? Wherever you let God in!" To seek to verify the claim that God cares for the world is precisely to miss the point; the experience of God's presence, of God's demand, is infinitely more overwhelming than any proof. The prophet's experience of God's call is self-verifying.[18]

I concede that this "constructivist" epistemology is much more my own extension of Heschel's thought than his own personal conclusions. But as an attempt to justify this extension, it is clear that Heschel dismisses the entire issue of verification as simply illegitimate for anyone who has had the direct, unmediated, and overwhelming experience of God's presence—as did the prophet. To question the objective reality of that experience, even to harbor the suspicion that it may be purely subjective or, even worse, illusory, is, however unwittingly, to deny the experience itself.

> This then is the order in our thinking and existence: The ultimate or God comes first and our reasoning about Him second. Metaphysical speculation has reversed the order: reasoning comes first and the question about His reality second; either He is proved or He is not real. However, just as there is no thinking about the world without the premise of the reality of the

world, there can be no thinking about God without the premise of the realness of God.[19]

The prophet never questions the reality of the God who speaks to him. Nor should the believer.

This notion of pathos is Heschel's metaphor for God, his image of how this transcendent, fundamentally unknown and unknowable God appears to the prophet. It is the prophet's perception of God, more than God's self-perception. My own theological assumptions force me to conclude that no human being knows what God is in God's essence—that is what makes God, God and me, a simple human being. I hasten to add that on this point, I write more for myself, not for Heschel. In many ways, Heschel's epistemology is an anti-epistemology, a denial of the very possibility of human beings knowing anything objectively about God. It is one of those many issues that I would have loved to pursue with Heschel, possibly to encourage him to confront some of the many issues that this approach raises.

The Bible records a rich, complex, and fluid system of metaphors to capture God's nature, reflecting the equally rich, complex, and fluid nature of one community's experience of God over many generations. Heschel's divine pathos captures the ground tone of this system—the underlying image that underlies all of the remaining more specific images in which God appears to this community. All of these other images— shepherd, judge, parent, lover, spouse, rock, military warrior, and the rest—assume what Heschel tries to capture in the term *pathos*.

HESCHEL'S ENDURING LEGACY

I suggested, at the outset, that Heschel's notion of divine pathos is both the impetus for his understanding of prophecy and also the core of his own mature theological inquiry. Ultimately, these two functions are one, for the prophet's self-understanding constitutes his own implicit theology, and his implicit theology is Heschel's. More than any other twentieth-century Jewish theologian—certainly more than Martin Buber, Franz Rosenzweig, or Mordecai Kaplan, to isolate the three other theological giants of the period—Heschel compels us to return to the Bible, to recapture biblical categories and to take them seriously.

Without the divine pathos, there would be no prophecy; but then, neither would there be a Bible, or a people Israel, or Torah, or covenant, or Jewish religion. The foundation of the entire enterprise is the awareness of a God who cares passionately for the world, for humanity, even for the cosmos as a whole.

Even more, my personal recollection of Heschel traversing the country and speaking out against war, racism, poverty, and oppression enables me, in my imagination, to recapture the image of Amos or Isaiah preaching the identical messages centuries ago. To many Americans who have only the slightest interest in theology, that image of Heschel marching with Martin Luther King Jr., in Selma, Alabama, endures to this very day— and because of that, the prophets remain alive. That may be his most enduring legacy.

But this writer is interested in theology. At various points in this chapter, I have suggested some of my personal frustrations with Heschel's work, and there are others that I have discussed elsewhere. What remains for me, the very words with which I began, is his remarkably insightful sensitivity to the religious experience. He was a creative theologian, a brilliant analyst of traditional Judaism, and a master of the classical literature. Above all, he was a superb phenomenologist of religion. He is at his very best when he traces the contours of the religious experience, the wrestling that occurs when God and human beings search, find, lose, and then rediscover each other once again. And nowhere does this skill emerge more clearly than in his work on prophecy. It displays Heschel at his very best.

Chapter 4

CREATION IN THE BIBLE
AND IN THE LITURGY

The major methodological assumption of this chapter is that in Judaism those portions of the liturgy that originate in the literature of the Talmudic period (ca. 100–600 CE) should be viewed as the extension, frequently the transformation, and, at times, even the subversion of biblical doctrines. We are fully aware that the Bible does not always speak in one voice on significant doctrinal issues. Yet, if the Bible represents the initial canonization of at least the core of the Jewish religious myth, then in postbiblical Judaism the extension of that process of canonization can be found most explicitly in the liturgy.

The liturgy uses biblical texts in many different ways. More than seventy psalms, almost half of the Book of Psalms, appear in their entirety somewhere in the liturgy.[1] Countless individual verses were introduced into later liturgical texts. Specific prophetic texts were used as *haftarot* accompanying the yearly Torah reading cycle on Sabbaths and festivals. But what interests us more are those liturgical passages, formulated by the Talmudic rabbis, that appropriate biblical themes by using distinctively biblical code words or phrases, or that in some other way echo biblical texts, thereby identifying themselves as biblically based.

The large majority of worshiping Jews, from the end of the Talmudic era to our own day, are much more familiar with these liturgical passages than with their original formulation in the Bible itself, certainly more familiar than with the contents of the Prophets and the Writings. (Of course, the yearly cycle of Torah readings on the Sabbath enables them to be totally familiar with the Pentateuch.) Without necessarily being aware of it, Jews encounter much of the Bible through the liturgy. These liturgical texts have played a decisive role in shaping the belief system of postbiblical Jews, more so than the more scattered and unfamiliar Talmudic homilies that also frequently transform a biblical doctrine in ways that echo or anticipate their transformations in the liturgy.

The difference between these two forms of expression is that the Talmudic homily is the individual statement of one rabbi in a specific historical context that can only rarely be recaptured today. In contrast, the liturgical formulation is much more of a consensual statement. Because it frequently uses the original, unpronounceable four-letter name of God, the precise wording of the statement acquired a halakhic, or legal, standing and therefore, had to win consensual rabbinic approval.

These liturgical texts should be studied not as texts to be read, but rather as activities to be performed.[2] The specific activity being performed here is what can be called "doing theology." Though we conventionally use the all-purpose English term "prayer" to designate all forms of worship, in Judaism worship is fine-tuned and subdivided into a number of different models. One familiar model, embodied in the daily *Amidah*, is petitionary prayer: we petition God for forgiveness, healing, and the rest. But another model, the one that interests us here, is the one in which the liturgy articulates a series of theological claims, much like in the Credo portion of the Roman Catholic Mass. Frequently, however, in its liturgical guise, a biblical doctrine undergoes a subtle transformation that lends it a new meaning. It is precisely this transformation that takes place within the liturgical passage we refer to as "doing theology."

Of these texts, we can ask a series of questions: Why did the Rabbis choose specific biblical phrases, verses, or passages for liturgical purposes? Why in this specific liturgical context? What happens to these terms in their new formulation? How do these transformations reveal the way the Rabbis read and understood the biblical text? Finally, how do these texts work for us, the worshipers? In this chapter, we will concentrate on texts that deal with the doctrine of creation. We will also compare the biblical and liturgical understandings of creation with a very different model in Jewish mystical literature, and suggest some methodological issues for further investigation.

On the question as to how these texts work for the worshiper, I will use a conceptualization suggested by anthropologist Clifford Geertz in his seminal "Religion as a Cultural System."[3] We sense, intuitively, that there is a tight relationship between liturgy and ritual, on the one hand, and the feelings and behaviors of those who worship and perform the ritual, on the other. But it is not intuitively clear just how that relationship is established and how it works. Geertz provides us with a conceptualization that enables us to deal with this question. Geertz defines religion as

> a system of symbols which acts to establish powerful, pervasive and longlasting moods and motivations in men by formulating conceptions of a general order of existence, and clothing these conceptions with such an aura of factuality that the moods and motivations seem uniquely realistic.[4]

My own preferred terminology is to refer to this system of symbols as "myth." A myth is a set of symbols extended and systematized into one coherent structure of meaning. A myth can articulate or describe that structure (a structural myth), or narrate how that structure came into being (a narrative myth).[5] It is a device through which an individual or a community organizes its experience of the world, or of one part of the world (as in the

Freudian psychoanalytic myth that attempts to make sense of human behavior), so that it forms a coherent whole. Following Geertz, myths are ordering devices. Rollo May provides an alternative definition:

> A myth is a way of making sense in a senseless world.... [M]yths are like the beams in a house; not exposed to outside view, they are the structure which holds the house together so people can live in it.[6]

Two points about these definitions: first, a myth is a selective, interpretive reading of "the real," designed to introduce or reveal an underlying, hidden structure or order that we can now see. And second, no myth is a photograph of the real. We cannot photograph, or even observe, the real without some preexistent structuring device. So much for the common distinction between a myth and "the facts"; without a myth, we are not even aware of what the significant facts are in the first place.

In the course of unpacking his definition, Geertz addresses the question of how precisely this "system of symbols" acquires that "aura of factuality" that makes "the moods and motivations seem uniquely realistic." His answer is that it is through ritual. He writes: "In a ritual, the world as lived and the world as imagined, fused under the agency of a single set of symbolic forms, turn out to be the same world."[7]

In ritual, which Geertz defines concisely as "consecrated behavior," the moods and motivations, the feelings and behaviors induced by the sacred symbols (or religious myths) and the general conceptions of an ordered world that the myths formulate, meet and reinforce one another.

I understand the liturgy that accompanies the ritual to be an integral part of that complex ritual activity. Ritual and liturgy differ in that they use two different languages, one behavioral and the other verbal. But in significant ritual moments, such as the Passover seder, the rites of passage, or the Christian Eucharist, these two languages are woven together to convey one set of meanings. At these moments, the mythic world and the real world of real people fuse and become one. It is ritual, then, that brings the mythic system into the life of the believer so that it can accomplish its function of ordering the world.

One addendum is necessary to our previous discussion of the relationship between liturgy and the Bible. Myths exist in time. They live and they die but, more frequently—because myths are singularly tenacious—they evolve and change. Portions of a myth can be discarded and new elements can be introduced. This is what we mean when we say that myths enjoy a certain plasticity. This is precisely what happens to some biblical versions of the classical biblical myth as it enters into the later liturgy.

My specific interest here is to study some liturgical passages that deal with the biblical accounts of creation. These creation narratives form an integral part of the canonical Jewish religious myth. They both portray the structure of the ordered, transcendent world that explains how the world we live in coheres and describe how that structure came to be. Our purpose is to understand how some liturgical passages reflect and transform the biblical texts that they invoke, and thereby extend and transform the body of the Jewish myth. We will use four such specific liturgical texts, all of which refer to biblical doctrines of creation.

THE *SHEVA BERAKHOT*

These seven benedictions that originate in the Talmud[8] form the major part of the liturgy that accompanies the Jewish marriage ceremony. Following the order in which they are recited under the huppah (wedding canopy) the most difficult of these seven benedictions is the fourth.[9] Its concluding words, in which we praise God as *yotzer ha-adam*, are identical to the concluding words of the benediction that immediately precedes it. The precise meaning of these concluding words is obscure. They could be translated literally as "creator of the man" or as "creator of mortals" (echoing

Genesis 1:26, where God creates *ha-adam* both male and female).
But in its broader context, this fourth benediction clearly refers to
the creation of the first woman (as in Numbers 31:35, where the
word *adam* is used to refer to women), while the preceding benediction lacks any specific gender connotation.

This benediction then represents a further narrowing of
God's creative activity. In the second, God creates all things; in
the third, God creates humankind. Now, in the fourth, God creates the woman, and through the woman, *binyan ade ad*, or eternal human posterity. That this text refers to the creation of
woman is explicitly conveyed by the term *binyan* (literally, "building" or "edifice"), an allusion to Genesis 2:22, where the verb
vayiven is used to describe God's fashioning (or building) of the
woman from the rib taken from the man. Through the children
born by the woman, the man achieves posterity or eternity.

The problem is with the three words *tzelem demut
tavnito*, on which much scholarly effort has been expended.[10]
The three terms all convey the general sense of image or "like-
ness." The human person was created in someone's image. But
whose image is being invoked here? The first two terms surely
do refer to God's image; they are used in Genesis 1:26 and 27 to
indicate that the first human person (or persons, depending on
how we read 1:27), was (or were) created in God's image.

But *tavnito* should not refer to God; it is much too physi-
calistic. Maimonides, in the *Guide of the Perplexed* (1.3) suggests
that *tavnit* means an object's (physical) shape, as in Exodus
25:8, where the phrase *tavnit hamishkan* refers to the shape of
the desert sanctuary, or in Isaiah 44:13, which refers to an idol as
having a *tavnit ish*, or "human [clearly physical] form." On this
basis, Maimonides insists that it can never be used to apply to
God, because God has no physical form. However, in 2 Kings
16:10, *tavnit* is used as a synonym for *demut*, and both refer to a
sketch, plan, or blueprint.

The conventional interpretation of the passage follows the
tenth-century CE Babylonian authority Saadia Gaon's reading,
which either transposes the *vav* from before the word *vehitqin*

earlier in the passage to a point immediately prior to the word *b'tzelem*, so that our phrase now reads *u'vetzelem demut tavnito hitqin lo mimenu binyan ade ad*.[11] Now, the three synonyms, *tzelem*, *demut*, and *tavnito*, refer to Adam, not to God. Or, without actually moving the *vav*, we simply read the text as if it were transposed. The text now begins by claiming that Adam was created in God's *tzelem*, or image, and then concludes that the woman was created in Adam's image. Since Adam was created in God's image, so was the woman.

Note also that the word *tavnit* foreshadows the word *binyan*, both stemming from the biblical (Gen. 2:22) *vayiven*, which refers to the creation of the woman. But what is unusual about the term *tavnit* is precisely its physicality. As David Flusser and Shmuel Safrai, Israeli professors of Jewish liturgy, emphasize, this formulation constitutes a rejection of any dualistic anthropology.[12] There is no reference here to a soul, to a *nefesh* or a *neshamah*, as these terms are understood in the later literature.[13] In the medieval philosophical tradition, the *tzelem* in which the human person was created was the faculty of intellectual apprehension.[14] But our text reflects a thoroughly biblical anthropology following Genesis 2:7, where God creates the human person by vivifying a clod of earth. The human person is composed of some physical matter that has been given a breath or spark of life. The anthropology is thoroughly monolithic.

This liturgical text then extends the biblical narrative in three ways. It teaches us that the first woman was created in the image of the first man; that it is through the woman that the man achieves eternal posterity; and that, in both cases, the image of God in man and woman is not exclusively spiritual, but also denotes the body. Leaving aside the much broader question of what, in the first place, the Bible means by claiming that the man was created in God's image, here at least it means some form of vivified matter.

The liturgical text also reflects a rabbinic dispute that stems from an ambiguity in Genesis 1:26. Here, "God creates *ha-adam* in God's image, in the image of God God created him," and then, "male and female God created them." Does this text refer, then, to one act of creation, or to two? Did God create *ha-adam*, and then the woman? Or did God create both man and woman in one act of creation, with the subsequent (Gen. 2:22) reference to the creation of the woman, simply indicating that God separated the original woman from the original man?

The rabbinic dispute[15] revolves around the two separate benedictions, the third and the fourth, dealing with the creation of the original human persons. That there are two such separate benedictions suggests that the rabbis understood that there were two separate creation acts here, one relating to the first man and the other to the first woman.

Using Geertz's conceptualization, how does this ritual work? Precisely by fusing the two worlds, the transcendent mythic world of the creation story and the actual, real world of the two people who are getting married. This is explicit in the sixth benediction, where the two people being married are identified with the first two human beings. In effect, then, two weddings are taking place simultaneously. The huppah becomes Eden, the couple becomes Adam and Eve, and the presiding rabbi becomes God. The Rabbis here echo the familiar midrash in which God prepares Adam and Eve for their wedding and pronounces the wedding blessings.[16]

Actually, three weddings are taking place simultaneously because the fifth benediction portrays the "wedding" of Zion and her children. Here, the huppah becomes Jerusalem, the couple becomes Zion and her children, and again, the rabbi becomes God who unites Zion and the people Israel. Two significant dimensions of the classic Jewish mythic structure enter our consciousness: the universal creation myth and the national Zion myth.

Finally, why did the Rabbis incorporate references to creation in the wedding liturgy? There are three possible reasons: First, they did so to echo the Mishnah where the Rabbis note that God created only one person from whom the entire world was populated; thus, every single human being (and now, this couple who will procreate) is potentially the source of an entire world.[17]

Second, they understood marriage in sexual terms. The wedding canopy symbolizes the marital bed, and for the Rabbis, sexuality means posterity, posterity means Jewish continuity, and continuity is important.

Third, the Rabbis include the creation references because the last of the seven benedictions is explicitly eschatological. The liturgy locates this marriage within the broadest possible temporal canvas of the myth, between creation and redemption. The Rabbis incorporate the very words of Jeremiah 33:10–11 with their reference to marriage. Jeremiah 32:2 enables us to date this entire passage within weeks prior to the destruction of the Temple. In this context, marriage is a metaphor for the eventual restoration of Israel to its land. Its thrust is eschatological. The liturgical use of this passage makes every marriage a redemptive act, effectively a statement of hope in the future at the moment of utmost despair. To establish that broad canvas, the Rabbis open the seven benedictions with creation and close with eschatology. Echoing Geertz, this is a striking example of ordering.

Finally, I believe that the breaking of the glass, the ritual that concludes the marriage service as a whole, is not at all as it is conventionally understood, a recollection of the destruction that was, but rather is an anticipation of the chaos that remains, a return to history, a breaking of the messianic spell.[18] Again echoing Geertz, it separates the two worlds, the mythic and the real, that had been momentarily fused. For just a moment, redemption was in the air; but we know that the world has not been totally redeemed, that chaos still rules "out there," and that this couple must now return to the unredeemed real world.[19]

My next three examples are drawn form the *Yotzer* (creation) benediction of the *shaharit* (morning) service.

YOTZER 'OR U-VORE HOSHEKH

These words form the opening core of the *Yotzer* benediction for the morning service.[20] We praise God "who fashions light and creates darkness, who makes *shalom* [which we leave untranslated for the present] and creates all things."

In Genesis 1:2, God begins by creating light. Darkness, together with deep waters, a mighty wind, and the earth in its state of *tohu vavohu* ("unformed and void"), exists before the creation of light. The liturgy, however, incorporates a different version of creation, one based on Isaiah 45:7: "I fashion light and create darkness, I make *shalom* and create evil—I Adonai do all these things."

First, then, in deliberate contravention of Genesis, the Isaiah text has God also creating darkness. God creates all things, light and darkness, good and evil, and not only these polarities but also probably everything in between. In other words, God really creates *kol eleh*, or "all these things." But though the liturgy has God creating darkness, Isaiah's word for "evil," *ra*, is dropped and replaced with the words *et hakol*, or "all things," taken from that concluding phrase of the verse, from *kol eleh*.

In formulating the opening benediction for the *Yotzer*, the Rabbis decided to use the Isaiah text to the effect that God creates light as an appropriate phrase for the beginning of the formal service at dawn. But the benediction could simply have read, *Yotzer or u'vore et hakol*, God "creates light and forms all things," omitting the reference to darkness.

Why, then, did the Rabbis include the claim that God also creates darkness, in explicit contravention of Genesis 1? I believe for three reasons: First, they did not want worshipers to puzzle over who created darkness; of course, God created darkness too. Genesis may not have said this, but they wanted to. Second, they were uncomfortable with the dualistic implications that anything coexisted with God before God's creation of the world.[21] Third, they also did want to make a statement about the source of evil, though they were more ambivalent about the issue than the author of Isaiah 45. In Isaiah, darkness is parallel to *ra*. This enables us to translate *shalom* not as the conventional "peace," but rather as "completeness," "harmony," or simply "cosmos," and *ra* as its opposite, "chaos." Since they assumed that the

41

worshiper might hear the echo of Isaiah, and since *hakol* also includes evil, they were able to make that point as well.

The biblical understanding of creation does not teach *creatio ex nihilo*, creation from nothing. That may have been a burning issue for medieval philosophers,[22] but in Genesis at least, creation is not something out of nothing, but rather cosmos out of chaos, with the chaotic or anarchic nature of the preexisting stuff captured in the theme of the "deep waters" and more particularly in the phrase *tohu va-vohu*. Rashi (on Gen. 1:2) accurately captures the sense of that phrase through his use of the early French, *étourdir*, which means "to swirl," or "to make dizzy." The Genesis narrative portrays God's creative work not as creating "all things," but rather as controlling, disciplining, ordering, or structuring the preexisting chaotic forces in the world.

The liturgical passage thus forms a way station between the Bible and the medievals. It does not invoke *tohu vavohu*, but it does include darkness within God's creation, and darkness can also be understood as part of that preexisting chaos, now part of God's creation.

We should not underestimate the theological power of this statement. Genesis 1 claims that God did not create darkness; it was there at the outset. What Genesis does claim (1:4) is that God separated the darkness from the light, or, in other words, placed boundaries about the darkness, as God does with the waters (1:9). In contrast, the Isaiah text has God creating darkness (and presumably the waters as well) and then proceeds to identify this darkness with evil, with the opposite of cosmos, with chaos. God then creates evil as well. In Genesis, God controls chaos; in Isaiah, God creates it. One can understand why the liturgy wished to dilute that claim. In fact, the substitution is discussed in the Talmud (Berakhot 11b) and is explained by the rabbinic preference for what may be loosely translated "more exalted language" (*lishna me'alya*).

Here is a classic example of liturgy as "doing theology." The worshiper is led through a complex theological exercise consisting of: first, Isaiah's departure from Genesis to the effect that God created darkness as well as light; second, the change from *ra* to *hakol*; third, the claim that God, too, is responsible for evil; and finally, that creation was, in a way, *ex nihilo*.

U'VETUVO MEHADESH BEKHOL YOM TAMID MA'ASEH VERESHIT

The claim here is that God, "in [God's] goodness, daily renews the work of creation." This phrase appears originally in the Babylonian Talmud, Hagigah 12b, which quotes Isaiah 40:22b as a proof text (reading the two verbs in that passage in the present tense). In our version of the *Yotzer* benediction the phrase appears twice: once near the beginning, and again, in a very slightly altered form, near the end. The effect of this second appearance is to restore the thematic unity of the benediction by picking up the thread of the opening words of the *Yotzer* benediction. Apparently, the later insertion of the extended angelology liturgy, which in our texts makes up the bulk of the benediction, required this second appearance of the phrase.[23]

The claim here is that God's work of creation is not a one-time event in the distant past, but rather an ongoing activity that continues daily, every day. This constitutes another transformation of the Genesis version. Genesis suggests that God created the world in one series of acts at the outset. Now, creation is not only a statement about how the world came into being at the outset, but also a statement of the created world's ongoing dependence on God's daily intervention.

How does the liturgy reach that conclusion? It does so, first, from the liturgical proof text Psalm 136:7, "Who makes [*l'oseh*] the great lights, God's steadfast love is eternal." The emphasis is on the present tense of the verb, *oseh* ("God makes"), and on the "eternal" quality of God's steadfast love. God then continues to create today, every day. Second, this conclusion is drawn from the daily experience of sunrise. The Rabbis understood that daily experience as a new act of creation all over again.

In this context, compare the *Yotzer* benediction with its parallel in *ma'ariv*, the evening service, which also celebrates God's creative work. First, it is intriguing to note that although the Rabbis chose to characterize God as *yotzer or* ("creates light") at dawn, they did not characterize God as *yotzer hoshekh* ("creates darkness") at evening. Even more, though in the morning they portray God as creating both light and darkness, none of this is echoed in the evening service. In its place, the emphasis is on God's daily maintenance of creation. Daily, God brings on evenings, changes seasons, creates day and night, removes light before darkness and darkness before light, causes day to pass and brings night, and separates day and night.[24] Creation is not a single event in the distant past, but a daily manifestation of God's power.

Finally, the single theme of the entire evening text is God as creator of distinctions. It then echoes forcefully the creation account of Genesis 1, where God is portrayed again and again as distinguishing between light and darkness, day and night, waters above and waters below, the Sabbath and the common days of the week. The emphasis is on creation as a process of bringing cosmos out of chaos. Distinctions or boundaries are intrinsic to the process of creating an ordered world out of a preexistent anarchy.

Though the opening of the *Yotzer* benediction is closer to the Isaiah 45 version of creation, the theme that God daily renews the work of creation coheres more closely with the Genesis version. If, as in Genesis, God does not create darkness but rather confines it within boundaries, then God must continue daily to control the chaotic forces in the world. That is why God must renew creation every day. But, if following Isaiah, where God creates the chaos, why the theme of daily renewal?

The key to this lies in the single word *u'vetuvo*. It is God's "goodness" that leads to God's daily renewal of creation. The original Hebrew for what we have interpreted as chaos is *ra*. God creates evil. But once God has created evil, then the contrary or balancing impulse in God, God's goodness, requires that God work constantly, daily, to ensure that the chaotic be kept under a measure of control. Hence, creation demands God's daily attention.

OR HADASH AL TZION TA'IR

The *Yotzer* benediction concludes with this supplication that God "cause a new light to shine on Zion." The thrust of the petition is clearly eschatological; this is precisely why it was so controversial. Saadia Gaon opposed its use: partly because it is a petition he felt was out of place in this part of the liturgy; but mainly because he felt it represents a confusion of categories. The theme of the *Yotzer* as a whole is God's creative work in nature. Hence its reference to God's creation of natural light in the opening and concluding words of the benediction. But the petition extends and transforms that theme by using God's creation of light as a metaphor for God's redemptive work. Its inclusion dilutes the integrity of the larger passage. To use another idiom, it confuses God's work in nature with God's work in history. That God also works in history is the theme of the next benediction in the sequence, the *Birkat HaTorah*, which praises God for choosing Israel and for the revelation of the Torah.[25]

But if we understand this liturgy as a case of "doing theology," and if we agree that it is not infrequent for rabbinic liturgy to transform a biblical doctrine, then this passage belongs perfectly. What it says in effect is that God's power ranges not only over nature but over history as well; that if God recreates nature daily, then God can recreate the fate of God's people on any day. In praising God for creating nature, we can also praise God for working in history. In fact, only a God who is sovereign over nature can be sovereign over history. The distinction between nature and history fades in the face of God's transcendent power over everything.

And this passage accomplishes all of this through the use of a singularly powerful literary device, whereby the light of nature becomes a metaphor for the light of God's favor.

CREATIONISM AS MYTH

My first encounter with the notion that religion has something to do with myth was in the magisterial, multivolume *Toledot Ha-Emunah Ha-Yisra'elit (History of Israelite Religion)*, published between 1937 and 1956, by the Israeli scholar Yehezkel Kaufmann. The opening chapters of this study are devoted to a comparative phenomenology of pagan and Israelite religions designed to document the author's thesis that monotheism could not have evolved out of paganism but, rather, constitutes a radical, revolutionary break with the pagan culture of the age. One of the differences between the two, Kaufmann maintains, is that whereas pagan religions are replete with myths, biblical monotheism is not.

Kaufmann can make this distinction because he defines myth as "the tale of the life of the gods."[26] The pagan god has a biography: he is born, he dies, he loves, he wars with other gods; his destiny is shaped by his interaction with these other gods and by their mutual dependency on a force that is superior to them all. In contrast, Kaufmann claims, the God of Israel has no biography: God is not born and does not die; God does not mate, and God is not challenged (except by human beings). God's will and God's power are sovereign and absolute over all of nature and history, not dependent on any prior force or power.

In retrospect, Kaufmann's definition of myth, though possibly in line with the state of scholarship on that subject decades ago, appears to us now as excessively narrow. Though we do continue to refer to narrative myths, our definition of myth now includes the notion of what we have called a structural myth, a phenomenological description in symbolic terms of an ordered world as it is, not only how it came to be. We have also expanded the definition of narrative myth to include stories of major, transformatory events that portray gods, or God, interacting with human beings in space and time. The biblical account of the revelation at Sinai in Exodus 19 is an example of that use.

The biblical accounts of creation are, explicitly, narrative myths and, implicitly, structural myths. They describe how the ordered world came to be, and they imply a portrait of what that world looks like. The most accurate description of that ordered world lies precisely in the benedictions that surround the daily recitation of the *Sh'ma*: the *Yotzer* blessing and the *Birkat HaTorah* before, and the *Ge'ulah* (redemption) blessing after. God reigns over all of creation, nature, and history, and maintains, daily, the created world; God is covenanted with Israel, having redeemed Israel from slavery and revealed a Teaching (*Torah*) that instructs the community on how it is to conduct its communal and personal life to please God; God rewards obedience and punishes transgression; God will again, in time, redeem that community and restore the original order of creation. The core of the structural version of the myth is the image of a transcendent, sovereign God who cares deeply about what transpires in nature and history.

One implication of this myth is that God abides "outside" the created world. At the beginning (in this liturgical version), there was only God. After creation, there was God and the world, and these two are distinct. That chasm is bridged in various ways: first, by God's constant concern for what goes on in the world; second, by the concrete expression of that concern in God's revelation of Torah; third, by God's interventions in history in the light of God's ongoing designs for humanity; and fourth, by human prayer.

That mythic model of creation is not the only one in Judaism. As discussed earlier, the sixteenth-century Safed mystics, disciples of Rabbi Isaac Luria, proposed a very different model: God creates by emanation, an explosion of God's own essential nature into a preexistent void. That emanated "God-matter" becomes the created world. This emanationist understanding of creation skirts two potential classic Jewish heresies, pantheism and dualism. It skirts pantheism by insisting that one facet of God's nature, *Ein Sof* (literally, "Infinity," not, as conventionally understood, "The Infinite One"), remains distinct from the world. It skirts dualism by insisting that ultimately these are simply two faces of the single God.

In this model, God is identified with the created world. The split between God and the world vanishes. The result is that what happens in the world also happens "in" or "to" God, not, as in the Bible, in the presence of God. If, as this mystical model teaches, the created world is "broken" through some primordial catastrophe that accompanied creation, then God too is "broken." The most imaginative metaphor for this state of God's brokenness is the "exile of the *Shekhinah*." In mystical literature, this suggests that the two aspects of God—God in Godself or God as Infinity, and God's presence in the created world—are split apart, only to be rejoined eschatologically. And if the world demands redemption, so does God, with the impetus for that redemptive process being Israel's performance of God's commandments. To put it somewhat concisely, in this model God is responsible for the state of brokenness in the world, and Israel for its repair.[27]

These alternative creation myths convey alternative images of the natural world and its relationship to God. In the mystical, emanationist model, the world is infused with the presence of God. God permeates creation, metaphysically. The created world becomes sacralized. We experience God by simply looking at the created world through the spectacles of this mystical model. To experience nature is to experience God.

In the biblical and liturgical model, God remains distant from what transpires in the world. God may care about the natural order, and God may command humans to care for it, but ultimately, God is not intrinsically or metaphysically affected by what transpires on earth. This is not to suggest that our behavior may please or anger God, but that God remains apart from the scene of human activity.

These two creation myths imply two different models for human activity. In the biblical-liturgical model, we are commanded to obey God's instructions on how to deal with the natural order, and hence to please God, for which we will be rewarded by bountiful crops, freedom from oppression by other nations, and a long and fruitful life. In the mystical model, our behavior has a sacramental quality. Every single divine command, even the most "humanistic" or interpersonal act, such as giving charity to the poor, when accompanied by an awareness of mystical cosmology and its understanding of redemption, not only redeems the world but also redeems God. To put it concisely, the first model recognizes the distinction between God's interpersonal commands, what may be called the realm of the ethical, and those commands that affect our relationship with God, the realm of ritual. In the mystical model, everything we do is ritual.

The mystical model is extraordinarily suggestive, but it is vulnerable on one significant issue. In effect, it denies the reality of the natural world. Nature becomes a shell that conceals (or reveals) God. For the mystic, enlightenment comes with the ability to "see through" the shells of our common experience and perceive God's presence in the world, which is the "really real," the ultimate reality. The mystic's relation to nature is intrinsically ambiguous. On the one hand, he venerates nature, but on the other hand, it is ultimately not nature itself that he venerates.[28]

Both of these models are mythic—as mythic as Darwin's evolutionary model with which all creationist models are conventionally contrasted. They are all attempts to disclose hidden or elusive patterns in our experience of the world in order to make that experience cohere and acquire meaning. It is precisely that mythic standing that makes it possible for proponents of the alternative models to speak to one another. None of them claims to be objectively true; each is a selective and interpretive version of "the facts." But without such interpretive visions, what we call "the facts" are simply a blooming confusion. Without them, we don't really know what "the facts" are in the first place. The covert message of the myths is not only a description of what happened aeons ago, but also a prescription as to where we are to locate ourselves within the created world, and how we are to live in accord with this vision.

Finally, though Jewish mysticism contributed much to Jewish liturgy, it did not substantially affect the liturgical tradition of creation, possibly because this liturgical version was firmly canonized centuries before the mystical model became popular, or possibly because of the pantheistic and dualistic implications of that model. With some relatively minor changes, that liturgical version remained securely anchored to the biblical version.

As Daniel Breslauer suggests in the title of his anthology *The Seductiveness of Jewish Myth*,[29] powerful, long-standing religious myths are extremely beguiling. They are properly indispensable, but they also contain within themselves the possibility of betrayal. Myths are betrayed when they are no longer understood as myths but as objective and factual. They then become idolatrous. The precarious stance of the modern believer requires that he accept the myth precisely as myth or, to use Tillich's language, as a "broken" and "living" myth, and therefore to mistrust it.[30]

IMPLICATIONS FOR PRACTICE

Finally, some thoughts on the implications of this discussion for the issue of liturgical change. The basic assumption of this inquiry is that in Judaism, the liturgy represents a primary locus for theological expression; here, Jews encounter Judaism's belief system. But this belief system was hardly static; as we have seen, it was transformed between the biblical and the rabbinic periods. Nor did this process end with the close of the Talmudic era. The image of an original, normative, enduring system of this kind persisting over generations is simply a fiction. To use our earlier terminology, the myth enjoys a certain plasticity.

This conclusion would seem to support the efforts of modern, post-Enlightenment Jews to continue to change the liturgy in the light of their own reformulations of Jewish beliefs. It would seem to justify, for example, the early Reform Jews' elimination of references to Israel's chosenness, the resurrection of the dead, the return to Zion, and the restoration of sacrifices from the liturgy.[31]

On the other hand, a convincing argument can be adduced in favor of a more conservative stance toward liturgical change. It is not unreasonable to attribute some "normative" authority to the biblical-rabbinical belief system and its liturgy. Jewish doctrines did continue to evolve in post-Talmudic times, but the liturgical impact of these further changes was relatively peripheral in comparison with those of the premedieval period. The structure of the core, daily, Sabbath, and festival liturgies and the rites of passage was basically canonized by that time. Further liturgical creativity, such as medieval liturgical poetry (the *piyyut*) or *kabbalat Shabbat*, the service that welcomes the Sabbath at sunset on Friday, took the form of additions to the basic structure, not changes within that structure.

Further, whether or not moderns believe as the authors of the biblical and rabbinic texts believed, there is at least a pedagogical value in exposing the worshiper to those original formulations. There should be one place in the worshiper's experience where that original version of the myth is articulated. The ensuing tension can be handled either outside the liturgical service, in the classroom, or by introducing explanatory comments that deal with the tension and justify the change "below the line," at the bottom of the page of the prayer book; or by providing the worshiper with various alternative versions of a specific prayer "above the line" in the service itself, with the original version included as one of these options.

Whatever position we take on this issue, what remains clear is that the liturgy represents the cutting edge of ideological or theological expression in Judaism. It is when the worshiper is confronted with a specific prayer book and the wording of a specific prayer that he or she must confront firsthand just what he or she believes and, therefore, where he or she belongs in the range of contemporary models of Jewish religious identity. That fact alone confirms our thesis that a primary resource for any authentic exploration of Jewish thought must include a close study of the liturgy.

CHAPTER 5

HOW WILL IT ALL END?

ESCHATOLOGY IN SCIENCE AND RELIGION

In retrospect, eschatology has been part of my theological agenda since I began to reflect on theology some fifty years ago. I recently came upon the essays I wrote for admission to rabbinical school back in the spring of 1954. To my amazement—I was then a rank undergraduate at McGill University—they were suffused with the issue of messianism. When I arrived at the Jewish Theological Seminary, one of my mentors, Professor Gerson Cohen (who later became chancellor of the Seminary) made an offhand remark to the effect that every significant Jewish movement had an eschatological impulse at its core. That remark stuck with me and remains one of many issues that I wish I could have explored with Gerson before his untimely death.

Eventually, that impulse culminated in my book-length study of Jewish thinking on the afterlife, *The Death of Death: Resurrection and Immortality in Jewish Thought* (Jewish Lights). My original plan had been to write a book on eschatology in general, but I soon realized that it was impossible to embrace the topic in one book. I then focused on what, to me, was the most interesting of the subtopics involved in Jewish eschatology—what happens to us when we die?

At the same time, I remained puzzled as to why eschatology was so significantly absent from the writings of my contemporaries in the field of Jewish theology. I recall with particular pain my late teacher Abraham Joshua Heschel's comments in a television interview that he gave just weeks before he died in 1972. Carl Stern of NBC asked him—Heschel didn't know that he was about to die—what do you think is going to happen to you after you die? Heschel responded, "I have so many things to worry about while I'm alive, I'll let God worry about what happens to me after I die." How could Heschel not think about what was going to happen to him after he died?

Interestingly, the one exception to this pattern was a book published in 1952 by Will Herberg, *Judaism and Modern Man*. It is probably not accidental that this was the book that brought me back to Judaism when I was at McGill. Herberg was a disenchanted Marxist, which explains why he was interested in eschatology and why he saw Marxist eschatology as an echo of the biblical model.

Equally puzzling to me is why Christian theologians are so preoccupied with eschatology. Why is it everywhere in contemporary Christian theology and so strikingly absent from the writings of twentieth-century Jewish thinkers? Still more puzzling to me is why our cosmologists and astronomers are so preoccupied with the question of how it all will end. It's almost as omnipresent in the writings of astronomers and cosmologists as it is in Christian theologians, and it has produced a new school of scientist-theologians, like Ian Barbour and John Polkinghorne, who try to graft a Christian eschatology onto their science.

Why do they care? Why is so much scientific money and energy poured into trying to understand how it will all end trillions and trillions of years from now?

WHY ESCHATOLOGY?

The term "eschatology" refers to that subfield of theology devoted to the discussion (*logos*) of the last things (*eschatos*). It was located within the field of theology because of the assumption that the "last things" would represent God's ultimate intervention in history. Today, we talk of secular eschatologies—Marxism, for example—and scientific eschatologies. Some would argue that Marxist eschatology is part of what makes Marxism a religion. So, perhaps, the term "secular eschatology" is an oxymoron after all.

But why the impulse to discuss the last things? Why are we curious as to what will happen at the end of time, or "after" the end of time, as if it is even possible to think of an "after" to the end of time? Why does all of this preoccupy us?

Speaking anthropologically, my sense is that it comes out of the human need to bring cosmos out of chaos, order out of anarchy. Human beings need structure. We structure space and we structure time. We create seconds, minutes, hours, days, weeks, months, years—what Heschel so felicitously named "the architecture of time." These structures bring order out of anarchy. Homogenized, structureless time would be chaotic.

Recently, as I was looking for a new academic calendar, I came across one that was composed of completely blank pages except for the date listed at the top. I said to myself, "What am I going to do with this?" I want a book that says 7:30, 7:45, 8, 8:15, 8:30, and so on, because if I have this blank page and I have to make an appointment, let's say for 8 a.m., where do I put it on the page? And, worse yet, what happens if I put it near the top and I end up having to make a 7:30 appointment? Do I put the 7:30 appointment below the 8 a.m. one with an arrow circling around?

Microscopically, we structure time. We need to know what time it is because otherwise we would be lost, we would be in a state of chaos. Macroscopically, we begin with creation and we end with the age to come. The Hebrew term *olam haba*, strictly speaking, is not the "world to come" but the "aeon to come." The word *olam* in Hebrew is ambiguous. It can mean "time" and it can mean "world." But when we refer to *olam haba*, as contrasted with *olam hazeh*, we refer to the age to come as opposed to this current age, the age of history—or, speaking from the perspective of science, from the big bang at the beginning to however the universe will end.

THE MIDDLE

One of the more mysterious claims I like to make is, if there is no beginning and no end, then there is no middle. And if there is no middle, then we don't know where we are; we can't locate ourselves in time. We are literally lost in a state of anarchy.

The attempt to wrest cosmos out of chaos is one of the classic definitions of religion. Clifford Geertz defines religion as "a system of symbols which acts to establish powerful, pervasive and long lasting moods and motivations in men by formulating conceptions of a general order of existence."[2] By this definition then, all eschatological definitions become, ipso facto, religious because they are ordering devices. They help us structure our experience. They provide the broadest possible frame for where we are in history, in nature, and in society. If we are preoccupied with creation, then we must, in a similar manner and for a similar reason, talk about eschatology. If we talk about the beginning, we have to define the end. Otherwise we don't know where we are.

On the other hand, stemming from a different impulse are what have come to be called utopian eschatologies, visions of an ideal state of affairs. These visions are impelled by the sense that the world in which we currently live is inherently flawed, and that human life as lived in this familiar world, is never totally fulfilled. Contributing to this sense, and speaking not out of logic but out of my very personal gut feeling, is the reality of death.

I've always felt that death is the ultimate absurdity, the ultimate eruption of chaos into a human life. I am aware that this is not a popular view and that there are many people who feel that any kind of death is a thoroughly natural and blessed event. It is the way nature revives itself and the way freshness and novelty enter into the world. When I read these descriptions of death, I feel like the tenured professor who has all of these untenured assistant professors waiting for him to move on so that they can become tenured professors as well. Death is natural, welcome, and blessed to these assistant professors.

If our lives are inherently flawed and unfulfilled, then it is thoroughly understandable for us to dream of an Eden. Now, we are no longer speaking of a beginning and an end, we are speaking of a specific kind of beginning and a specific kind of end, an Eden at the beginning and an Eden at the end. Time and history are cyclical. We always return to the beginning.

BEGINNINGS AND ENDINGS

In the biblical account, creation in Genesis 1 is not *ex nihilo*, something out of nothing, but rather something out of something. In Genesis 1:1, there were a lot of somethings out of which God fashioned the world: there was water, there was darkness, there was wind, and there was *tohu vavohu*—what my colleague Yochanan Muffs translates as "chaos shmaos." Therefore, God's initial creation was not *ex nihilo* but rather bringing order out of anarchy.

The whole account of creation, the whole Genesis 1 creation myth, is a structuring myth: God divides, God separates waters above and waters below; earth and sea; night and day; light and darkness; animals, vegetation, fish, birds, and human beings. Everything is ordered. And at the end, the climax of creation, is the Sabbath. On the Sabbath, the seventh day, God rested and the world was perfected. This is interrupted, of course, by the twofold story of rebellion—Adam and Eve and then Cain. Structurally they are one story or two versions of the same story. Both are displacement stories: Adam and Eve wanted to be God, Cain wanted to be his brother. God responds by saying, "if you want chaos, I'll give you chaos," whereupon exile and death enter into creation, and history begins its course, a course that will end with the restoration of an eternal Sabbath at the end of days. Every Sabbath that we enjoy in history is a recollection of the cosmos that was, and an anticipation of the cosmos that will be. It is both a reminder of God's creation—*zekher lema'aseh bereishit*—and a foretaste of the age to come—*me'ein olam haba*.

Gerson Cohen used to refer to the Sabbath as a surrogate eschatology—a whiff, in historical time, of what the perfectly ordered world might be like at the end. There are other surrogate eschatologies in the Jewish tradition, for example the last momets of the wedding service, when Jeremiah 33 is invoked. Here too, there is a messianic whiff in the air because those verses were uttered when Jeremiah was in jail and the Babylonians were at the gates, ready to destroy Jerusalem. God reassures the prophet: "Don't worry, people are going to get married again in the streets of Jerusalem." Marriage then becomes a surrogate eschatology, and the breaking of the glass at the end of the marriage ritual is a return to history. It reintroduces the chaotic element and the couple turns and goes back into the congregation to face history once again.

The same thing happens at the climax of the Passover seder when we bring Elijah, the messenger of redemption, the herald of the Messiah, into our homes. The story of redemption has been told, and we have come out of Egypt once again. Eschatology is alive and well in our dining rooms. Then we open the door and look outside to see that the world is not yet redeemed. This again marks our return to history. This back-and-forth continues throughout our liturgical year.

Biblical eschatology combines these two impulses. It stems from a need to define a beginning and an end to our experience of time, and it possesses a utopian quality. It corrects the flawed nature of our lives in the here and now and permits us to dream of an age when the flaws will disappear.

COSMOLOGY

According to cosmologists, the world will end ten thousand trillion, trillion, trillion, trillion, trillion years after the big bang (which occurred, roughly, 15 billion years ago). According to one account, after the epoch of proton decay, the only large objects remaining are black holes that eventually evaporate into photons and other types of radiation. At this point, only waste products will remain—mostly photons, neutrinos, electrons, and positrons wandering through a universe bigger than the mind can conceive. Occasionally, electrons and positrons meet and form atoms larger than the visible universe is today. From here into the infinite future the universe remains cold, dark, and dismal (*Time*, June 25, 2001). That forecast is based on the assumption that the universe will continue to expand, which is, I believe, the reigning assumption today.

However, until recently, the assumption was that gravity would eventually overtake the expanding universe and the forces unleashed by the big bang, causing the universe to fall back upon itself, and ending with the "big crunch" and a return to the point of singularity. This may set the stage for another big bang starting the process all over again. This is cyclical time with a vengeance.

There are even less optimistic scientific eschatologies concerning our own planet. We could be hit by an asteroid as we were 65 million years ago when the dinosaurs became extinct. Or, there could be a supernova explosion in our galaxy that would damage our planet with highly damaging radiation. And, of course, there is the mounting concern over global warming, the evidence for which is now "unequivocal,"[3] as well as all the possible pandemics that we are told might still be unleashed. However, the very processes of cultural evolution, which may bring some of these to pass, also have the potential to provide us with the resources to intervene and limit their effects.

What strikes me about these forecasts is that most deal with inanimate matter—stars, planets, and the sun. This is appropriate for physicists and cosmologists because these are the subject matter of their disciplines. Humans are irrelevant to these eschatologies; from the cosmic perspective the presence of humanity in the universe is trivial.

JEWISH ESCHATOLOGY

There is no underestimating the influence of classical Jewish eschatology. It effectively shaped Christian and Muslim eschatologies, its two daughter religions, as well as much of the thinking in the West, Marxism, for example. Jewish eschatology was an evolving process. In its most highly developed form, probably during the first few centuries of the common era, it had three dimensions: a universal dimension, a national dimension, and an individual dimension. What is the ultimate destiny of the world? What is the ultimate destiny of the Jewish people? And, what is the ultimate destiny of the individual human being?

The universal dimension is the oldest and the most enduring. Isaiah's vision from the eighth century BCE is of a world at peace, with social justice, universal recognition of the one God— the God of Israel—and people streaming to Zion to learn Torah from Israel (Isa. 11:1–10). Despite the changes that have characterized all of Jewish thought from antiquity to this day, and despite the denominationalism that has shaped Jewish life throughout the ages, this dream has remained at the center of Jewish eschatology to this very day.

The other two dimensions have not had the same good fortune. On the national level, in the early rabbinic period after the destruction of the Second Temple in 70 CE, the vision was that Israel would eventually return from exile, as it did after the destruction of the First Temple. Israel would become the master of its own destiny, rebuilding Jerusalem and the Temple, reinstituting the sacrificial ritual, and teaching Torah to the other nations of the world. That vision has died except among circles of religious Zionists, largely the victim of emancipation and the Enlightenment movement of the early nineteenth century. Exile is no longer considered a punishment, and the restoration of the Temple, if prayed for, is a dream deferred to the indefinite future. We'll let the Messiah worry about that one.

Finally, for the individual, in the Pentateuch itself, death is final. Later, at the very end of the biblical period, two doctrines emerge. The first, found in only two biblical texts, Daniel 12 and Isaiah 25–26, is the resurrection of bodies from the earth. The other, the eternity of the soul, is straight out of Plato and not found in Jewish sources until the early rabbinic period. It states that when we die our bodies are buried, but our souls survive in God's company. At end of days, when the messiah will come, God will lift our bodies from the earth and reunite them with our souls. We will be reconstituted as we were during our lifetime on earth and will come before God for judgment. That conflated notion, spiritual immortality together with bodily resurrection, remained canonical until the nineteenth century with some significant exceptions, notably Maimonides, who was too good an Aristotelian to accept the idea of resurrected bodies. However, it too was killed by the Enlightenment. Today bodily resurrection is pretty much ignored, whereas spiritual immortality remains very much in fashion.

This complex scenario, all three dimensions together, will be brought about by the advent of the Messiah, literally "the anointed one." Either an idealized human being or a semidivine being, the Messiah arrives either by God's will or by the inherent processes of an increasingly devoted spiritual humanity.

There are two striking contrasts between these two eschatological visions. The first is that the human factor, ignored in the scientific eschatologies, and properly so, is at the very heart of the Jewish vision. It is in the dream of a world at peace, the end of exile, and the ultimate conquest of death. At the same time, it has no interest in the fate of stars and moons, or of photons and neutrinos. And if it does, it is interesting to note how marginalized it is. There are apocalyptic visions in some of the prophets: Amos 5 and Zechariah 14 speak of a "Day of the Lord," a cosmic catastrophe where day becomes night and night becomes day and the entire cosmos is overturned. These apocalyptic scenarios portray a cosmic revolution that will touch both nature and history.

But these scenarios are marginal to the preeminent eschatological vision in Jewish sources. These sources echo the second creation story, found in Genesis 2 and 3. This creation myth, in contrast to the first in Genesis 1, emphasizes God's creation of the human person and places the rest of creation—the garden, the animals, and the vegetables—at the service of humankind. Jewish eschatology echoes this second creation story. It tries to recapture, at the end of time, the Eden that God created before the fall. As in Genesis 2–3 where God creates the world to serve humanity, so the dominant eschatological vision locates the human dimension at the heart of this age to come.

The second major difference is that the scientific eschatology, at the cosmic level, is totally predetermined. It is set in motion by the big bang and will run its course come what may. Whereas in the biblical account, the end-time will be determined by the will of God, either when the world will have sunk into a state of abominable evil, or, as in a different tradition, when the world will have achieved a level of sanctity. God will then send the Messiah to put the divine seal on a world now perfected. Still a third tradition, the kabbalistic myth of the sixteenth-century mystic Rabbi Isaac Luria, assigns the task of redemption to Israel. Now, the performance of the commandments with the proper mystical intent will repair the flaws in creation, thus redeeming the world and even redeeming God. The path to redemption is human, though the resources, the commandments, are God's gift to us.

My major theological argument for an afterlife, whether as resurrection or spiritual immortality, is based on the assumption that God must be more powerful than death. If at the end, death wins out, then death is God and we should worship death. My text is that popular folk song with which we end the Passover seder, "Had Gadya." It is the story where a father buys a goat for two *zuzim*; the cat bites the goat, the dog bites the cat, the stick hits the dog, the fire burns the stick, the water douses the fire, the cow drinks the water, the slaughterer slaughters the cow, and the angel of death slaughters the slaughterer. But the author knew not to end it there. He adds one last verse in which God slaughters the angel of death. In the hierarchy of power, God is even more powerful than the angel of death and, at the end, death too shall die.

THE EMOTIONAL DIMENSION

The scientific description of how it will all end, quoted above, provides a precise, clear, and coherent description of the end-time: "cold, dark, and dismal." "Cold and dark" can be taken as a literal description—cold because it will be physically cold, and dark because of the absence of light. But dismal? Dismal is a feeling and, likely, reflected how the author felt on reading or contemplating what these cosmologists said.

Recently, I was struck by something I found in the traditional liturgy, in the *Kedusha* of the morning service for Sabbath and festivals. It can be translated as follows:

> O our sovereign. Please manifest yourself from your abode and reign over us because we are longing for you. When will you reign over Zion? Soon, in our own day, for ever and ever. May our eyes see your kingdom as it is expressed in the song of David, your anointed one. God will reign forever from generation to generation, Hallelujah.

This was one of those passages I've been reciting since I was a kid, but only recently was I struck by its poignancy, by the plaintive quality of a community that is waiting for God. Where are you? When are you coming? We're longing for you.

HOPE

I first discovered the theological valence of hope in the work of the Christian existentialist philosopher Gabriel Marcel, on whom I wrote my doctoral dissertation. Since then, I have discovered hope everywhere in Christian sources. But, interestingly enough, despite "Hatikvah" (literally, "The Hope," the national hymn for the State of Israel)—which is not exactly a rousing religious or theological statement—it is nowhere in contemporary Jewish writings. Hope is not wishful thinking; it is not easy optimism. Marcel calls it hope against hope. Hope when the tests results are all positive, when the statistics are all against you, when everybody around you says "Stop denying." I portray this in medical terms because existentially, in our lives, it's precisely in those situations when we find swelling from within us a yearning, a hope, from some indeterminate source that somehow we'll make it. Where does that hope come from? Why is that inbred in us? To me, this is a theological and metaphysical statement about something deeply rooted in the human person. Part of my guess about its origins comes from the rush to label it denial: "Face the reality"; "it's finished"; "give up hope." The rush to deny hope is the best testimony to its weight and gravity. On a cosmic scale, it is in confronting all of the imperfections in this world, all of the flaws that challenge us on a day-to-day basis and all of the unfulfilled dimensions of our personal lives, that we hope. The ultimate hope is eschatological hope. Somehow, somewhere, there will be an age when these flaws disappear.

THREE CONCLUDING POINTS

First, why the difference in emphasis between Christian and Jewish eschatology? Why is it omnipresent in Christianity and so subdued in Judaism? I remain puzzled, but—and this is an imperfect answer—perhaps it is because halakhah, the system of commandments that the religious Jew is committed to perform, provides the Jew with a realized eschatology. If the goal of an eschatological description is to describe a structured world, then it seems to me that halakhah provides such structure in the here and now. It is something that cannot be appreciated by reading a book. The only way one can appreciate it is by living it. And, in doing so, one is provided with a very powerful sense of how the commandments lend structure to every moment of one's waking life. And, that's a gift.

That is the reason why, when I talk about eschatology, people say to me: "Forget about it, Judaism is a this-worldly religion. We're not concerned about what is going to happen afterward, we're just concerned with what happens in the here and now." And, of course, this is true. But, we can say that it is a this-worldly religion because Judaism has this very powerful structure at hand. My sense is that Judaism has this realized eschatology in the here and now.

I'm aware of the fact that Christianity also has a realized eschatology, and that "Christ is risen." Not *has* risen but *is* risen and is present in the life of the Church and in the life of the believing Christian. However, my sense remains that there is a qualitative difference in the day-to-day life experience of the Jew.

Second, all eschatological language is inherently and invariably mythic in the academic sense of myth. Rarely has there been a time when science and religion have had so much in common. The ancient conflict between science and religion is properly behind us. Both disciplines now realize that they deal with realities way beyond the very possibility of any form of human experience. And both are doing the same thing—trying to explain the world we see by referring to a world we do not see. Both find the ultimate explanation for the immediately visible by postulating a world that is invisible and accounts for why things are the way they are. That is what myths do—they deal with the invisible to explain the visible.

A number of years ago, The Jewish Theological Seminary gave an honorary degree to an Israeli astronomer. As the faculty was roaming around prior to the procession, I walked over to him and said: "Can I ask you a question? It's the first time I've ever been able to talk to an astronomer. Was the big bang loud?" "Of course not," he replied, "there was no air so there was no sound." Then he asked, "Who are you?" After I told him I was a professor, he asked what I taught. I said "theology." At this point, he smiled and said "You know what? Big bang is much more theology than it is science. Both are poetry."

I subsequently discovered that an airplane's "black box," which retains the record of an aircraft's maneuvers and provides crucial data in plane-crash investigations, is not black. This is obvious; if it were black, you wouldn't be able to find it after a crash. It's orange. So black boxes are not black, and big bangs are not loud.

Finally, American microbiologist Professor Robert Pollack, in his review of *The God of Hope and the End of the World* by British theologian John Polkinghorne, suggests three possible models for the interrelationship of science and theology: either the neutral acceptance of both science and theology; or the presumption that one of the two holds the more important reality; or, last, the active acceptance of both at once. Pollack favors the last of these, as does Polkinghorne and most of the representatives of this relatively new school of scientists-theologians, which is largely made up of Christian thinkers.

I must confess, however, that I favor the first. My sense is that these are two equally valuable master stories dealing with equally significant realities that, for the most part, do not intersect. The reason for this is hope. There is no room for hope in contemporary cosmology. And if there is no room for hope, then my life has become absurd. Absurdity is the final verdict. Therefore, it is my conviction that eschatology has to serve as the cornerstone of all theology. Without hope, human life is meaningless. Without hope, creation is meaningless.

The evidence of history is very ambiguous. On one hand, I have that incredible violin solo in the "Benedictus" of Beethoven's *Missa Solemnis*, which I can hear daily and cry each time. There is the creativity that I feel dwelling within me as I write and the sheer joy that I experience when I teach.

But then, there is that incredible incident when a tree falls on a car speeding down the Saw Mill River Parkway on a beautiful, warm spring day. There is no thunder, no lightning, no storm, no wind. Yet, a tree falls as the car drives underneath it. The tree hits the front of the car; two parents are killed, while the young child strapped into the backseat survives. There is the twelve-year-old I visit at Memorial Sloan Kettering who is dying of leukemia. There are hurricanes, holocausts, and our unbelievable inability to prevent famine and mass killings in Africa. Will it all end in a whimper or with a bang? Is it all pointless?

Polkinghorne understands this. He writes:

> If [the universe] simply ends with a bang or collapse or the whimper of decay, it runs into incompleteness. Is the cosmos, after all, as pointless as Stephen Weinberg believes, so that its story is really a tale of chaos? Are the deep order of the world, and the fruitfulness of its history, hints of its being a creation, or are they just happy accidents in a meaningless process? Are human intuitions of hope windows into a divine reality, or are they comforting illusions that offer us delusive support as we battle to survive? If the universe really is God's creation, the ambiguity of its past history and present prospects will have to be resolved in its final end. In the "Four Quartets," T. S. Eliot struggled with how meaning is to be found in the co-inherence of beginning and ending. "In my beginning is my end." The reason that eschatology is such an indispensable element in theological thinking is that it responds to the question of the total meaning fullness of the present creation, a meaning that can only be found beyond science's extrapolation of contemporary history.[4]

CHAPTER 6

BEYOND *WISSENSCHAFT*

THE RESURRECTION OF RESURRECTION IN

JEWISH THOUGHT SINCE 1950

In *The Death of Death* (Jewish Lights), my book on the subject of resurrection and immortality in Jewish thought, I summarized the historical development of these ideas in Judaism as follows: With the exception of three brief passages (Isaiah 25:8, 26:19, and Daniel 12)—all relatively late in the biblical corpus—the Bible denies any form of life after death other than some form of shadowy persistence in what is termed *sheol*.

In the early postbiblical period, two doctrines of the afterlife become progressively more prominent in rabbinic and apocryphal texts: the resurrection of the body and the immortality of the soul. These two doctrines are soon conflated in rabbinic texts, which describe how the soul separates from the body at death and journeys to God, while the body disintegrates in the earth. At the end of days, according to the Rabbis, the body and its soul will be reunited and the individual human being, reconstituted as during life on earth, will come before God in judgment.

With some prominent exceptions (for example, in the writings of Maimonides), this conflated doctrine, in one form or another, becomes canonical until the early nineteenth century, when bodily resurrection is dismissed by all but the more traditionalist wings of the religious community, leaving spiritual immortality as the sole acceptable doctrine for modern Jews. The clearest indication of this change is found in the liturgy of the early and later reformers, German and American, where the phrase *mehaye hametim* ("who gives life to the dead") is removed from the *Gevurot* blessing in the *Amidah* in favor of some alternative formula (*mehaye hakol*, "source of life").

During the second half of the twentieth century, this trend begins to be reversed. Quite suddenly, bodily resurrection is not only reconsidered in liberal theological circles but there are those who even claim it to be preferable to spiritual immortality. The idea begins to make its way into the liturgy of American Reform.

What accounts for this recent and rather unexpected reversal in the fate of the doctrines of resurrection and immortality?

As noted, the most explicit rejection of bodily resurrection can be traced in the platforms, programmatic statements, theological writings, and liturgies of classical Reform Judaism, first in Europe and later in America.[1] It was echoed in the thinking of Mordecai Kaplan and in the liturgies he created for the Reconstructionist movement;[2] in a much more muted form, it can also be discerned in the theological writings (though not in the liturgies) of America's middle-of-the-road Conservative Judaism.[3] In the 150 years separating the dawn of the Jewish Enlightenment and the middle of the twentieth century, there was no serious consideration of the notion of bodily resurrection by thinkers from the liberal wing of the Jewish community. Since 1950, however, that doctrine has returned to the liberal theological agenda, as advocated in the writings of a number of eminent American Jewish theologians.[4]

The first of these is Will Herberg, whose *Judaism and Modern Man* was widely read at the time of its publication in 1951. What may be the richest chapter in the entire book is Herberg's discussion of eschatology, in which he reviews the doctrines of the resurrection of the body and the immortality of the

69

soul.[5] Herberg terms the former "outrageous"—but indispensable—while dismissing the latter as rooted in the antihistorical and otherworldly outlook of Greek and Eastern thought.

Resurrection is indispensable, Herberg claims, first, because it teaches that man's ultimate destiny "comes to him solely by the grace and mercy of God," not by virtue of his possessing an immortal soul; second, because it teaches that what is destined to be fulfilled is the "*whole* man—body, soul, and spirit"; and third, because the whole point of the doctrine is that "the life we live now, the life of the body, the life of empirical existence in society, has some measure of permanent worth in the eyes of God." This doctrine, then, is an affirmation of the value to God of history and society and of the only life human beings can know, that of embodied individuals. Finally, for Herberg, the doctrine is a "symbol," not the "literalistic pseudo-biological" fantasy either of the traditionalists who accept it, or of the reformers who reject it.

Arthur A. Cohen, who (like Herberg) was strongly influenced by the writings of Martin Buber and Franz Rosenzweig, also concedes that the doctrine of resurrection is "unpersuasive," "alogical," and "antirational." Yet it is precisely because of its unpersuasive nature that the doctrine must be accepted, he argues, because it is a "miracle that God works for the individual." More specifically: "What fails within nature and dies is restored in the kingdom, transformed, strained of the agitation of the flesh, and purified by miraculous grace." In short, it is a statement about God's ultimate power: "God bestows upon the dead a unity analogous to that which he has won for himself." A God who is truly God must be able to work such paradoxes.[6]

Richard Levy, a representative of the more traditionalist wing of Reform, argues that Reform should reconsider the doctrine for three reasons: "It is faithful to the nature of our being as creations of God; it is compatible with the basic covenantal promise that has bound our people with God ... ; and by its connection with the messianic promise,[7] it binds us to *Eretz Yisrael* in a manner that political and cultural Zionism fails to do." In a more general way, Levy argues that Reform should reaffirm the doctrines of Judaism as they were known by Jews who lived prior to the Enlightenment.[8]

Steven Schwarzschild, also of the Reform movement, argues as well for bodily resurrection because it asserts "what is nowadays called the psychosomatic unity, or the embodiedsoul [*sic*]/ensouled-body, of the human individual and the infinite ethical tasks incumbent upon him or her."[9] Herschel Matt, a close friend and disciple of Will Herberg's, echoes all of Herberg's arguments. Belief in resurrection is required because "to believe in the Creator-God ... is to trust in a fulfillment of our life that is beyond history." He believes in resurrection because the doctrine affirms that the body is no less God's creation, because the notion of a bodiless soul runs counter to one's experience of oneself, and because it affirms the significance of one's existence within society. Finally, echoing Herberg's reference to the doctrine as a "symbol," Matt calls it a "myth."[10]

Before turning to Eugene Borowitz, arguably the reigning theologian of American Reform, it is worth considering another recent reaffirmation of resurrection, this one an article written in 1992 by Michael Wyschogrod, a prominent Orthodox theologian. It is not surprising that an Orthodox theologian should reaffirm a traditional Jewish doctrine. What is significant about Wyschogrod's article is that he submits this traditional doctrine to a systematic and rigorous theological defense. Moreover, this defense echoes many of the arguments provided by the more liberal thinkers considered thus far—mainly, that belief in resurrection is demanded by the Jewish concept of God. Wyschogrod insists, in brief, that "because God is a redeeming God, it follows that death cannot be the last word.... Either death wins or God saves."[11]

It is in the writings of Borowitz, however, that we find perhaps the most dramatic example of the recent turnabout in the fate of the two doctrines of resurrection and immortality. A prolific author and teacher of generations of Reform rabbis, Borowitz was a moving force in the composition of the 1976

Centenary Perspective, the third of American Reform's historic platforms. Within this platform is a statement on the afterlife that reflects a slight change in emphasis from a parallel statement in the earlier Columbus Platform of 1937. In the words of the 1937 statement, "Judaism affirms that man is created in the Divine image. His spirit is immortal." The 1976 statement removes the advocacy of spiritual immortality in favor of some more ambiguous form of eternal life: "Amid the mystery we call life, we affirm that human beings, created in God's image, share in God's eternity despite the mystery we call death."[12] In two extended elaborations of that 1976 statement, one a separate book-length commentary on the Centenary Perspective published in 1982[13] and the other contained in his *Liberal Judaism*, a comprehensive statement of his personal theology published a year later, Borowitz confesses that while he has no knowledge of what awaits him after his death, he is yet "inclined to think that my hope is better spoken of as resurrection than immortality for I do not know myself as a soul without a body but only as a psychosomatic self."[14]

Unlike Reform Judaism, throughout its entire history the Conservative movement has published only one statement of principles. Titled *Emet Ve-Emunah: Statement of Principles of Conservative Judaism*, the document was composed in 1988 by a joint commission of academicians, rabbis, and laypeople who represented all streams of thought within the movement. Though originally presented at a conference of the movement's Rabbinical Assembly, *Emet Ve-Emunah* has never achieved the canonical standing of Reform's platforms: it was never subjected to a movement-wide discussion, nor was it ever formally voted on. Nonetheless, it reflects the consensus of a representative body of Conservative Jews. As a member of the commission, I authored the draft text on eschatology that appears in *Emet Ve-Emunah* as "Eschatology: Our Vision of the Future," where it is noted that the two doctrines of resurrection and immortality of the soul have been understood in a widely varying manner, by some as literal truths, by others "in a more figurative way."[15]

Finally, we should note two full-length books, one stemming from Reform and the other from the Jewish Renewal movement. The first, *What Happens after I Die? Jewish Views of Life after Death*, edited by two Reform rabbis, begins with a brief overview of traditional Jewish teachings on the issue and concludes with eight cautiously agnostic personal statements.[16] The second, Simcha Paull Raphael's *Jewish Views of the Afterlife*, draws heavily from the Jewish mystical tradition, contemporary thanatology, Buddhist and Hindu teachings, the transpersonal school of psychology, and the writings of Elisabeth Kübler-Ross, the Swiss psychiatrist best known for her study of death and dying. It includes a thorough summary of traditional teachings on the afterlife, including the doctrine of resurrection, but places a greater emphasis on the spiritual dimensions of life after death.[17]

To summarize, the principal arguments for the recent reaffirmation of the doctrine of bodily resurrection are both theological and anthropological. The theological argument suggests that God, in order to be really God, must be stronger than death. If death wins out, then death is God and we should worship death—which is inconceivable. Although this appears to be a broadly based argument for some form of life after death, it is more an argument for bodily resurrection than for the immortality of the soul. In the latter case, God does not have to do anything; the soul is immortal because of its very nature. It simply never dies. But resurrection demands an aggressive expression of divine power. That is precisely why it appears liturgically in the second blessing of the *Amidah*, appropriately called *Gevurot*, or (God's) power.

The anthropological argument is more directly related to resurrection. It insists that we are intrinsically related to our bodies, that in fact we are our bodies, that without our bodies we simply would not be. Therefore, whatever God has in store for us after our death must also affect our bodies. This argument affirms our psychosomatic identity; it is a deliberate refutation of any dualistic view of the human person. At the same time, it also affirms the significance of history and society, in which our embodied selves are located.

Finally, throughout this material, we find references to the fact that the doctrine should not be interpreted as a biological statement but rather as a symbolic or mythic statement— where "myth" is understood in its more academic sense as a complex pattern of meaning that lends coherence to a body of experience.[18]

In attempting to account for the recent reconsideration of the doctrine of bodily resurrection, the place to begin is the American Reform movement, which has experienced a rather remarkable change in rhetoric over the past several decades. That movement's transformation is but one dimension of a much broader phenomenon affecting the forms of Jewish religious expression in America during the past half century, as will soon be discussed.

BEYOND CLASSICAL REFORM JUDAISM

American Reform Judaism today is very different from what it was half a century ago. That change is manifest, among other things, in its affirmation of Zionism, its acknowledgment of the indispensability of Hebrew as the authentic language of religious Jewish expression, its eagerness to embrace traditional forms of Jewish learning, and its advocating the introduction of traditional Jewish rituals in Reform homes and synagogues.

On a programmatic level, evidence of Reform's internal transformation can be discerned by comparing the founding document of American Reform, the Pittsburgh Platform of 1885, with a proposed new platform that came under intense discussion in 1998–1999 before being adopted in a revised form at the Central Conference of American Rabbis in 1999.

The 1885 platform recognizes in the "Mosaic legislation" a "system of training the Jewish people for its national life in Palestine." However, it accepts as binding "only the moral laws

... and such ceremonies as elevate and sanctify our lives," refusing to accept those laws that are not adapted "to the views and habits of modern civilization." It also rejects "all such Mosaic and rabbinical laws as regulate diet, priestly purity and dress, originating in ages ... altogether foreign to our mental and spiritual state." It affirms that "we consider ourselves no longer a nation, but a religious community, and therefore expect neither a return to Palestine, nor a sacrificial worship under the sons of Aaron." Finally, it asserts that "the soul of man is immortal," but it rejects "as ideas not rooted in Judaism the beliefs both in bodily resurrection and in Gehenna and Eden [Hell and Paradise] as abodes for everlasting punishment and reward."[19]

As noted earlier, between 1885 and 1999, American Reform produced two further statements of principles, the Columbus Platform of 1937 and the Centenary Perspective of 1976, each marked by a progressive attenuation of the more stridently liberal claims of the Pittsburgh Platform. For example, the 1976 statement advocates "creating a Jewish home centered on family devotion ... private prayer and daily worship, daily religious observance, keeping the Sabbath and the holy days, celebrating the major events of life." The Columbus Platform echoes the 1885 platform in affirming spiritual immortality, but in contrast with its predecessor (and in common with the Centenary Perspective), it is silent on bodily resurrection.

In 1998, Richard Levy, the president of the Central Conference of American Rabbis (CCAR), proposed the formulation of a new platform for Reform Judaism. In preparation, he wrote "Ten Principles," which he expounded at length in an interview appearing in the Winter 1998 issue of *Reform Judaism* (vol. 27, no. 2, pp. 14–22). From the outset, these principles provoked intense discussion. Indeed, an editorial comment in the magazine warned readers that much of what Levy suggested constituted a "radical departure from the earlier platforms" in calling "for the reclaiming of some traditional practices rejected by our Reform forefathers and for embracing new pathways to holiness and social justice."[20]

In the interview, Levy deplored the continuing influence of the 1885 platform. He advocated that Reform Jews "listen to the call of *mitzvot* [commands]." He noted that even the Centenary Perspective used the term "obligation" instead of the Hebrew term. Moreover, they should acknowledge the authority not only of "our individual understanding of what is holy"—a reference to Reform's classical insistence on individual autonomy in determining belief and practice—but also of "the ever-growing body of interpretations by *Kenesset Yisrael,* the eternal community of the Jewish people." In his new guidelines, Levy explained, "Jewish life-cycle, ritual, and holiday observances are emphasized more than ever before. We are encouraged to observe *Shabbat*" (not, as previously, "the Sabbath"). Levy also enjoined his fellow Reform Jews to "to read, pray, study and speak in Hebrew." Referring to Leviticus 19, he noted that the text "shows us the way to *kedushah* [holiness] ... through *mitzvot.*" And in what may be the most radical departure from previous statements of principles, he called as well for a serious consideration of kashrut, both as an expression of "the spiritual dimension of what we consume," and because "a kosher diet ... can also respond to ethical injunctions."

These are but snippets of a much more extended discussion that touches on theological issues (the authority of Torah), divisive issues in the American Jewish community (patrilineal descent; the status of the gay and lesbian community), and the traditional Reform emphasis on social action. Toward the end of the interview, Levy is asked if his "right-of-center" positions might estrange him from the majority of Reform rabbis. His response is that, whereas the original Pittsburgh Platform essentially told Reform Jews what "you *don't* have permission" to do (for example, kiss the tzitzit, or ritual fringes, during the recitation of the *Sh'ma* prayer), the fact that more Reform rabbis are now doing so is liberating their congregants to "experience more ways of living a holy life."

Countering Levy in the same issue (pp. 23–27) is Robert Seltzer, a rabbi and professor of Jewish history at Hunter College and at the City University of New York Graduate School. The title of his response, "This Is Not the Way," forecasts what is to follow. Seltzer begins by alerting Reform Jews that they must "guard against turning Reform Judaism into Conservative Judaism." An increase in piety and traditionalism may obscure the essence of Reform Judaism, which is that Reform beliefs and practices ought to be "rationally consistent, intellectually coherent, and subject to critical inquiry." The 1885 Pittsburgh Platform, Seltzer claims, "is not as outdated as Rabbi Levy contends," even though it clings to a faith in the essential goodness of human beings and inexorable progress in a way that "appears naive in light of the horrors of the twentieth century." Levy's draft document, in contrast, "errs in the opposite direction, expressing a certain cultural pessimism." Moreover, Seltzer continues, any new statement of principles must guard against the "tendency to turn the hands of the clock backward instead of forward." As evidence of this proclivity, Seltzer attacks Levy's endorsement of kashrut, which for most Reform Jews, "is no litmus test of Jewish identity or spirituality."

The debate over Levy's proposals raged within the movement both before and during the CCAR convention of 1999. An editorial comment in the following (Spring 1999) issue of *Reform Judaism* described various reactions, some of them published and others appearing on the movement's web pages. (A rough survey indicates that those opposing Levy's proposals outnumbered those supporting them by a ratio of at least two to one.) Among the views appearing in *Reform Judaism* was that of Eric Yoffie—the current president of the Union for Reform Judaism and arguably the preeminent spokesman for American Reform—who "questioned the creation of a new set of principles at this time." Over time, Levy's "Ten Principles" were revised six times before being adopted, in significantly attenuated form, at the 1999 convention.

In its final version, Levy's original ten principles have been expanded to thirty principles that are divided into three broad topics: God, Torah, and Israel. They include a number of references

77

to the performance of the "*mitzvot* (sacred obligations)" as a way of responding to God, some of which "demand renewed attention as the result of the unique context of our own times" (for example, "*Shabbat* ... calls us to culminate the workweek with *kedushah* [holiness], *menuchah* [rest], and *oneg* [joy]"). Significantly, there is no reference to the dietary laws, perhaps the most controversial of Levy's suggestions. Regarding immortality, the section on God concludes with the following statement: "We trust in our tradition's promise that, although God created us as finite human beings, the spirit within us is eternal"—a curious amalgam of the previous statements of 1937 and 1976.[21]

Although a considerable divide separates Levy's original principles from the ones that were finally adopted, the fact that a prominent Reform rabbi even considered proposals of this kind is significant, as is the fact that they were given serious consideration and received a certain amount of support. Even the rhetoric of the final, drastically toned-down text shows how far American Reform has strayed from its origins.

Similar indications of change are evident at the annual summer study *kallot* (retreats) sponsored by Reform's Commission on Jewish Growth. Meeting in various locations around the country, these four- to five-day retreats attract several hundred lay members of the Reform movement. Participants worship twice daily, and *kippot* and *tallitot* are omnipresent on men and women; as a guest participant, I have been asked several times to instruct men and women on how to don *tefillin*. Although the Reform liturgy is used, services are conducted almost exclusively in Hebrew. The meals are not kosher, but pork products and shellfish are avoided and vegetarian alternatives are always available. Shabbat is spent in worship, study, singing, and rest, and always concludes with the *havdalah* ceremony. On one occasion when the retreat coincided with Tisha B'av (a traditional communal fast day), a number of participants joined me in breaking the fast at day's end. Particularly interesting is the rhetoric employed at such retreats, which indicates that both the lay and rabbinic leadership of the *kallot* consider the retreats' participants to be the model Reform Jews for the movement's future. Although the number of participants is not large in proportion to the size of the movement, I have observed similar patterns of religious observance in many Reform congregations where I have visited as a weekend guest.

BEYOND *WISSENSCHAFT*

As noted, the transformation of American Reform is but one instance of a much broader change in the character of American Jewry as a whole. Although noted by many scholars, that broader transformation is more elusive since it is not reflected in formal programmatic statements. Nonetheless, what is inescapable to any serious observer of American Jewish life today is the continuing and growing search for specifically Jewish forms of what is conventionally called "spirituality."

The modern spiritual impulse finds various means of expression in Jewish society. There is the emergence of the Jewish Renewal and *havurah* movements; the striking liturgical and ritual creativity among Jewish feminists; the flourishing synagogues on the model of Manhattan's B'nai Jeshurun, where hundreds of worshipers sing and dance their way through a *kabbalat Shabbat* service. There is the oft-noted concern for what Judaism has to say about environmental and ecological issues and the flowering of Jewish Lights Publishing, whose motto is "words for the soul, made in Vermont." There is also the renewed popularity of the neo-Hasidic writings of Martin Buber and Abraham Joshua Heschel, alongside the writings of Reform's Lawrence Kushner and the late Aryeh Kaplan—and, more generally, the fascination with popular forms of Jewish mysticism and Hasidism. In its more extreme form, the search for spirituality is marked by a tendency to syncretize Judaism with Eastern religions such as Buddhism. All of this, of course, reflects a much broader cross-cultural phenomenon that perhaps can best be captured by the following anecdote. Visiting one of

Manhattan's "super-bookstores," I asked to be directed to the section containing books on religion. I was shown to two shelves marked "Religion." But immediately next to them, I found five floor-to-ceiling shelves labeled "Spirituality," which contained a generous selection of writings not only by Buber and Heschel, but also by the noted Israeli scholars of Jewish mysticism, Gershom Scholem and Moshe Idel.

The new worldview may be regarded as a Jewish expression of what has come to be called "postmodernism" (although that term is even more elusive than "spirituality"). It is marked by a religious romanticism, a suspicion of rationalist models of theological inquiry, and an emphasis on the emotional, affective dimension of the individual's relationship with God over the more rational or structured expression of that relationship. To use traditional polarities, the stress is on *kavanah* (inwardness) rather than *keva* (structure),[22] aggadah rather than halakhah (narrative over law). In consequence, the dominant scientific-technological-rationalistic outlook of the past century is now viewed as inadequate for dealing with what might be broadly called "meaning of life" issues.

A similar spirit has begun to transform the academic study of Judaism. Since the dawn of the Enlightenment, the reigning paradigm for the study of Judaism was *Wissenschaft des Judentums*, literally the "science of Judaism," identified by the eponymous school that emerged in nineteenth-century German Jewish academic circles. *Wissenschaft* emphasized the critical, dispassionate, or "scientific" approach to the study of Jewish texts and institutions, subjecting Judaism to the same scholarly criteria that were applied to other ancient cultures or bodies of literature. The more personal, subjective, faith-oriented stance of the academician was to be ignored; for the purposes of scholarly inquiry, the goal was to discover the scholarly "truth" concerning the issue at hand, whatever its source or its implications. In the study of ancient texts, for example, *Wissenschaft*'s goal was to come as close as possible to the *p'shat*, or literal meaning of the text—the original intent of its author or authors, as opposed to its accumulated homiletical or midrashic layers. Finally, the enterprise as a whole was thoroughly imbued with historicism: the assumption that everything Jewish had a history; the attempt to trace the historical evolution of any given Jewish text or institution through the ages; and the religious and historical impact of Judaism's encounter with successive surrounding cultures. *Wissenschaft*, in short, was a thoroughly relativizing and inherently secularizing enterprise.[23]

In fairness to the generations of scholars who pursued that enterprise, their approach to the study of Torah served a noble purpose. They were convinced that the scientific study of Judaism was indispensable in order for Judaism to be perceived (both by Jews and non-Jews) as congenial with the temper of modernity. The yeshiva style of Jewish learning was an impediment to this broader goal: for Judaism to adapt successfully to the modern age, it had to be open to the clear light of Western, scholarly methodologies.

By the end of the nineteenth century, *Wissenschaft* had come to be enthroned in the first centers for advanced Jewish learning in America, namely, the Reform movement's Hebrew Union College in Cincinnati (founded in 1875) and the Conservative movement's Jewish Theological Seminary of America in New York (founded in 1887).[24] Both the founding faculties and the curricula of these early rabbinical schools were exemplars of *Wissenschaft* principles, which in turn suggested an implicit model of the American rabbinate. In effect, these seminaries were superb graduate schools. Their stated purpose was to create rabbis; after all, what other forms of religious leadership did the American Jewish community require at that time, and what other goal could induce the community to fund these schools? Nor were there academic positions awaiting their graduates. Nonetheless, these rabbis were meant to be miniature versions of their teachers, who themselves were appointed because of their academic qualifications. Very few faculty members had served as rabbis of American congregations.[25]

In hindsight, it is easy to characterize this enterprise as totally dysfunctional. But in its historical and cultural context, it was quite appropriate; the schools and their faculties were doing what they did best. Early leaders of the Reform and Conservative movements were also convinced that their seminaries would serve as the next link in the long chain of Torah centers originating in Jerusalem and Yavneh and continuing in the academies of Babylonia (and later, in Western and Eastern Europe). They sensed that no great Jewish community had ever survived without a significant center for the study of Torah, and they had begun to realize that the great European academies were, for one reason or another, soon to become extinct. The future lay in America. Consciously or not, they assumed that neither East European Orthodox Judaism nor its yeshiva style of learning would make a successful transition to the New World. Of course, we now know that they were wrong on both counts. Nonetheless, this model of rabbinic education persisted until the 1950s.[26]

Together with many other factors, preeminently the move to suburbia and the growing acculturation of American Jewry, this academic model of the rabbinate played a decisive role in shaping the prevailing model of American Jewish congregational life. It was embodied in the classical "cathedral synagogue"—a large sanctuary, seats arranged in theaterlike rows, a high, frontal bimah, and a formal, highly choreographed service led by the rabbi and cantor accompanied by choir and organ, with the congregants relegated to the largely passive role of spectators. My own observations, confirmed by anecdotal reports of adult Jews who were raised in these settings, suggest that the sermons delivered by these "cathedral synagogue" rabbis studiously avoided topics that might be called "religious." Instead they were devoted to general topics such as anti-Semitism, Zionism, Jewish education, or current affairs (and especially, from the 1960s onward, such matters as the Holocaust, Soviet Jewry, and the Israeli-Arab conflict). Far less in evidence was any discussion of God, Torah, mitzvot, prayer, Jewish ritual life or, more generally, "meaning of life" issues such as alienation, illness and death, the dissolution of marriage and the family, sexuality, or the ambiguities of the moral life. Few rabbis could teach what they had not been taught in their years of training, namely, what Judaism had to say about all of these issues. Their education had emphasized what the classical texts had meant to their authors, not what they could mean to them or to their congregants.

It is clear that the new search for spirituality on the part of American Jews represents a vigorous and explicit rejection of the cathedral synagogue model. Old-style rabbis and their synagogues have been forced to reach some measure of accommodation with new forms of expression; the alternative is that their congregants will simply go elsewhere. The transformations in American Reform Judaism as outlined earlier are but one indication of this broader transformation in American Jewish religious life.

More directly related to the agenda of this article is the impact of all of these changes on recent developments in the enterprise of American Jewish theology. In accordance with the *Wissenschaft* model, theology was taught as merely one dimension of Jewish intellectual history. To the extent that rabbinical students were taught theology at all—the curriculum was heavily weighted in favor of the study of biblical and rabbinic texts—the emphasis was on what the great Jewish thinkers of past centuries had to say. The new model, in contrast, encourages students to evolve their own working theology, informed not only by historical Jewish philosophers but also by modern thinkers such as Martin Buber, Franz Rosenzweig, Mordecai Kaplan, and Abraham Joshua Heschel, along with younger disciples such as Emil Fackenheim, Will Herberg, Eugene Borowitz, and Harold Schulweis. It has also led to an appropriation of the language of myth and symbol as a way of characterizing theological thinking and language.

It is specifically the last of these matters that touches on the issue of resurrection. Reformers of the nineteenth century rejected the notion of bodily resurrection because it offended the rationalist, critical temper of their time. The only way they could understand it was as "the literalistic pseudo-biological" fantasy dismissed by Will Herberg—which of course was the way it had been understood and accepted by traditionalist thinkers throughout the ages. Yet as we have seen, it is precisely the "unpersuasive," "outrageous," "antirational," "alogical," "paradoxical," "symbolic," or "mythic" character of the doctrine that recommends it to the new generation of theologians discussed above.

The doctrine of bodily resurrection is one dimension of the broader Jewish eschatological myth. Both eschatology and the doctrines of creation deal with aeons that lie beyond direct human apprehension. They provide the widest framework of meaning for Jews try to make sense of their own historical experience, which lies in between these two "beyonds." Put somewhat differently, they help Jews understand "where they are now" in history, and thus lend a measure of integrity to the vastly larger canvas of human experience. Although the doctrine of resurrection may seem to describe events that will take place at the end of time, it speaks just as clearly about how we can make sense of our lives in the here and now. But none of this can be captured literally. To attempt a literal explanation is inevitably to trivialize.

According to the technical terminology employed by Protestant theologian Paul Tillich, all of eschatology (including the doctrine of bodily resurrection) should be understood as a "broken myth"—"broken" in the sense that its mythic character is acknowledged. Yet this broken myth can remain very much "alive" and functioning.[27] To borrow a term coined by the contemporary French philosopher Paul Ricoeur, accepting or even welcoming this myth is to step into a state of "second" or "willed naïveté." Through it, we recapture an almost childlike awareness of how the entire world coheres. At the same time, it is a willed naïveté because it follows the awareness that this picture of the world is not literally or objectively "true," and because believers "will" themselves into taking this next step in their personal faith journeys.[28]

The history of Jewish philosophy and theology has amply demonstrated the influence of intellectual developments in the world at large. Hence it is not surprising that the issue of the afterlife is also high on the agenda of contemporary Christianity. To cite but one example, in 1994, John Hick (arguably the most accomplished of American Protestant philosophers of religion) published his *Death and Eternal Life*. Hick's claim that without some belief in immortality, "any religious understanding of human existence ... would be radically incoherent" has apparently struck a chord among his Jewish readers.[29]

THE IMPACT OF THE HOLOCAUST

Finally, the transformation in Jewish religious and theological consciousness in the past few decades can also be seen as a consequence of the growing impact of the Holocaust. More than any other event, the Holocaust has taught us to be humble about human powers and impulses, to be skeptical about the imperialism of reason and science. None of these, we now realize, is competent to deal with the most significant dimensions of human existence. The Holocaust, precipitated by a culture that embodied the highest achievements of modernity, has led to a profound disillusionment with the perceived accomplishments of the past two centuries.

We have also become aware that mathematical systems rest on axioms that are themselves improvable; that physics must acknowledge a dimension of indeterminacy in trying to understand the material world; that astronomy also deals with entities and events that elude direct human perception and verification.

I also cannot but believe that the sight of the emaciated bodies in the liberated concentration camps, alongside the mounds of ashes in the crematoria, contributed to a renewed appreciation of the reality and finality of death, specifically our own inevitable death. One cannot be detached about death.

Here, more than ever, the entire body of assumptions that underlie the *Wissenschaft* approach to the study of religion must declare itself impotent. We must contemplate death. Unless we deal with our death, we cannot even begin to deal with our life. And if theology does not deal with the significance of human life in the face of death, it has avoided its central issue.

The Holocaust, moreover, has taught us something about the preciousness of the human body. We may not be *only* our bodies, there may be dimensions to our selves that are not reducible to bodily existence, and we may choose to call that dimension of our selves "soul." But we are clearly incarnate beings, and our experience of our bodies is very much integral to our experience of our selves. We may want to insist that something of us persists after the death of our bodies. But the doctrine of bodily resurrection can become one way of acknowledging the simple truth that when our bodies die, we die, and that if God is to affect our destiny even after we have died, God must deal with our bodies as well.

The recent reconsideration of Jewish teachings on the afterlife that I have traced here is clearly a work in progress. Predicting its eventual outcome is precarious, since it is very much a product of broader cultural changes whose trajectory is unpredictable. But it is also quite clear that the devaluation of this entire body of Jewish thinking over the past two centuries has come to an end. That in itself is a major statement about the current state of private faith in American Jewry.

Part Two

TORAH

Chapter 7

THE JEWISH PHILOSOPHER
IN SEARCH OF A ROLE

Two issues dominate the agenda of Jewish philosophy today. They are, more accurately, metaphilosophical issues in the sense that they deal not so much with substantive questions, like the nature of God, but more with the Jewish philosophical enterprise itself in our contemporary setting. The two issues are closely interrelated; the second can be dealt with only in terms of our responses to the first. Neither is totally new, but each has gained added urgency because of the specific conditions of Jewish life today. Finally, both have been largely ignored by contemporary Jewish philosophers.

The first is the attempt to define the specific tasks and unique responsibilities that the contemporary setting poses to the Jewish philosopher, and raises the broader issue of the role of Jewish philosophy in the process of contemporary Jewish self-definition. The second is the attempt to define parameters of authenticity for a contemporary Jewish philosophical statement. What makes any such statement authentically Jewish? What would make it inauthentic? Which Jewish philosophers should be taught, preached, or discussed? Which should be ignored or dismissed? And who decides?

This issue raises the broader question of authority in Jewish philosophy.

For the purpose of these analyses, the term "Jewish philosophy" will be used to indicate the broad range of ideological issues raised in the search for a positive Jewish identity. For many of us, some of these issues will be more narrowly theological in the sense that they will assume that Jewish identity has to be understood in religious terms.

The most revealing fact about the place of philosophy in Judaism is that no compilation of the body of commandments that are incumbent on every Jew includes among its number a mitzvah that an authentic Jew should "do" philosophy. Maimonides begins his *Mishneh Torah* with the principle that there is a First Being and that to acknowledge this principle is a mitzvah.[1] Given what we know about Maimonides' philosophical predilections, his intention was undoubtedly to stipulate that the mitzvah is not simply to acknowledge God's existence but actively to prove it through the use of reason. The fact remains that Maimonides' approach is highly idiosyncratic. As we well know, it is entirely possible to acknowledge God's reality without having reflected on what we mean by God and how we know that God exists. In fact, most Jews whom we would call "religious" are so in this nonreflective way. What is striking about Judaism is precisely the extent to which it is possible to be a "religious" or, preferably, an "authentic" Jew without having anything resembling an explicit theology or without dealing with the philosophical issues that it implies. Until fairly recently in Jewish history, authenticity in Judaism was determined by adherence to mitzvot. The authentic Jew was the observant Jew. This makes Judaism the polar opposite of a religion such as Christianity. The central Christian act is an inner act of faith: that Jesus is the son of God (or alternatively, God Himself become flesh) who walked among men, was crucified, was resurrected on the third day, and will return at the end of days. The Christian is required to make this act of faith to be "justified" or to "become right" with God. If he or she does not believe in this way, he or she is simply not Christian. Philosophical reflection, then, is intrinsic to Christianity simply because the content of this belief system, what the Christian believes, demands clarification and reformulation through reflection. That is why many forms of Christianity insist on articulating the substance of Christian belief as the Credo, which is an integral part of the Christian liturgy, or in the form of dogmas or precise formulations of doctrine that the Christian must explicitly accept as true in order to be an authentic member of the Church. It need not be said that Christianity also expects its adherents to live in a certain way, and, for its part, Judaism's emphasis on observance assumes a host of beliefs that also demand clarification and ongoing reformulation. But it is patently clear that the emphasis in the two traditions is reversed.

This phenomenon should go far toward explaining the relatively peripheral role that the formal philosophical enterprise has played in Judaism. The keynote is sounded by the eleventh-century French exegete, Rashi, in his commentary on the very first verse of Genesis. Rashi elects to quote an earlier rabbinic homily[2] to the effect that the Torah should have begun with the twelfth chapter of Exodus, which contains the first commandment addressed to Israel in its entirety (the Passover sacrifice). One has to pause at the state of mind that prompts such a suggestion in the first place. The very assumption that the nonlegal portions of the Torah (for example, the story of creation in Genesis 1) do not belong within revelation boggles the mind—at least the mind of the Jewish philosopher. But consider the following: How many genuinely influential philosophical works were written by Jews between the time of Philo in the first century BCE and Abraham Joshua Heschel or Mordecai Kaplan in our own day? We would be hard pressed to count beyond twelve to fifteen. And even if we add portions of the Bible such as the first chapter of Genesis, Job, Ecclesiastes, and Proverbs, the homiletical material included in the Talmud or the anthologies of midrash, and the writings of Jewish mystics and the Hasidic masters, some of which deal with philosophical issues in their own characteristic vocabulary, it would still all add up to a

91

fraction of the energy expended by Jews over the same period of time in the exploration of the Jewish legal tradition.

Even more striking are four further characteristics of the later (that is post-ninth-century CE) philosophical literature. First, there is its remarkably transient quality. Maimonides' *Mishneh Torah* is considered an authoritative codification of Jewish law to this day. Yet while his *Guide of the Perplexed* may be acknowledged as the pinnacle of medieval Jewish philosophy, it is hardly consulted by the perplexed of our day. In fact, it has even been argued that Mordecai Kaplan, whose thought was forged in the 1920s and 1930s, has little to say to a post-Holocaust generation of Jews. Second, it borrows extensively from the philosophical style of the non-Jewish world in which it was composed: Saadia from the Islamic Kalam, Ibn Gabirol and Abraham Ibn Ezra from medieval neo-Platonism, Maimonides from medieval Aristotelianism, Herman Cohen from nineteenth-century German idealism, Franz Rosenzweig and Martin Buber from twentieth-century, continental existentialism, and Mordecai Kaplan from American naturalism. In fact, it seems that its main function in each generation is to provide a reading of Judaism in terms of the philosophical vocabulary of the period in which it was written. Third, it is a remarkably pluralistic enterprise. Take any issue, even one as central as the nature of God. Apart from the fact that God exists, there is little that one can find in common on it in the thought of Maimonides, Isaac Luria, Martin Buber, Mordecai Kaplan, and Abraham Heschel. Finally, and most significantly, the preeminent works in Jewish philosophy were written in a language other than Hebrew: Philo in Greek; Saadia, Yehudah Halevi, Ibn Gabirol, and Maimonides in Arabic; Cohen, Rosenzweig, and Buber in German; Kaplan and Heschel in English. Each of these thinkers was eminently capable of writing in masterful Hebrew; in fact, many of them composed other lasting works in Hebrew—for example, Maimonides' *Mishneh Torah*, Halevi's liturgical and secular poetry, or Heschel's scholarly work on rabbinic theology. But they chose to write their philosophical works in the language of some other civilization in which they were obviously also at home.

This configuration literally begs for an explanation, and our first clue may well lie in this passage from Maimonides' own Introduction to his *Guide*. Why is he writing this book? He answers:

> Its purpose is to give indications to a religious man for whom the validity of our Law has become established in his soul and has become actual in his belief—such a man being perfect in his religion and character, and having studied the sciences of the philosophers and come to know what they signify. The human intellect having drawn him on and led him to dwell within its province, he must have felt distressed by the externals of the Law and by the meanings of the above-mentioned equivocal, derivative, or amphibolous terms, as he continued to understand them by himself or was made to understand them by others. Hence he would remain in a state of perplexity and confusion as to whether he should follow his intellect, renounce what he knew concerning the terms in question, and consequently consider that he has renounced the foundations of the Law. Or he should hold fast to his understanding of these terms and not let himself be drawn on together with his intellect, rather turning his back on it and moving away from it, while at the same time perceiving that he had brought loss to himself and harm to his religion. He would be left with those imaginary beliefs to which he owed his fear and difficulty and would not cease to suffer from heartache and great perplexity.[3]

To whom, then, is this volume addressed? To the Jew for whom identification with Judaism and its teachings can no longer be taken for granted, to the Jew who is painfully aware of other ideological options, who is both Jewish and yet thoroughly at home in the intellectual currents of the non-Jewish world at large and in a language other than Hebrew. In short, it is addressed to the intellectually "marginal" Jew. We use "marginal" here specifically to designate the Jew who stands on the margin that separates Judaism and some other civilization, and not in the contemporary sense of the Jew whose Jewish identity is remote and fragile. Maimonides was certainly not "marginal' in this latter sense; he was, however, in the former sense. If we may generalize from Maimonides, Jewish philosophy flowers when Judaism itself becomes problematic, when it can no longer compel allegiance through its own internal dynamics, when it is no longer self-validating. And, we may assume, the one who feels the marginality of his condition most acutely is the philosopher himself. That is precisely what impels him to write. He may permit his concerned contemporaries to look over his shoulder but he writes primarily for himself, to resolve his own personal perplexity about where he stands in the face of the challenges of his day. The legitimate task of Jewish philosophy, then, is "apologetics" in the best sense of the term: to provide a coherent, internally consistent and sophisticated defense of Judaism in terms of the conceptual scheme and vocabulary of the particular age—in short, to make the case for Judaism, precisely at a time when such a case has to be made. And since the nature of the challenge from the outside world is constantly changing, both the substance and the vocabulary in which Jewish philosophy is articulated must change concurrently. Hence the ephemeral nature of all such formulations. Hence, also, the decision to write in the lingua franca of the day instead of Hebrew. It could not be assumed that the intended audience would have mastered Hebrew—further evidence of its "marginality."

If this analysis has merit, we may be able to explain why Jewish philosophy flowered in those historical periods when Jews participated in an intellectually open society. The Islamic and Christian world between the tenth and fifteenth centuries provided the paradigmatic instance of such a setting. Jews got into philosophy in the Middle Ages because both the Christian and Islamic conditions of the age encouraged them to share this experience. The very presence of three competing religious traditions, each claiming exclusive truth, impelled believers of all traditions to step back and reflect on the phenomenon of religion itself. Not only had Judaism, Christianity, and Islam become problematic to each community of believers, religion itself had become problematic. It is not surprising, then, that the first in the line of great medieval Jewish philosophers, the tenth-century Saadia Gaon, does insist that contrary to our opening claim, in his age it is very much a mitzvah to do philosophy. Saadia's contemporaries, indeed, faced a bewildering number of alternative religious options. First, there were Judaism, Christianity, and Islam. Each of these was further split into a traditionalist camp that insisted on a literal understanding of scripture and a modernist camp that was prepared to modify its teachings to accomodate the new philosophical winds. In fact, Greek science and philosophy had been rediscovered and had produced a crop of skeptics who denied, in principle, the validity of all forms of revelation. Oriental cults abounded, and the Jewish community was also confronted by a vigorous and articulate sectarian group, the Karaites, who challenged the authority not only of the Talmud but, also, of its acknowledged interpreters who sat at the head of the Babylonian academies, the most prominent of whom was Saadia himself.

Is it any wonder, then, that Saadia and his contemporaries were impelled into philosophy? Judaism had, indeed, become problematic, and, Saadia insists, Jews must resort to philosophy for two reasons: first, in order that reason may establish and verify those religious claims that have been given by revelation alone; and second, in order to answer the attacks on Judaism on the part of competing ideologies.[4] In short, Jews must do philosophy because they could no longer function intuitively as Jews.

It is clear that our situation in twentieth-century America is very much a replica of Saadia's age. We, too, live in a veritable supermarket of ideologies, each clamoring for adherents. American Jewry is intellectually sophisticated and upwardly mobile.

Jewish identity is entirely voluntary, and much of contemporary culture argues against any form of religious identification as anachronistic, and against the preservation of ethnic ties as destructive of a more broadly based "love of humanity." Assimilation and intermarriage are rife. America, too, then, is the paradigmatic open society and we are all paradigmatic marginal Jews. We are all painfully aware of other ideological options. In such a cultural context, it is again a mitzvah that reflective and articulate Jews once again step back and look afresh at what it means to be a Jew in terms of the conceptual scheme and vocabulary of our own day and, in the process, address the specific challenges to Jewish identity that are being posed by the competing ideologies of our generation.

There is one additional factor that should impel a flowering of Jewish philosophy in our day. Our generation has experienced two momentous historical events: the European Holocaust and the creation of the State of Israel. In the past, events of such magnitude have always sparked an outpouring of philosophical creativity as thinking Jews struggled to integrate their new historical experience into their thought patterns as Jews. Two notable examples come to mind: the destruction of the First Temple in 586 BCE and the expulsion of the Jewish community from Spain in 1492. Each of these events forced the participant and succeeding generations to rethink the ground rules of Jewish existence. Though it predates by a few years the destruction of the First Temple, Jeremiah 29 is a letter addressed to Jews already in exile, and it represents an attempt to formulate how they are to live, think, and worship as Jews in exile and without a Temple. This letter is an explicit contradiction of Deuteronomy 28:36–15, which warns that the exilic experience will be totally destructive of all attempts to live fruitfully and to worship as Jews. Jeremiah disagrees and orders the exilic community to do just that. In other words, the reality of the event, when it finally occurred, exposed the inadequacies of the earlier ideology and impelled the creation of a totally new one.

Similarly, the expulsion from Spain forced the Jewish community to struggle anew with the twin themes of exile and redemption. A few generations later this struggle led to the mystically inspired theology of Isaac Luria, which sees exile not only as a historical event in the life of the Jewish people, but also as a metaphysical symbol denoting a fault in all of creation, affecting even God, who is portrayed as sharing in Israel's exile. The work of redemption is now assigned to the individual Jew whose every action becomes potentially redemptive—not only of Israel, but also of the world, and even of God. Momentous historical events, precisely because they are unprecedented, expose the inadequacies and anachronisms of our ideological consolidations and force us to struggle to reformulate them so that we may respond to our own historical experience as Jews.

The role of Jewish philosophy may also be set forth in traditional terms, by suggesting that it be understood as midrash. Midrash is commonly understood to designate a brief homily, usually of Talmudic origin and designed to teach some truth that a contemporary homiletician will then expound and elaborate into a sermon. But this is an excessively narrow sense of the term. In its broad sense, midrash denotes a process—the process of exegesis and interpretation by which the meaning of an ancient text is expounded beyond its original plain or literal sense (*p'shat* or "simple" meaning) to convey ever-new layers of meaning. Sometimes the text is a specific scriptural word or verse. A legal passage, through halakhic or legal midrash, may yield an entire body of laws; a narrative passage, through aggadic or homiletical midrash, may yield a homily bearing on some moral, theological, spiritual, or national issue facing the community.

It is not too much of an extrapolation, however, to expand this view by suggesting that a philosophy of Judaism in its entirety may be understood as a midrash where the "text" becomes the total body of prior traditional teaching. Thus, rabbinic Judaism as a whole may be understood as a midrash (or, more accurately, a series of overlapping midrashim) on Scripture, as can Maimonides' *Guide*, the *Zohar*, Lurianic kabbalah, Kaplan's *Judaism as a Civilization*, or Heschel's *God in Search of Man*. In these latter instances, the "text" is Scripture plus rabbinic literature (which, because of its scope and centrality is awarded a role just about equal to that of Scripture) along with selected later formulations of Judaism. Heschel, for example, draws heavily from the Talmud, from medieval philosophy, from mysticism, and from Hasidism; all of these together form his "text." Jewish intellectual history, then, can be understood as an evolving and overlapping set of midrashim on an ever-expanding "text," itself a midrash.

A midrash is a temporary consolidation. It represents an ideological plateau, the outcome of an extended struggle to rethink and rewrite an ideology that has been recognized as out of date. Every midrash exists in a state of tension. On the one hand, it is rooted in the past, on a "text" understood either narrowly as Scripture or broadly as a previous midrash; on the other hand, every midrash is directed to a new historical situation, one that is by definition unprecedented—for otherwise why would we need a new midrash? An effective midrash, then, is inherently unsatisfactory; it tends to be offensive to the traditionalist (who doesn't feel the need for a new formulation in the first place) and inadequate to the liberal (who is prepared to distance himself more radically from the text). Furthermore, since the Jewish people is very much within history, all of these consolidations are inherently ephemeral and quickly outdated. They may well linger long after they have served their immediate purpose; it is always safer to hold on to the past, and the task of evolving a new consolidation is an enormously difficult and painful adventure—until we are shocked out of our complacency by the realization that our children consider us anachronistic.

What difference does it make if we refer to our philosophical consolidations as midrash? Preeminently, it enables us to recognize them as decisively influenced by the historical and cultural contexts in which they arise. They are all cultural documents, shot through with human appropriation, testimonies as much to the concerns and vocabulary of the specific age as to the eternal, ongoing "truths" of Judaism. We are thus liberated to do in a much more conscious and deliberate way what Jews have been doing all along. We can recognize not only the legitimacy but even the imperative to do midrash.

But then another, more significant question presses itself upon us. What are the theological implications of this understanding of midrash? Specifically, what are the implications for a theology of revelation? Our claim is that in each generation Jews felt free to reformulate the intellectual context of their tradition in terms of the conceptual scheme and idiom of their time. What gave them the authority to do this? And what authority did they accord to the original formulation of the content of Jewish belief in the Torah? If all formulations of Jewish thought are as much the product of human appropriations as they are of divine revelation, should we then not do away with the notion that there is an "ideal" (in the Platonic sense) Judaism—an original, pristine formulation of Torah that embodies the very words of God, floats above the historical experience of the Jewish people, out of which all further formulations emerge through the simple unfolding of the implications of the original, ultimate truth? The ultimate theological implication of this view is that even the original revelation itself must be seen as the product of divine and human interaction, as both God's *mattan Torah* and man's *kabbalat Torah*. Abraham Heschel captures this interaction when he insists: "As a report about revelation, the Bible itself is a midrash."[5] All further formulations of Jewish thought, then, are midrashim on an original text that is itself midrash.

The issue of revelation is crucial because our understanding of revelation determines the authority of Torah on matters of belief and practice. And on the issue of revelation, there are only two possibilities: either Torah is the literal word of God (the dogma of verbal revelation) or it is not. If it is not, we then recognize a substantive human contribution to the formulation of Torah and thereby construe its authority in an entirely different light. Midrash, as we have described it, becomes a continuation of a process that was present from the very outset. Torah itself, then, is properly midrash.

It is no accident that among contemporary Jewish theologians it was Heschel who hit on this formulation. He was a theological supernaturalist, but he also inherited from his Hasidic ancestors a conviction that God is beyond human conceptualization. After all, what kind of God would God be if *I* can understand God? Heschel was forced to confront the intrinsic inadequacy of all human characterizations of God. The naive literalist understanding of revelation was unacceptable not because it demeans human beings (as a Mordecai Kaplan might claim) but because it demeans God! Torah, then, could not be the literal word of God. It was a human appropriation of some more primitive content that, in its purity, is inaccessible to us. Heschel's monumental *Torah Min Hashamayim B'aspaklaryah Shel Hadorot*[6] offers wide-ranging documentation that this view of revelation permeates the literature of Talmudic Judaism as well.

A more contemporary formulation of this claim would be that all theological statements, particularly those that refer to God qualities and manifold relationships with creation, have to be understood as myths.[7] In a preliminary way, to say that all theological claims are myths is to say that they must not be taken as literal, precise renderings of the realities to which they refer. Popular usage to the contrary, however, neither are they to be understood as deliberate fictions. Myths use material from everyday experience, from the realm of time and space, to enable us to talk about that which is totally beyond direct human apprehension. They are partial, impressionistic constructs or accommodations and they are indispensible, for human conceptualization and language are totally incapable of capturing the reality that we call the essence of God. The issue is not myth or no myth, but, rather, which myth. If God is to figure in our scriptures, theologies, liturgies, and rituals, if God is to participate in the life of the community of believers, God's essence has to be concretized in the form of myth. The Torah itself, then, has to be understood as the original complex record of the Jewish religious myth through which our ancestors interpreted their historical experience.

A myth, like a midrash, has a life span of its own. It lives and it dies; that is, it loses its power to do what great myths uniquely can do: create a community, establish identity, generate emotion, reveal unsuspected truths about the world and the human experience, and motivate to action. But rarely does a myth in its entirety die, for then the community will also die. More frequently, portions of the myth die for segments of the community. When this happens, a vital and healthy community will then set about to revise or rewrite its myth. That is precisely what happened when Job's personal experience led him to conclude that the received tradition, which stipulated human suffering as God's punishment, was simply inadequate. In effect, that portion of the biblical myth died for Job, and the voice out of the whirlwind should be understood as proclaiming a new—equally mythical—understanding of God's complex relationship with creation. Harold Kushner's *When Bad Things Happen to Good People* is a contemporary paradigm of the same process, as is the enterprise of Holocaust theology.[8] In the latter instance, the process is still in a preliminary, fragmentary stage; witness the fact that we have neither a liturgy nor a set of rituals that are Holocaust specific. Great myths always have the power to generate liturgy and ritual; Passover is the primary example of that process.

It should be apparent from the above that much of what can be said about midrash applies equally well to religious myths. They are two ways of describing the same process. Most important for our purposes here, a myth—like a midrash—comes into being out of the encounter between a community and its distinctive historical experience. Both are the way in which that community reads its historical experience. That reading is then embodied in the community's scriptures, liturgies, and rituals, which, in turn, function to train future generations to read *their* historical experience through the prism of the community's distinctive myth. Scripture, then, is the first stage in a process of myth writing and rewriting that extends throughout the historical experience of the community.

By definition, then, it is precisely the "marginal" member of the community, as we have defined the condition of "marginality," who first feels the incipient death throes of portions of the myth. However crudely or negatively expressed, his or her dissatisfaction with the received tradition jars the community out of its complacency and alerts it to the need to engage itself once again in the revision of the myth or midrash.

Three issues, then, define the Jewish philosopher's role in the process of Jewish self-definition in our day. Two of these are classic; one is unprecedented. An open intellectual setting renders every myth or midrash exposed and vulnerable because other options are glaringly accessible. And momentous historical events are uniquely capable of rendering even the most successful of them anachronistic. These dimensions are classical. What is unprecedented, however, is the uniquely modern collapse of the dogma of verbal revelation and, with it, the sense that the Torah can serve as an explicit standard of authority on all matters of belief and practice. Once this happens, we are forced to confront in a new light precisely what claim the received tradition has on our lives. To be precise, what is new here is not the process of midrash or remythologizing; our historical survey has shown that this process is familiar and well established. Rather, what transfigures the enterprise is the uniquely modern selfconsciousness, the awareness of the *fact* of history, that destroys fundamentalisms of every kind.

For if the Torah itself is a myth or a midrash, if there is no such thing as a pristine reading of Judaism that carries within itself its own warranty of ultimate truth, how do we determine which of the later consolidations are authentic? What standard or criterion can we use? And who decides? One who has a question in Jewish law knows how to find an authoritative answer. What is the ultimate seat of authority in matters of Jewish thought?

The task of revising the Jewish myth or midrash in every generation has invariably fallen to Jewish philosophers for it is they who personally and most acutely experience the state of "marginality" and the accompanying dissatisfaction with the received tradition. That is undoubtedly the reason why even the most creative among them has usually been viewed with suspicion by the established authorities of the day—and, in Judaism, the "established authorities" have always been the recognized masters of the halakhic tradition in every generation. This suspicion—and, on occasion, for example, with Maimonides in his day and Mordecai Kaplan and even, to a degree, Abraham Heschel, in our day, "suspicion" is a considerable understatement—can easily be understood.

Ultimately, the philosopher and the halakhist represent two different constituencies. The halakhist speaks for those Jews who are totally at home with their Judaism and its halakhah, who either tune out the challenges from the intellectual world outside, or simply do not feel challenged as Jews and, hence, have no need to defend or justify what they stand for. The philosopher, on the other hand, speaks to the Jew whose Judaism is in question, who is not totally at home in the Hebrew language, which we must understand as symptomatic of a much deeper sense of not feeling at home with his Judaism. The halakhist can only wonder what the fuss is all about and can only be shocked at the foreign cast that his Judaism acquires as a result of the transformations wrought by the work of the philosopher.

But these tensions notwithstanding, Jewish philosophy is an enormously powerful weapon, doubly powerful because of the flexibility and pluralism on which it thrives. It may well be an elitist enterprise, created by the few for the few; it may easily become dated; it may well strain the implicitly accepted boundaries of authentic Jewish teaching. But, overriding all of these considerations, it serves in every generation to enable countless Jews to remain Jews precisely at a time when the halakhists could not do so on their own.

Today, in our situation in America, it is once again an enterprise whose hour has come. It can no longer be considered a luxury. The elitist few have now become the many. In fact, the problem is no longer to find Jews who feel the problems, but, rather, to persuade these Jews even to consider the answers that are being suggested by the philosophers of our day. That may be the greatest challenge of all.

CHAPTER 8

AUTHORITY AND PARAMETERS IN
JEWISH DECISION MAKING

What is the authority of Torah in our lives? From a theological perspective, the basis for determining the authority of Torah in matters of belief and practice rests on how we understand revelation. Regarding revelation, there are only two possibilities: the traditionalist position and, for want of a better name, the liberal. The traditionalist insists that there is a tight congruence between what God wants us to know of God's will and what the Torah tells us about God's will. The liberal insists that no such congruence exists, that there is a gap between whatever God revealed (or reveals) and what is recorded in Torah.

Thus Norman Lamm, one of the clearest exponents of the traditionalist position, insists that God "willed that man abide by His commandments and that that will was communicated in discrete words and letters." He continues: "The divine will, if it is to be made known, is sufficiently important for it to be revealed in as direct, unequivocal, and unambiguous a manner as possible, so that it will be understood by the largest number of the people to whom it is addressed." Hence he accepts "unapologetically the idea of the verbal revelation of the Torah." "To deny that God can make His will clearly known is to impose upon Him a limitation of dumbness that would insult the least of His creatures." Finally, "given the above, it is clear that I regard all of the Torah as binding upon the Jew."[1]

In short, if God cares enough to give us the Torah in the first place, we must assume that God has the power to communicate precisely what God wants us to know. To deny this is to deny God's power—in fact, to deny God. For the traditionalist, the criteria for authenticity in Judaism are therefore both halakhic and theological. It follows that halakhically correct conversions performed by liberal rabbis are not acceptable to a traditionalist Jew, because they follow the halakhah but for the wrong reasons, that is, not as revealed by God in discrete words and letters. For this position, then, authority in Judaism rests explicitly with God, whose will is revealed in the text of Torah.

THE LIBERAL POSITION

In contrast, as soon as Abraham Heschel writes, "As a report about revelation the Bible itself is a midrash,"[2] he has taken a decisive step out of the traditionalist camp. His further conclusions that "what reached the ear of man was not identical with what has come out of the spirit of the eternal God,"[3] that "Judaism is based upon a minimum of revelation and a maximum of interpretation,"[4] and that "the source of authority is not the word as given in the text, but Israel's understanding of the text"[5] amply confirm that judgment. If the words of Torah are not God's words, then they must be human words. There is no middle ground here.

I choose Heschel as representative of the liberal camp because he is commonly identified with the more traditionalist wing of modern Jewish theologians. Even stronger cases can be made for the liberalism of Franz Rosenzweig and Martin Buber. Rosenzweig claims that "'He [God] came down [on

Sinai]'(Exod.19:20)—this already concludes the revelation; 'He [God] spoke' is the beginning of interpretation, and certainly 'I am.'"[6] And Buber even rejects Rosenzweig's suggestion that "God is not a Lawgiver. But He commands."[7]

In these statements of the liberal position, the human community does not possess God's explicit will: in Heschel, because God's will has to pass through the screen of human comprehension and language; and in Rosenzweig and Buber, because God does not explicitly reveal God's will in the first place. In Mordecai Kaplan's thought, the liberal position reaches its most radical conclusion. For Kaplan, God's will is thoroughly identified with the human community's "discovery" of salvational patterns in human beings and in nature.[8] In short, for Kaplan, God wills whatever the human community says God wills. But in principle, the very same claim could be made for Heschel, Rosenzweig, and Buber. In all of these formulations, the human community determines the content of Torah and becomes thereby the locus of authority. That is the distinguishing mark of all liberal theologies of revelation.

This liberal approach to defining authority is also evident in Solomon Schechter, who claims that "it is not the mere revealed Bible that is of first importance to the Jew, but the Bible ... as it is interpreted by Tradition." He continues, "It follows that the center of authority is actually removed from the Bible and placed in some living body, which, by reason of its being in touch with the ideal aspirations and the religious needs of the age, is best able to determine the nature of the Secondary Meaning." This "living body" is Schechter's "Catholic Israel"— the consensus shaped by committed Jews in any one generation. Schechter writes that God may have chosen the Torah, Moses, and Israel, yet "God's choice invariably coincides with the wishes of Israel."[9] This striking formulation surely helps us understand why, in 1909, Schechter invited the young Mordecai Kaplan to teach in his school.

THE HUMAN DIMENSION: SUBVERTING GOD'S WILL

The gap that exists between what God wanted or wants us to have as the text of revelation and what we do indeed have is created by the substantive human contribution to the formulation of Torah. The traditionalist tends to eliminate such a human dimension; the liberal tends to acknowledge or even welcome it. But the issue is more complicated than this simple dichotomy might suggest, because the Torah itself seems to provide a basis for subverting God's explicit authority over its contents, thus making God's verbal revelation theoretically irrelevant.

The basis for this subversion lies in a number of texts that I refer to as the "best interest of Judaism" clause, by analogy to the "best interest of baseball" clause in the rules of Major League Baseball, which gives the commissioner the right to make any ruling, if, in his estimation, it promotes the "best interest of baseball." This authority is granted the commissioner, however, by the owners of Major League Baseball teams, who wrote the rules and retain the right to hire and fire him.

The "best interest of Judaism" is addressed in several passages. Deuteronomy 17:8–11 describes how difficult cases are to be presented to "the magistrate in charge at the time," and of the responsibility not to "deviate from the verdict ... either to the right or to the left." Rashi emphasizes that we go to the authorities "*in charge at that time*," even if they are not on the level of previous authorities, for all any generation has to draw upon is the authorities of its own day. The closing words of Exodus 23:2, as interpreted by the Rabbis, provide the biblical basis for majority rule in all such judicial proceedings.[10]

Even God cannot argue against the rabbinic majority in matters of law. This is the point of the Talmudic story concerning the ritual status of Akhnai's oven. Rabbi Joshua uses the phrase that the Torah "is not in heaven" (Deut. 30:12), to reject God's verbal intervention on behalf of Rabbi Eliezer in his dispute with the rabbinic court. In this case, God is later reported to have laughed and said, "My children have defeated me (Baba Metzia 59b).

In these celebrated instances, Torah, or, more precisely, God, has granted the rabbinic court the explicit authority to determine how the Torah rules in any specific case. This leads Eliezer Berkovits to conclude that "once the Torah was revealed to the children of Israel, its realization on earth became their responsibility, to be shouldered by human ability and insight.... Having left its heavenly abode, it had to be accommodated to the modest cottages of human uncertainty and inadequacy."[11] And again, "once a Jew accepts the Torah from Sinai, whatever it teaches him in his search for its meaning and message is the word of God for him.... The subjective human element is not to be eliminated from the acceptance of the Torah."[12] Note that Berkovits deliberately leaves the specifics of revelation and Sinai undefined.

Joel Roth concludes his discussion of this same issue as follows: "The scope of rabbinic authority knows no theoretical bounds. As the sole normative interpreters of the meaning of the Torah, Torah means whatever the rabbis say it means. And to whatever they say it means, in every generation, God agrees, even if, in some 'objective' realm, He disagrees with their interpretation."[13] In another context, Roth concludes, "ultimately, then, it seems incontrovertible that the sages do possess the right to abrogate the Torah both actively and passively ... both temporarily and permanently."[14]

WHAT MAKES A RABBI?

The decisive issue, then, is "Who is a sage?" or "Who is a rabbi?" and what qualifications should such an authority possess? Roth concludes that a rabbinic authority must be academically qualified and must possess such nonacademic qualifications as those cited by Maimonides: wisdom, humility, fear of God, hatred of unjust gain, love of truth, respect, and an upstanding reputation.[15]

Above all the authority must possess *yir'at ha-shem* (fear of heaven).[16] For Roth, *yir'at ha-shem* entails a commitment that the Torah as *grundnorm* (the basic norm grounding the authority of Torah as a whole) is "the reflection of the word and will of God and that the sages of the Torah are the sole legitimate interpreters of the *grundnorm*.... Positing the *grundnorm*, however, does not entail any specific theological stance regarding the manner in which it reflects the word and the will of God."[17] Once again, the specifics of revelation are left open, while the qualifications for becoming an authority are shown to be highly subjective.

Even in the traditionalist camp, the ultimate authority for the system rests with the human community. I insist on "community" here, as opposed to sages or rabbis, because authorities are not self-designated. A sage or rabbi receives authority from a community of Jews when it turns to that authority with its questions and is prepared to accept his or her answers and live by them. Seminaries and yeshivot may ordain, but a rabbi becomes a rabbi when a community elects that person to serve as its rabbi or turns to that rabbi for instruction. *Empowerment flows from the community to its authority.*

Also required is a fundamental congruence between a community and its authority on the parameters within which decisions on belief and practice will lie. Rare is the authority whose decisions stretch significantly beyond the boundaries his or her community is prepared to accept. Equally rare is the community that turns to an authority whose decisions will stretch its parameters.

A traditionalist response to this analysis would claim that the rabbinic interpretation of Scripture was itself revealed at Sinai as the Oral Torah, so that, in fact, it is God's authority, not the community's, that lies behind these rulings.[18] It would also claim that this Oral Torah is exhaustively canonized in the Talmud, which is why the Talmudic resolution of a halakhic issue has far greater authority than that of a later sage. Thus the Talmudic authorities could legislate that we praise God for having commanded us to light the Hanukkah candles (*Shabbat* 23a), though Scripture records no such explicit commandment;[19] whereas many contemporary traditionalists insist that we must not similarly praise God for having commanded us to say the Hallel psalms on Israeli Independence Day. In short, the early authorities could, but we can't.

ON THE COMMUNITY'S ROLE
IN DEFINING PARAMETERS

When the human factor enters our picture of halakhic authority, an element of relativism and subjectivity is inevitable. To put it in another, possibly less gracious way, authority becomes politicized.

Thus, the casual use of the terms "the halakhah" and "the halakhic process" is unfortunate. Each of these phrases implies there is an *objectively* determined set of parameters that defines what is "within" or "outside" the halakhic system, within which all decisions for a community that acknowledges the binding power of halakhah must lie. But if the community is the ultimate authority for what constitutes the word and will of God, it is clear that no such objective set of parameters is even possible. To put this another way, there are no intrinsic parameters; or, rather, the parameters are established and continually set anew as decisions are made by the decisor or community. We can only trace the parameters up to this point; where they fall in the future depends on the next issue to be considered, which is determined consensually by the community and its decisor.

That the subjective model I have presented is empirically the case is obvious among both liberals and traditionalists. The Conservative movement accepts the marriage of a *kohen* and a divorcee despite Leviticus 21:7, which explicitly forbids such a marriage,[20] yet abides by the ruling of Leviticus 18:22 that homosexual relations remain forbidden.[21] Similarly, the supposedly monolithic traditionalist community is riven with subjective disagreement over such issues as the religious legitimacy of the State of Israel, of a secular college education, or of participation with liberal movements in any activity that touches on halakhic or other religious issues.

It should be clear that there are no intrinsic parameters for decision making. The community determines the parameters as issues arise. There is nothing surprising or particularly upsetting about this pattern. What is disturbing is the attempt to conceal the process by insisting all along that any community is or is not "a halakhic community." That phrase has no clear meaning that I can discern.

HALAKHIC INNOVATION

Here is a concrete example. When a groom places a ring on his bride's finger, the traditional liturgy has him recite the formula: "Behold you are consecrated unto me with this ring according to the law [ritual? practice?] of Moses and Israel." Today, in a double ring ceremony, the bride customarily says something to the groom as she places the ring on his finger. Frequently, she recites a halakhically innocuous passage, such as a verse from the Song of Songs, but in the search for a more egalitarian ritual or liturgy, other couples under rabbinic guidance have used liturgical formulas that more closely approximate what the groom has recited to the bride. Some rabbis now permit the bride to recite the traditional formula, using the masculine form of the Hebrew in place of the feminine.

This is clearly a significant departure from the tradition since it subverts the traditional Jewish understanding of marriage, in which the groom alone is the active partner; he acquires the bride but she is totally passive. It then further offends the tradition by dubbing this new practice as being also "according to the law of Moses and Israel," which, traditionalists insist, is simply not the case.

But the issue is precisely who is "Moses and Israel" here? Whatever Moses' role may have been in transmitting God's revelation to Israel, the fact that the liturgy acknowledges "Israel" as holding an equal role in determining the content of revelation raises the issue of who is "Israel"? And if we acknowledge that "Israel" represents the community that lives in history, then we have acknowledged the role of our own community as representing "Israel." We then have the authority to claim that this new practice is "according to the law of Moses and Israel."[22]

The halakhic process is simply far more fluid and ambiguous than we usually acknowledge. Speaking broadly, American religious Jewry is made up of multiple overlapping halakhic communities, ranging from Satmar (a sect of Hasidism) on the far right to left-wing Reform and even the UJA–Federation "civil religion" community on the far left,[23] each with its own authority figure(s). Some of these overlapping communities form coalitions (Reform, Reconstructionist, Conservative, Modern or Centrist Orthodoxy, and the rest). These coalitions are more or less stable or fragile, depending on the issue. The ongoing process of shaping the parameters of each community or coalition is inevitably heavily politicized, as it properly should be.

We usually bemoan the fragmentation of the community, but we should not. If anything, the pluralism, fluidity, and even the tensions within and among our communities are signs of the vitality of people who care about the issues and are prepared to invest themselves and their energy in shaping them. For this we should be grateful.

CHAPTER 9

ON THE RELIGIOUS EDUCATION

OF AMERICAN RABBIS

RABBINIC EDUCATION IN AMERICA

There are three commonly accepted dimensions to the education of an American congregational rabbi: the academic, the professional, and for want of a better word, the "religious."[1]

The first two are easy to define. The academic dimension refers to the bodies of knowledge and linguistic and textual skills that a rabbi must acquire to function as an authority on Judaism: the ability to speak, read, and comprehend modern Hebrew; the skills needed to understand a body of classical Hebrew and Aramaic texts—primarily biblical and rabbinic (the Babylonian Talmud, the anthologies of midrash, the liturgies, and the later codifications of Jewish law)—along with a knowledge of the contents of significant portions of these texts; and a basic general knowledge of Jewish history, theology, and philosophy, and of medieval and modern Hebrew literature. Whatever other roles the modern American rabbi may play, he or she is expected to be a master of the broad field of Jewish learning.

The professional dimension includes homiletical, pedagogical, counseling, pastoral, and administrative skills. There is a theoretical component to mastering some of these skills (for example, curriculum development or psychoanalytic theory), but it is clearly subservient to the practical.

The religious dimension is much more elusive. It may be taken as the cultivation and refinement of a perspective that views the world as manifesting a singular "order of existence," understands said order as reflecting the presence of God, is powerful enough to motivate the individual to shape his or her life experience in response to that presence, and instructs the rabbinical student as to how to transmit that perspective to a congregation of American Jews.[2] In other educational circles, this dimension is referred to as "religious formation," but I have never heard that phrase used in regard to Jewish education.

Of these three, by any criterion of measurement, it is the academic dimension that monopolizes the curricula of modern rabbinical schools. There is nothing inherently new or surprising about this emphasis. Judaism has always prized learning, largely because it understands God's will to have become recorded in sacred texts. Jews must study these texts to ascertain what it is that God demands of us in any life situation. From the very outset, then, rabbinic authority has been rooted in intellectual and scholarly accomplishment. The impact of modernity on this model has been felt in the broadening of the curriculum beyond the mastery of sacred texts alone, by the introduction, in some circles, of new scholarly methodologies, and by the addition of the professional dimension to rabbinic education.

The introduction of this professional dimension was itself the result of the reshaping of the rabbinic role in the modern setting. Essentially, the American rabbi assumed the pastoral, clerical, and administrative functions of Christian clergy. For many years this professional dimension was accorded at best a grudging recognition by rabbinical schools. It was usually relegated to a few courses in the last year of study. More recently, it has come to be recognized as crucial to the student's sense of professional integrity and is now accorded a much more central place in the curriculum.[3]

It is also clear that neither of these two dimensions presents a formidable educational challenge. We know, or can easily discover, how to conduct an advanced academic program and how to teach professional skills; we simply have to decide on our goals and shape our curriculum accordingly.

In contrast, the very existence of a religious dimension to rabbinic education is just coming into awareness and is a source of considerable bewilderment. To be more precise, the bewilderment applies mostly to the institutions on the left or liberal wing of the religious spectrum, to those schools that are committed to a critical or scientific approach to the study of Judaism. In the context of the contemporary American Jewish community, it applies preeminently to The Jewish Theological Seminary of America in New York (the fountainhead of the Conservative Movement in American Judaism), the Reconstructionist Rabbinical College in Philadelphia (the youngest of the three, the school that reflects the late Mordecai Kaplan's naturalist reading of Judaism), and the Hebrew Union College–Jewish Institute of Religion with its campuses in Cincinnati, New York, Los Angeles, and Jerusalem (which trains rabbis for American Reform congregations).

Of these three schools, for more than three decades, I have been associated, exclusively with The Jewish Theological Seminary—as a student, administrator, and professor. The analysis that follows, then, inevitably reflects my personal experience. My sense is that it applies equally well to HUC–JIR and less to RRC, but I cannot claim to speak of their programs with any degree of authority.

The schools that represent the right, or traditionalist (commonly called "Orthodox"), wing of the Jewish religious spectrum—primarily a number of yeshivot, or academies, most of them transplanted to America from their Eastern European settings during the first half of this century, and, to a certain extent, the modern Orthodox, or, as its leadership prefers, centrist Rabbi Isaac Elchanan Theological Seminary, affiliated with Yeshiva University in New York City—are not at all bewildered.

They are spared because they share a number of theological and ideological assumptions: Both the Written Torah, that is, Hebrew Scriptures (primarily the Pentateuch), and the Oral Torah, as recorded in Talmudic literature (which constitutes the authoritative interpretation of Scripture), were directly (either verbally or propositionally) revealed to Moses at Sinai. This body of teaching contains God's final and exclusive word for Israel on all matters of belief and practice. The study of this literature, then, is itself an act of worship, for its goal is to uncover the will of God for the infinite details of the Jew's life experience at all times. This setting views this entire body of teaching—including the post-Talmudic (that is, post-sixth-century CE) legal material that extends, elaborates, explains, and codifies the earlier material—as retaining a singular integrity, unaffected by historical, cultural, sociological, or economic considerations. In other words, it is perceived as representing one internally coherent and consistent body of discourse. This body of material, then, can be taught only by instructors and with the help of exegetical resources that share all of these assumptions.

Finally, these traditionalist schools are clear on what constitutes a religious or authentic Jew, and hence the goal of the entire enterprise. That goal is to create a Jew who is committed to fulfilling the explicit will of God as embodied in this sacred tradition, throughout his (but not her, for these schools will not ordain a woman) life experience, and who has the skills needed to persuade and enable his congregants to do the same.

To put this another way, in these traditionalist circles, the academic and religious dimensions of rabbinic education coincide. The academic program is the instrument of religious education. The entire enterprise is endowed with explicit religious significance.

This traditionalist model of rabbinic education has exhibited a singular resiliency; with relatively minor modifications, it has been in place from the Talmudic era to this day. When it began to be questioned, it was not, at least at the outset, questioned because of its purely theological assumptions. That came later.

What came first, during the nineteenth-century European *haskalah*, or "Enlightenment," was the application of those critical or scientific modes of scholarship to the study of Judaism. The primary result of this extended inquiry was to introduce the *fact* of history into the study of all Jewish texts and institutions. Everything Jewish was discovered to have had a history and thus to have been shaped by the ever-changing, broader cultural contexts in which the Jewish community has participated to the present. Even the Bible itself was now seen as embodying manifold reflections of its pagan, Middle Eastern setting. The Talmud and its later elaborations were replete with borrowings from Hellenistic civilization, from medieval Jewish institutions, from Christianity and Islam. Every area of Jewish law, from the very outset in the biblical and Talmudic eras, was viewed as influenced by and responding to economic, sociological, and cultural considerations.[4]

In short, Torah (in the extended sense as the entire body of Jewish religious instruction from the Bible to the present) was no longer viewed as a single, internally coherent, and consistent body of discourse, floating above time and history, but rather as deeply enmeshed in the life experiences of Jews in different geographical and cultural settings, doubtless shaping these experiences, but also responding to and being substantively affected by them as well. Torah itself implicitly came to be viewed as cultural document. As such, it could legitimately be studied with all of the tools and resources available to study any cultural document. Effectively, the study of Torah became secularized.

EARLY SEMINARY YEARS

The founding faculty of The Jewish Theological Seminary was deeply committed to this mode of study. They shared this commitment with the faculty of the Reform Hebrew Union College, which predated the founding of the Seminary by more than a decade. What precipitated the break with American Reform Judaism and led to the founding of the Seminary in 1886 (and eventually, to the Conservative movement) was largely the respective positions of the two founding groups in regard to Jewish law, particularly to the ritual law. Reform Judaism, in its landmark Pittsburgh Platform of 1885, viewed all of the ritual law of the Torah as anachronistic, valid in the earlier, more primitive stages of Jewish national history but now an obstacle to the "spiritual" development of Judaism in a modern American setting. The founders of the Seminary, in contrast, viewed the law in its totality as remaining the preeminent form of Jewish religious expression. True, this body of law may well have evolved over time in response to changing historical conditions and should, in fact, continue to do so. But in principle, the founders affirmed the law as binding, and their approach to Jewish legal development was evolutionary, gradualist, and cautious—in short, "conservative."[5]

The generations of students who came to study at the seminary, then, were exposed to a conflicted message. In the classroom they were taught, implicitly again, that Torah is a cultural document that can be studied with all of the tools available to Western scholarship. ("I teach Torah at the Seminary much as I might teach it at Harvard.") But concurrently, and programmatically, Jewish law remains binding in all of its detail, as if it were explicitly revealed.[6]

This conflicting message could be maintained because the Seminary's founding faculty studiously avoided doing theology. Solomon Schechter, president of the Seminary from 1902 until his death in 1915, wrote a masterful survey of rabbinic theology, and at great length, on the ideology of the Seminary and of the movement that it was in the process of creating. But he reveals almost nothing about his personal theology. Most important, he says nothing about his own understanding of revelation, that theological issue dealing explicitly with the question of religious authority.[7]

Of the early seminary faculty, only Mordecai Kaplan (who taught from 1909 to 1963, when he left to join the competing Reconstructionist Rabbinical College) followed the educational assumptions of the school to their theological and programmatic conclusions and propounded a thoroughly naturalist view of the emergence of Judaism. In broad strokes, Kaplan taught that Judaism is not only a religion but the evolving religious civilization of the Jewish people. God is the process within the natural order that promotes salvation; revelation is the discovery, by a human community, of what makes human life more and more abundant, creative, and value filled. In short, the authority for determining the shape of Judaism in any generation has always been, and continues to be, the caring and committed community. Thus, Torah is legitimately a cultural statement. Theology, ideology, and eventually, program (for what the community originally created, the community can continue to reshape) become aligned.[8]

But Kaplan was the exception. By and large, his colleagues remained pious Jews who pursued their scholarly inquiries in the modern style. If it occurred to them to ask why Torah should retain any authority whatsoever in their lives if it was accessible to secular tools of investigation, that question was never posed in the classroom.[9]

Essentially, then, for most of its first century (1886–1986), the rabbinical school of the Seminary was such in name only. It was, in fact, an extraordinary graduate school for advanced Jewish studies. Long before doctoral programs in Jewish studies were in place in major American universities, and, in fact, long before the Seminary itself began to offer a formal doctoral program (1970), students who never had any intention of becoming congregational rabbis came to the Seminary because it was the only place where they could acquire a first-rate, graduate-level education in the broad field of Judaica. Many of these men were later to populate departments of Jewish studies in universities in America and abroad. (Women were first admitted into the Seminary's rabbinical school in 1983.)

But with the questioning of the traditionalist model, and the eventual collapse, for many Jews, of its theological foundations, the nexus between the academic and religious dimensions of rabbinic education dissolved. What then was to become of that religious dimension? If Torah is indeed a cultural document, to be taught with secular tools, how is it to be taught in a religious setting? In fact, what, then, is Jewish religious education? Clearly more than texts, skills, and bodies of knowledge. But what is this "more"? And how are the culture and curriculum of a rabbinical school different from those of a graduate school?

THE SHIFT TO A RABBINIC CURRICULUM

In retrospect, it is stunning that for the first eight decades of the Seminary's existence, these questions were rarely explicitly confronted.[10] But they eventually became unavoidable.

First, on the most practical level, in 1970 the Seminary established its own graduate school, offering master's and doctoral degrees in Judaica. But the Seminary is a small (some five hundred students) institution, and its faculty teaches in all of its programs. What criteria, then, are to be used in the hiring of faculty? Is academic excellence sufficient? Are the instructors' personal religious commitments to be taken into consideration? If so, how are these to be measured? Can an instructor be hired only for graduate school courses, or only for rabbinical school courses? And what happens when financial considerations lead to cross-registration between graduate and rabbinical students in the same Bible or Talmud course, and when a number of graduate students are not even Jewish?

Second, Seminary instructors and students began to be aware of the possibility that Judaism could be taught as "religion." The study of religions had become a discipline in the academic world at large—primarily in Protestant seminaries, university departments of religious studies, and in the social sciences—but until the seventies, these developments had had only minimal impact on scholars of Judaica. Jewish religion, it was now beginning to be acknowledged, is much more than texts, laws, theologies, liturgies, and institutions. A "religion"—any religion—is a unique and complex entity that can be studied as such, according to certain canons of scholarship that have won acceptance in the scholarly world at large.[11]

Finally, the Seminary administration and faculty began to acknowledge the existence of a persistent dissatisfaction, on the part of its rabbinic alumni and students, with the training they had and were receiving at the Seminary. Part of this dissatisfaction, it was felt, was endemic to professional education across the board and referred to the relative neglect of the professional dimension. But a good deal of it applied to the faculty's perceived failure to go beyond the purely academic demands of the curriculum.

A rabbinic graduate of the 1960s, in a personal conversation, put it this way: "On Yom Kippur [the Day of Atonement] I stand before a congregation of three thousand Jews. It occurs to me that I know everything *about* this holiest of days—all the relevant biblical and rabbinic texts, all the liturgies, the historical background of the day, its theology, the laws that pertain to its observance, and reams of homiletical material. But what I don't know—what I was never taught at the Seminary—is the difference this entire experience is supposed to make for my congregants out there. How is it all supposed to affect them, transform them, make them different at the end of the day than they were at the beginning? How am I supposed to translate and to transmit the meaning of this experience in terms of their existential situation?"

To officiate at a funeral, then, is more than a matter of saying the right words and making the right gestures. It is to address the issue of our mortality. To officiate at a wedding is to address the issues of love, intimacy, and sexuality. To visit a hospital bed is to address suffering and pain. To preach on Yom Kippur is to speak of anxiety, guilt, and the possibilities of growth and rebirth. What does Judaism have to say about any of these existential issues? More important, what does it have to say to a community of modern American Jews? And how are these messages to be transmitted in the endlessly varied settings in which a rabbi participates?

No one questioned the Seminary faculty's mastery of the academic disciplines of Judaism. But it is one thing to teach the historical setting(s) of the Book of Isaiah with minute attention to the textual variants, the higher critical apparatus, and the plain-sense or literal meaning of the text. It is quite another thing to distill Isaiah's message for a contemporary congregation of Jews. The faculty did the first superbly well, but it generally avoided the second. That task would have required instructors to step out of their academic role, to put themselves into the text, to speak out of their own existential situations, as one human being to another, or as one religious Jew to another. Whatever the original function of the strong textual orientation of the Seminary curriculum, it was clearly serving a secondary, and (from the instructors' perspective) welcome, purpose as well: it allowed them to distance themselves from their material and from their students. The text came between the two.

But now a host of new problems arose.

First, what is a religious Jew? What model are we trying to create? Some years ago, reacting against the careless use of the term "spirituality" in Jewish circles, I suggested that we can discern three different models of Jewish spirituality: the behavioral, the pietistic, and the intellectual. Each of these was proposed as an answer to the question: What does God demand of a Jew above all? Is it a certain behavioral pattern (obedience to the law), inwardness or intense emotion (as in mystical or Hasidic circles), or is it the intellect, study, the mind (as in Maimonides)?[12]

In retrospect, that inquiry seems to me to have been mislabeled. I fixed on the term "spirituality" out of an impatience with the current interest in that particular form of religious expression. I suggested that most Jews who preach "spiritual" Judaism assume a univocal definition of that term, what I identified as the pietistic model, and I then proceeded to question the exclusivity of that model in Judaism. I would have been more honest had I simply insisted that spirituality as it is popularly understood is not a Jewish value in the first place. Among other problems, it reflects a dualistic view of the world and of the human person, which normative Judaism has generally decried.

What I was searching for in that inquiry was, more accurately, a phenomenology of religious authenticity in Judaism. Who is the authentically religious Jew: The Jew who meticulously observes all of the laws? The Jew who feels God's presence most intensely? Or the Jew who devotes his life to the study of God's will? Of course, ideally, all of these should come together; in fact, they are usually in tension, and anyone Jewish usually feels most comfortable with one of the three over the other two.

But each of these models demands its own curriculum, its own set of educational strategies and pedagogical techniques, a distinct faculty, and a school with a distinct culture. Is it possible to get a faculty to agree on any one of these models? My sense is that in the traditionalist academies referred to above, there is a general agreement on the supremacy of the behavioral model of authenticity. The other two models are not ignored, of course, but then alternative models of this kind rarely are. We are dealing with emphases, not exclusivities.

But without this agreement on educational goals, little in the way of Jewish religious education can take place. And it is quite clear that such a consensus will be much more difficult to arrive at in a faculty that is selected primarily for its academic excellence, not for its religious commitments, and particularly in a school that takes a highly nonintrusive stance toward its faculty's private lives.

What further complicates the issue, then, are three long-standing cornerstones of the Seminary's mission: its commitment to academic excellence, its insistence on measuring that achievement by the canons of the American academic community, and its commitment to an essentially academic model of the rabbinate.

It is well-nigh impossible to overestimate the power of these three commitments in the culture of the Seminary. On the first, a simple glance at the roster of names, past and present—Solomon Schechter, Louis Ginsberg, Alexander Marx, Saul

Lieberman, Mordecai Kaplan, Shalom Spiegel, Abraham Joshua Heschel, and my contemporaries Judith Hauptman, David Kraemer, Joel Roth, Seth Schwarz, David Roskies, Anne Lapidus Lerner, just to single out a few—confirms what was frequently repeated in Seminary circles: "The cardinal Seminary sin is shoddy scholarship."

On the second, not only the Hebrew Scriptures but also the Talmud was taught in rabbinical school classes with all of the methods of lower (textual) and higher (source or documentary) criticism.[13] The application of these methods to Scripture is hazardous enough, but their application to Talmudic literature is even more potentially heretical.

In Judaism it is not so much the *p'shat* or plain sense of the biblical text that carries religious value, but rather its Talmudic interpretation. The Sabbath, for example, as it is concretized in the life experience of the Jew, is hardly a biblical institution. It is the Talmud that defines what modes of work are to be avoided, what liturgies to be recited, and what rituals performed, and that weaves the metaphorical web (Sabbath as Queen, Sabbath as Bride) that makes the observance of the day such a rich experience. To suggest that the Talmudic elaboration of the Sabbath law from its biblical and early rabbinic sources is marked by serious gaps and ambiguities and that the later codifications of this legal material may well reflect misunderstandings of the earlier rabbinic sources themselves;[14] that specific laws may reflect sociological or economic influences;[15] that the very methods of Talmudic exegesis of Scripture were borrowed from Hellenistic exegetes of Homeric literature[16]—all without engaging in the "reconstruction" of the text as sacred literature—can only play havoc with the religious sensibilities of students. And then, to insist that despite all of this classroom experience, rabbinical students and their congregants-to-be are expected to observe and teach the Sabbath law as binding simply compounds the confusion.

It should also be noted that the Seminary faculty has always enjoyed total academic freedom, as befits an American academic institution. Mordecai Kaplan, for example, whose naturalist reinterpretation of Judaism and its programmatic implications were very much at odds with the ideology of the leadership of the school and of just about all of his colleagues, nevertheless taught his own material to rabbinical students for more than five decades. When he left, it was at his request. Equally disruptive, it was not uncommon for the Seminary to invite a prominent, secularist Israeli scholar to serve as visiting professor in rabbinical school classes, providing, of course, that his scholarship was beyond reproach.

The third of these cornerstone commitments—the commitment to an academic model of the rabbinate—flowed naturally from the first two. Almost to a person, the Seminary faculty embraced the intellectualist model of authenticity referred to above. In the culture of the Seminary, the model Jew was the scholar, the best of rabbinical students were to be encouraged to enter academia, and only those who could not make it in the academic world would enter the congregational rabbinate. The hierarchy was well nigh explicit, and on occasion, it even led to a sly disparagement of the accoutrements of the rabbinic role. Certain interpretations of biblical texts, for example, would be dismissed, in class, as "sermons."

But even the congregational-rabbi-to-be was expected to be a well-grounded generalist in Judaica. Thus the heavily academic texture of the curriculum, the relegation of professional skills courses to its periphery, the refusal to consider "softcore" subjects such as the sociology of the Jewish community or congregational studies as worthy of course time. In fact, the Seminary's academic emphasis, particularly its emphasis on the mastery of the Hebrew language and of Talmudic texts, was one of the qualities that would distinguish it from the Hebrew Union College, whose graduates, it was believed, were never exposed to this intensive training.

If it is impossible to overestimate the power of these three basic Seminary commitments, it is equally clear how much they militate against any simplistic definition of what religious education might look like in a setting of this kind. It may be possible

126

to claim that the faculty's commitment to scholarship in the scientific mode was, in fact, a modern transformation of the intellectualist model of religious authenticity and that these scholars' inquiries were as much a religious quest as those of the traditional exegetes,[17] but that understanding was rarely apparent to their students, hardly ever emerged in the actual classroom experience, and was never explicitly articulated or defined. Finally, the exclusivity of this model in Seminary faculty circles served to distance those rabbinical students who did not share that model.

Despite these obstacles, the issue of the religious dimension of rabbinic education remains *the* Seminary issue, addressed in faculty meetings and in student forums, discussed at length in the self-evaluation material that was prepared for our reaccreditations in 1986, 1996, and 2006, and again and again in classroom settings. Most important, it has led to a thorough revision of the curriculum of the rabbinical school, in the 1989–1990 and 2006–2007 academic years. There is also near-universal agreement that these changes must never be bought at the price of sacrificing the school's strong academic orientation, the academic superiority of its faculty, its commitment to critical scholarship, or its academic model of the rabbi. The school will never abide that, nor should it be asked to. The culture of the Seminary is firmly established and generally esteemed; if anything, the scholarly demands that the lay community is making of its rabbis today are higher than ever before. Almost all American lay Jews now have a college education; large numbers of them are competent professionals or academicians. They expect their rabbis to be masters of their field, as they are of theirs.

But this new model will make unprecedented demands on the faculty. It will lead, in particular, to a significant reassessment of the authority structure in the classroom. The classic curricular structure, particularly its strong textual emphasis, invested instructors with clear and unambiguous authority. Their mastery of their disciplines, of the texts and tools required to read them, served as their power base.[18] The educational enterprise that followed was inherently infantilizing. In fact, one of the mysteries of the original Seminary style of rabbinic education is that it used an infantilizing educational experience to create an authority figure. Not unexpectedly, the graduates of this structure transposed it to the congregational setting, except that now, they did the infantilizing. Just look at the design of the large, suburban cathedral-style synagogue: The rabbi stands in front of and above the congregants, who are seated below in long, immobile pews and who sit, stand, turn to the proper page, read in English or in Hebrew, in unison or responsively—all in response to their rabbi's instructions—and who listen quietly and passively to the sermon that is preached to them.[19]

The new setting demands that instructors go beyond the explication of the text and expose their own personal struggle with its existential significance. There is no questioning the leveling of the authority structure that ensues whenever this takes place. The classroom becomes the arena for shared inquiry. To the extent that the faculty is transmitting the mastery of a discipline, its authority remains intact, but when it steps out of that traditional Seminary role and begins to wrestle with issues of meaning, its authority rests more in its prior engagement in a process than in any form of mastery. That enterprise is infinitely more hazardous. It requires a readiness to be personal; to put one's own agenda, feelings, achievements, and failures into the arena; to change one's mind; to explore, retreat, advance again, frequently without a clear vision of the outcome. It demands a good deal of charity and an ability to live with the possibility that there may be a number of equally tentative and legitimate outcomes to the inquiry. In short, it represents a new and anxiety-making experience.

This process does not have to take place in every class, nor should every instructor be expected to engage in it. But it has to take place somewhere, and the curriculum of the rabbinical school, *from the outset*, has to be shaped around those settings where it is *designed* to take place—not as an appendix to a lecture, or as an afterthought, or in extracurricular discussion groups, but at the heart of the teaching process itself. That is what distinguishes the curriculum of a rabbinical school from that of a graduate school.

This transformation of the authority structure in the rabbinical school will lead to a similar and parallel transformation in the congregation. In fact, this transformation is already taking place—for example in the emergence of the new *havurah*-style setting for worship (worship takes place in a library or classroom, seats are movable and all on the same level, intimacy and community are encouraged, the service is democratic and participatory) and in the replacement of the traditional sermon with a question-and-answer session or discussion of the biblical readings, with the rabbi asking questions and *listening*, as well as speaking.

GOD AS AN EVOLVING SYMBOLIC SYSTEM

Finally, on the substantive issue itself, I can do no more—or no less—here than what I attempt to do in the classroom, which is to trace how I myself struggle to resacralize my tradition without sacrificing the critical perspective that remains precious to me.[20]

My teachers in this enterprise have been Clifford Geertz, Paul Tillich, and James Fowler. Geertz's "Religion as a Cultural System" remains the single most impressive attempt to capture what a religious perspective on the world is designed to accomplish, namely, to formulate "conceptions of a general order of existence" through a system of symbols that engender "powerful, pervasive and long-lasting moods and motivations."[21] Tillich's *Dynamics of Faith* opened my eyes to the structure of the act of faith and the indispensability and power of religious and theological symbols and myths.[22] Finally, Fowler's *Stages of Faith* made it possible for me to understand my own theological journey—in particular, how I was able to move from his stage 4 to stage 5, from the individuative-reflective faith of my Seminary years and after, to the conjunctive faith that I am now trying to teach, or, in Tillich's language, to affirm Torah as the classical and authoritative formulation of a "broken," but very much "living," myth.[23]

This crossroad between Fowler's stages 4 and 5, the focus of this entire inquiry, is precisely where most of my students are stuck. I understand my task as the attempt to get them over this hurdle, to convey to them the full exhilaration and liberating power of Paul Ricoeur's "second naivete."[24]

I am most clearly aware of this sense of liberation when I deal with the issue of God in Jewish theology. For reasons that should be obvious by now, the discomfort that most Conservative rabbis feel when asked to preach or teach the Jewish concept(s) of God is amply justified. Looking back at my own teaching experience, I now understand that though I have always taught the classical Jewish literature on God, that is all I did. I taught it at a distance: the classical proofs, the experiential and existential approaches; Maimonides and mystics on God; Heschel, Buber, and Kaplan on God; and the rest. It was a safe, academic exercise.

More recently, I have begun to teach the Jewish concept of God as a complex system of symbols that changes and evolves before our very eyes—I have used the metaphor of a kaleidoscope—as we move from Genesis through the prophets, the Psalms, Job, and the rest of the Bible, and on through the Talmudic aggadah, the classical liturgy, and the later philosophical and mystical literature to our very day.

To speak of God as an evolving symbolic system permits me to ask a host of new questions: Why these symbols and not others? Why the pervasive masculine imagery in the liturgy and not the feminine? Why is God portrayed as creating? as revealing? as redeeming? Why do some of these symbols persist and others die? Why does the system change? Why, for example, is the God of the early Genesis narratives so quick to punish, while the God of the prophets is so patient and eager for repentance? And why is God so vulnerable, so caring, so frustrated, so incapable either of achieving God's goals or of abandoning them, despite God's vaunted power? Why the difference between the harshness of the Samuel-Saul encounter in 1 Samuel 15 and the pathos of the last verses of Jonah? Why is the Book of Job in the canon? What books did not make it, and why? What of the silences? And all of these questions increase and multiply as we move beyond the Bible to the later tradition.

Once the Jewish image of God is portrayed as a complex and evolving paradigm, not as what God is in some essence but rather as the way my ancestors read their experience or mapped their world, all of these questions become legitimate. And then I can also ask: Which of these symbols are alive for me today, which are not, and why? What can I appropriate and transmit, and what do I reject? Effectively, I do for myself what the authors of Job and Jonah did with their received tradition, and I invite my students to do the same. In that spirit, for the most part I no longer ask my students to write research papers. Instead, I require personal position papers on a variety of theological issues: God, revelation, eschatology, the problem of evil and the rest, and then subject these position papers to class discussion. The format demands that they be as personal in their writing as I am in my teaching.

This inquiry draws on the best of modern critical scholarship. It retains its academic character. But it is also imbued throughout with issues of personal meaning, and the teaching experience itself becomes a model of doing theology.

Fowler claims that stage 5 is "unusual before mid-life." That was true in my case, and it may account for the resistance of some students. We are all too painfully aware of the seductive quality of absolute systems and of our need for authoritarian models, whereas this approach puts a premium on individualism, pluralism, the inherently relative nature of all religious claims, personal responsibility, and extended periods of indecision as the process of appropriation and rejection works itself out. But many students have been able to emerge from the experience with a renewed sense of personal integrity and to begin their rabbinical careers with the confidence that their religious and intellectual commitments are at one. That integration, long the hallmark of rabbinic education in traditionalist settings, now reappears within a radically different and novel mindset.

AUTHORITY AND AUTHENTICITY IN JUDAISM

This exposition of Judaism as a complex symbolic and mythical system forces us to confront the twin issues of authority and authenticity in Judaism. Once we deny any literalist understanding of revelation and acknowledge the community's substantive role in shaping its content, these two issues acquire a new urgency. For, first, what criteria does the community invoke in determining if a particular reading of Judaism is, or is not, authentic? Obviously not fidelity to the original revelatory content, for that is also the creation of a community of Jews. But then what? And second, since we have no ultimate authoritative body to pass on contemporary theological statements, who decides? Even more pressing for this conceptualization that accepts the inevitability of theological individualism, how does the community exercise its function?

I now address these issues in class by using the classroom inquiry model that I have sketched above as a paradigm for how Jews have dealt with them in the past. My theological assumptions are grounded in some well-established traditions that acknowledge the indeterminacy of meaning of the revelation at Sinai. According to one of these, at Sinai the divine voice was split into seventy voices, one for each of the seventy nations of the world;[25] according to another, mystical tradition, the divine voice was heard differently by each of the six hundred thousand Jews present at the foot of the mountain.[26] An even more radical suggestion is conveyed by Gershom Scholem in the name of Rabbi Mendel of Rymanov, who claimed that all that was revealed at Sinai was the *aleph*, the first letter of *anokhi* ("I [am]"), the first Hebrew word of the Decalogue. Scholem notes that the *aleph* is nothing more than the position taken by the larynx when a word begins with vowel. "To hear the *aleph*,"

Scholem continues, "is to hear next to nothing; it is the preparation for all audible language, but in itself conveys no determi-
nate, specific meaning. Thus ... Rabbi Mendel transformed the
revelation on Mount Sinai into a mystical revelation, pregnant
with infinite meaning, but without specific meaning."[27]

But despite this indeterminacy of meaning, as the process
of canonization worked itself out, what emerged from Sinai was
one sacred text. Certain readings of revelation were accepted,
others rejected; certain documents were considered authoritative, others not; certain books were canonized, others not. The
dynamics of the process are lost, but if it was not the work of
God, then it had to be the work of the community. Of its leadership? Perhaps—but then it is the community who vests its leadership with the authority to make these decisions.

Still later that sacred text itself became subject to multiple
interpretations. Paradigmatically, look at a page from the
Miqraot Gedolot (literally, the "large Scriptures"), the authoritative, published version of the Hebrew Scriptures. The layout of
each double page includes a few verses of the scriptural text, and
surrounding them, two Aramaic translations, five medieval commentaries, and another five supercommentaries. Effectively,
then, we read Scripture through the eyes of our ancestors, and
we can choose from among them—either the eleventh-century
Frenchman Rashi (an acronym for Rabbi Solomon ben Isaac) for
the literal meaning mingled with an anthology of rabbinic homilies, or Rashi's student, the twelfth-century Samuel ben Meir, or
the twelfth-century Spaniard Abraham Ibn Ezra for a philologi-
cal perspective, or the thirteenth-century Spaniard Moses ben
Nachman for more mystical or philosophical insights, or the late-
fifteenth-century Italian Obadiah ben Jacob Sforno for a more
scientific or critical perspective. All of these varied voices are on
the page, all in dialogue with one another, all offering different
perspectives on the text—which remains one and singular. But
again, who determined which of these exegeses made it onto the
page, if not the community—simply by the process of deciding
who it would read and who it would ignore?[28]

Catch the tension, then, between individual and community, between unity and diversity: one God, one prophet (Moses), but multiple revelatory voices; one Scripture but multiple interpretations; one community but multiple understandings of the text.[29]

And if the criterion for authenticity is neither fidelity to God's will or to the original revelatory content, then we have no alternative but to appeal to the criteria we use to determine mythic truth. A myth is true if it does the things that great myths have always done: open up levels of reality that are otherwise closed to us, unlock hidden dimensions of our own being, explain how our experience of the world "hangs together," help us cope with the predictable and unpredictable crises of living, stimulate loyalty to our community, give us a sense of rootedness or belonging in the world.[30] A vital, living community in an almost intuitive way will screen out those readings of revelation that fail to accomplish these purposes and retain those that do. The process is subtle, complex, messy, and anxiety filled; it may take generations to work itself out—and the committed traditionalist will shun this portrayal like the plague—but for many of us, it is the only way.

Finally, who decides? Everyone—that is, every Jew who has a stake in the outcome, which is nothing less than the continued vitality of Judaism as a religion.[31]

The classroom inquiry is a microcosm of that process. On any one issue, I begin by teaching what I consider to be the most significant options available from within the tradition, and then proceed to teach how I deal with these options in working out my own position. Students then write their own personal statements, and the inquiry comes to a focus in those sessions where a number of these papers are circulated to the entire class for open class critique. In the course of the discussion, positions are clarified, modified, reformulated, and sometimes abandoned. My goal is to enable each student to emerge from the course with a coherent, defensible, personal theology. The interplay between the individual student and the class becomes the paradigm for what transpires in the community at large.

I have been urging my students to use this model as a way of teaching Jewish theology in their own congregational settings. My sense is that our laypeople have theological concerns and are capable of serious thought, provided they are given the resources and a modicum of encouragement and legitimation. That sense of legitimacy is absolutely crucial to Fowler's stage 5, but rabbis will never be able to transmit it to their congregants unless they have it themselves. That achievement remains the key test of an effective rabbinic education.

CHAPTER 10

TEACHING THE *AKEDAH*

My friend and colleague Joe Lukinsky was responsible for one of the most transforming educational moments I have ever experienced in decades of studying and teaching.

For years, Joe and I have shared an interest in the notion of myth: what myths are, how they work, how they shape communities, and how they give birth to rituals that capture the myth in a concrete and vivid form. Myths can be both secular and religious; for example, I recall with particular delight Joe's extended discussion of the mythic quality of baseball. I first encountered the notion of theological and religious myth (and symbol) in Paul Tillich's *Dynamics of Faith*,[1] a book that has played a decisive role in shaping my personal theology to this day. The term "myth" is now omnipresent in the literature of the social sciences and in literary criticism. Of course, by "myth" I do not mean a fiction, legend, or fairy tale, as the term is understood in popular culture; not "myth" as opposed to "facts" or "reality," but rather a pattern of meaning. Myths are the various ways in which we connect the discrete data of nature or history so that they become a coherent statement of what the facts mean. Without such a pattern of meaning, we would not even know what the relevant facts are in any single explanatory inquiry. But the patterns—precisely because they are patterns—isolated by a specific myth are far more elusive than any of the specific facts the myth tries to explain; myths enjoy a singular degree of subjectivity and imagination, which is the source of their strength and their perceived "fictional" quality.

One day some years ago, Joe invited me to attend a workshop on mythic reenactment to be conducted by a friend of his, Professor Sam Laeuchli, then affiliated with Temple University. Laeuchli had developed a technique of reenacting or dramatizing ancient tales—for example, from ancient Greek literature and from the Bible—to probe more deeply into the meaning of these texts.[2] This time, the story to be reenacted was the *akedah*, the binding of Isaac, as narrated in Genesis 22.

I walked into a classroom to find chairs arranged in a circle, with three chairs in the center of the circle. A group of about twenty students had assembled—most of them doctoral students in education from Teachers College, Union Theological Seminary, and The Jewish Theological Seminary. (I was then associate professor of Jewish philosophy at JTS.) Sam spoke briefly at the outset, explaining that he would select three students to play the central characters in the story: Abraham, Isaac, and God. At a signal from him, the three characters would enter into the story and into their roles and begin to talk to one another. There were no intrinsic limitations to the discussion; it could go in whatever direction the characters wished to take it. The point was to fill the many yawning gaps in the biblical narrative. The rest of us were to sit in the circle around them. We could not intervene in the dialogue, but we would have periodic "press conferences" in which we could ask the three participants why they said what they said, what they felt when they said it, and how they understood the story.

Sam snapped his finger and we were off. "God" began, as in the Bible, by commanding Abraham to bring his son to a certain mountain and to bind Isaac as an offering. But contrary to the biblical narrative, our Abraham protested, and our God had to defend his command. Suddenly, I was no longer in a bleak classroom on Broadway. I had entered into a magical realm of mythic space and time, an eternal present, where a primordial, prototypical drama was working itself out. The very spare, bare-bones quality of the biblical narrative, the lack of detail, and the absence of adjectives and of references to feelings—all helped give the proceedings an unreal quality. Unreal, but at the same time, transformative. To say that I was totally absorbed is an understatement; I was transfixed.

The biblical tale is indeed replete with gaps. Where was Sarah? Why doesn't she appear anywhere in this story? What were the "things" (or "words") that preceded God's command to Abraham (in 22:1)? Could they be related to Abraham's expulsion of his concubine, Hagar, and their son, Ishmael, recorded in the chapter immediately preceding this one? Why a three-day journey? What did Abraham feel during these three days? What did Isaac feel? Did they talk to each other, apart from the brief exchange recorded in the text (22:7–8)? Is Abraham's answer to his son a lie, or did he know something that we don't know? Who were the two lads who accompanied the father and son? Why are there two separate angelic speeches at the end? Why angels in the first place, and not God, as at the outset? At the end of the story, we are told where Abraham went, but what happened to Isaac? Isaac doesn't reappear in the biblical narrative until chapters later. And more and more and more. (Recently, in teaching this text, I asked my students to list all the unanswered questions in the narrative. They came up with more than fifty.)[3]

As the drama proceeded, I found myself progressively drawn into the circle, identifying with the personalities, sharing the tension. This was, most, emphatically, not like grading a research paper. I was assaulted with waves of emotion, chiefly anger at our "God," a student at Union Theological. When our Abraham challenged God over the sheer cruelty and absurdity of God's demand, this God responded by insisting that he was God, he was omnipotent, he could demand whatever he wished, and Abraham had to obey. Our Abraham simply capitulated and fell silent. This infuriated me, and with a passion that surprised me, I began to feel that this God had it all wrong!

I voiced my anger at this portrayal of God during the press conference. Sam listened quietly, and then responded, "Okay, let's do it again, and this time you [pointing to me] play God." I protested: I am a professor, not a student; I am an observer, not a participant; I came to learn, not to teach, and so on. He simply led me to my chair in the center, and this time, added a fourth chair for Sarah ("Let's make it a little more interesting!"). He chose a new Abraham and Isaac, and we began again.

Before I (now playing God) could say a word, our Sarah jumped in: "Abraham, it's early in the morning. Where are you and Isaac going?" "To sacrifice our son." "Are you out of your head!?" "It's not my idea. It's his"—pointing to me. Whereupon my Sarah, also from Union, poured forth two thousand years' of accumulated rage at God's (and Christianity's) oppression of women. She must have screamed at me for about ten minutes.

I prayed that Sam would snap his finger so that we could step out of character and so that I could recover and assemble my thoughts before responding. But no such luck. Sarah ended up sobbing, and everyone turned to me. I was terrified. To this day, I'm not completely sure from which level of my being my response came. What I said was something along the following lines: "Look, Sarah. Everybody thinks that I am omnipotent, that I get whatever I want to get here on earth. But in reality, I am a total failure. I have created twenty generations of human beings since Adam, and I have yet to find one human being whose loyalty to me is unquestioned. For the ages, I desperately need to point to one person whose loyalty I was able to win. Please don't stop Abraham. Please let him go on his mission. I need Abraham. Trust me!" I went on in this vein for what seemed to be hours. Mercifully, Sam's finger snapped.

I learned more theology from that moment than from years of reading and reflection. It launched me on an almost decade-long inquiry into the ways in which God is imaged in our classical texts. My methodological assumption is that no human being can grasp God's essential nature in thought or in language. If God is truly God, then God transcends human comprehension. If God is really God, then I, a mere human being, cannot even begin to comprehend God's nature. The alternative, namely, the conviction that God is as God is pictured, is to drift into idolatry. God, then, is not "really," objectively or literally, as God is portrayed in our traditional texts. God is certainly not corporeal, despite the references to God's "mighty hand" (Exod. 13:3). God is not literally male or female. God does not have an inner life; God doesn't really get angry. God is also not in space or time. Our options, then, are either idolatry, or worshipful silence in the face of the transcendent mystery, or the recognition that all characterizations of God are—here, pick your terminology—symbols, metaphors, constructs, or myths. The last of these options is the only one that modern students of religion can adopt.

In itself, that assumption is not at all heretical. It is shared by, among others, Maimonides in the very first pages of his *Mishneh Torah* (book 1, *Basic Principles of the Torah* 1:9–12), who insists that all physical and emotional descriptions of God in the Torah are metaphors or analogies. But I probably break with Maimonides in my belief that these images of God were crafted by human beings, here by our ancestors, and that they emerged out of the wide range of human experiences of how God appeared to them, and continues to appear to us in the course of our varied life experiences. My sense is that Maimonides probably believed that God revealed the metaphors. But I believe that our images of God are human projections, our own, very personal fantasies of what God must be like, if we are to account for the feelings that we experience at those moments when God appears most present to us.

Setting aside the epistemological issues involved in the claim that human beings experience God's presence in their lives—a crucially important issue but one that we will not explore here[4]—my major task is to collect and trace the evolution of these images throughout our literature, from the Bible, the Talmud and midrash, the classical liturgy, medieval philosophy and the kabbalistic tradition, through to Mordecai Kaplan, Martin Buber, and Abraham Joshua Heschel. My conclusion is that our tradition has preserved a wide-ranging, evolving, and fluid system of characterizations of God—fluid because the metaphors come and go, change and recur, are abandoned and then reappear or are replaced, not only within the texts, but also within the liturgical year and in the course of a human life. My image of God on Yom Kippur is very different from my Tisha B'Av image. The God I experienced when I was twenty is different from the God I experienced when I turned sixty. The images can also be positive or negative, laudatory or condemnatory, nurturing or abandoning, loving or cruel and capricious; the God of Psalms 23 or 91 is not the God of the first two chapters of Job or of Genesis 22. And there is precious little inner consistency within the system; the metaphors are frequently in tension with one another. Frequently, we can even catch the transformations of a specific metaphor in later strata of the traditional texts. For example, note the change in Jonah 4:2 of God's self-description in Exodus 34:6–7. Here, the author of Jonah stands the Exodus image on its head. The process is thoroughly subversive.[5]

My charge to my students is that they identify the image in a particular text and then enter into the experience, particularly the feeling and tone, of the person who wrote the text. I ask: What is (or are) the feeling(s) about God expressed in the text? How does the metaphor capture or express the feelings? Why is the story written precisely this way? How else could God have been portrayed? What difference would this have made in the telling? And then: How does God feel about that portrayal? How do you feel about it?

My final requirement is that the student write a personal theological statement reflecting his or her own characteristic image of God. My point is that we have the right and the responsibility to continue the centuries-long process of trying to capture how God appears to humans, now to us, today, in our own cultural and historical context. No footnotes. No bibliography. None of the typical scholarly apparatus. Just a personal statement of what the writer believes. I have conducted workshops of this kind in school and adult-education settings around the country, and I have collected dozens of such statements from students of all ages, rabbis, teachers and laypeople, both men and women. How about this one: "God is Fred Astaire to my Ginger Rogers." Or: "After the Holocaust, God is like a rat caught in a maze.... No, better still, after the Holocaust, God is the maze." The first was from a rabbinic colleague, the second from an eleven-year-old! Both led to some of the most fascinating theological discussions I've had in years.

Now, when I teach Genesis 22, I ask my students to retell the story from the perspective of some character in the tale or elsewhere, in some other voice—God, Sarah, Isaac, Abraham, Hagar, Ishmael, the two servants, the donkey, the ram, Job, a Holocaust survivor. (One student chose to tell the story in the voice of the knife!) The results are mind boggling. My feelings of guilt at how my students frequently stand the biblical story on its head are assuaged by the extraordinarily rich transformations of the biblical tale in the hands of the rabbinic midrashim. If the midrash could insist that Abraham actually killed his son, who was then resurrected by the tears of the angels flowing over his face—all in explicit contradiction of the Bible—then we should be able to tolerate our own modern spins on the text. Midrash also arises out of the gaps in a text. What I want from my students is for them to write their own, modern midrashim on this text.

The image of God that I discern in the *akedah* narrative is vulnerability. That God has a vulnerable side I had learned from my teacher Abraham Joshua Heschel—though that association did not occur to me until well after the workshop. As mentioned in an earlier chapter, Heschel writes at length of God's "pathos"—God's passionate caring, reaching out, involvement with the world. The divine pathos, Heschel claims, is the ground-tone of all of God's relationship with human beings. But to care for someone is to be vulnerable; we can only be hurt by someone we care about. That's why I was so much opposed to the image of the macho God described by The Union Theological Seminary student. To me, the God of the *akedah* is a desperate, needy, pleading, and vulnerable God. This is a God who has ceded to Abraham the power to make God really God.

This may be a way of "doing theology," but it is a very different way of conducting the inquiry from the ones usually employed in academic circles. For me, it represents the difference between teaching theology to graduate students and to rabbinical students. The former discussion takes place in a classical academic context; the inquiry is detached, objective, historical, and critical. The latter is an existential experience. We may begin with the dispassionate inquiry, but we should then go beyond it into the issue of personal meaning. Now that we know what the text meant to the author, we should ask what it means to us. That's what rabbis today should be asking when they preach the biblical text before their congregants on a Sabbath morning.

That insight impelled me to begin to teach theology to rabbinical students in a very different way. In my early years, I used to teach as I was taught. The professor stood apart from the text; the text effectively interposed itself between the instructor and the students. From my teachers, I learned everything about the text—its provenance, its setting in ancient Near Eastern culture, its accuracy, its probable dating—everything but what the text meant to my teacher in the most personal way, or what it might mean to the rabbinical student, or how this meaning was to be conveyed to a congregation of lay Jews. Why is this text there in the first place? Why do we read it again and again? How can it change our lives?

Not for a moment do I even want to imply that my education at the Seminary was anything but an intellectually exhilarating experience. My teachers were the greatest scholars of

Judaica in the whole world. I gobbled up everything they had to offer and spent six years on a perpetual academic high. But too often, at the end of a class, I was left with, "So what! What am I supposed to do with this text now?" (To be fair, this critique did not apply to all my teachers; certainly, Mordecai Kaplan, Shalom Spiegel, and Heschel himself did address issues of meaning—but they were the exceptions to the rule.) Since I never served a congregation, I was never forced to deal with these questions until I began to teach rabbinical students. That's when I began to realize that I was failing them.

What I learned from my experience was to go beyond the text into the living experience that generated the text in the first place. For the very first time, I understood Genesis 22 from God's perspective, not the anonymous narrator's. I had now entered God's persona as I understood it out of my own experience. I have used this method in teaching other texts in our classical literature and to help my students do the same, so that they in turn may help their students to lift the story off the printed page and into their hearts.

I also realized that if I was going to ask my students to pursue this method, I would have to do it myself, precisely in the classroom, in their presence. That meant putting my self, my own feelings, into the inquiry. If I wanted them to personalize the discussion, I had to set the example and do it myself. It was only much later that I came to the realization that what I was doing stretched the reigning teaching paradigm in our school. I was reshaping what I understood as the school's overemphasis on cognitive learning. I was redressing the balance between the cognitive and the affective. I never demean the cognitive material. We are frequently dealing with students who come to us without any serious background in Judaica and Hebraica, and in five or six years we are expected to transform them into authoritative spokespersons for Judaism. That by itself is an impossible task. But for rabbis-to-be, the affective issues should have an equal place in the curriculum and in their teaching and preaching. They will have to counsel families on the death of a child, or in preparation for a wedding, or when the primary wage earner is unemployed for an extensive period. How can we ignore the affective dimension of the rabbi's work at such times?

That change of emphasis has a number of critical implications. First, faculty in our schools are hired and promoted according to Western, academic criteria, chief among which is the publication of scholarly books and articles, with footnotes, bibliographies, and the rest. Professors are not hired for their personal religious sensibilities. The absence of such a sensibility would never disqualify a candidate, but scholarly limitations of some kind always will. I am, then, questioning the accepted criteria for academic standing in our school. Second, how does one grade a personal theological statement or a modern midrash? Third, most of my courses are cross-registered in both the rabbinical and the graduate schools. Graduate students are not expected to be "religious"—Jews or anything else. (I handle that issue by agreeing to accept a classical research paper from these students in place of the more personal theological statement.) But I insist that the rabbi is not a mini-professor. He or she must be a religious role model for a congregation of Jews. That role model does demand serious, Western-type learning, but it also demands much more—a grasp of what it means to be a religious Jew and of what it takes to create a congregation of religious Jews.[6]

I have never had the nerve to conduct a reenactment workshop with my own students. In fact, before concluding that workshop, Sam warned us against doing this: "It's much more complicated than it looks." Indeed it is! Serious ethical and psychological implications simmer close to the surface. This is, most emphatically, not an opportunity for group therapy, but it is abundantly clear that role-playing awakens a wide range of private, emotional issues. The leader must be aware of this and act quickly to protect the participant from himself.

That Joe Lukinsky inspired me to transform the way I teach theology is probably the least of his many accomplishments. But for that, I owe him my profound gratitude.

145

PART THREE

ISRAEL

CHAPTER 11

JUDAISM AND THE
SEARCH FOR SPIRITUALITY

What is a "spiritual" Jew? The attempt to frame a Jewish definition of spirituality is a troublesome issue.

Most of us share the common assumption that spirituality is a value; whoever has achieved it enjoys our esteem. We have also witnessed Jews denounce other Jews for their lack of spirituality and we bemoan its absence.

On the other hand, the term is one of a number of terms—"sacred," "soul," "holy" are others—that have been emptied of content by centuries of abuse. It is frequently invoked to create a mood of religiosity that is often at variance with the feelings of the speaker, the community being addressed, or the situation in which it is used. It smacks of sanctimoniousness, religion at its most vapid.

On a more serious level, there is a question as to whether "spirituality" as it is currently understood is an authentic Jewish value in the first place. It reflects a dualistic view of the human being that is more Platonic and Christian than biblical and rabbinic. It implies a debasement of the human body as at best trivial, and at worst, a prison for the nonmaterial spirit that is the "real" person and the locus of this person's value. It denies the

149

meaningfulness of human activity in the social and interpersonal realms of this world; the authentic believer must then escape this world through a mystical flight of the soul into some other supernatural world that alone is "true" or "real." It leads inevitably to an otherworldly eschatology that postpones the fulfillment of human aspirations until after the death of the person and the collapse of the social order. In other words, is not the current search for spirituality one more example of the attempt to bring to bear Western (read: Greek and Christian) categories of thought on Jewish (read: biblical and rabbinic) forms of religious expression, and hence to be dismissed? That is one way of looking at it. On the other hand, is it wise or even possible to tell our contemporaries that Judaism is not interested or has no room for what they understand to be a genuine religious value? How do we respond to their quest? How do we participate in what they see as a serious religious inquiry?

We can neither dismiss the issue nor uncritically buy the commonly accepted, univocal definition of spirituality. A third option is to broaden the frame. This option assumes that those religious traditions with long and successful careers have embodied within themselves a variety of models of spirituality that speak to the variety of human tempers and the wide range of cultural situations encountered in the course of their history. It is precisely this plurality of models that has guaranteed their ongoing vitality and effectiveness in mobilizing the commitment of adherents over centuries.

If valid, this approach has to assume a more neutral definition of spirituality, one that does not prejudge what its characteristics are to be. Let us then define "spirituality" as that which, according to the believer, God demands above all. God demands many things: forms of behavior, emotions, a set of beliefs or intellectual formulations, and more. However, by "spirituality," we are trying to get at that form of religious expression which the believer considers indispensable. It is the ultimate focus of religious energy, that dimension which acquires supreme emphasis. It defines the authentic believer. The spiritual Jew is the ideal embodiment of Judaism. Clearly this definition of spirituality is not commonly accepted. However, unless we want to dismiss the entire issue as irrelevant or capitulate to a definition that reflects what is in fashion in any one era, my sense is that this third neutral option is the only one available to us.

We should turn then to the history of Judaism as a religion, in search for those models that Jews in the course of their historical experience sought to embody. First, a brief phenomenological description of three such models. I do not claim that these three are exhaustive. However, I do find them all to be classical and authentic forms of Jewish spiritual expression as I have defined it. Each reveals a deliberate process of selection. Each emphasizes one form of expression over others. None ever denies or excludes others; to do so would be to take oneself out of the community. Rather it is a matter of setting up a heirarchy of values, of choosing one form to be most important, to be the one that God wants most of all. The others remain desirable, but in a secondary way. One value is ultimate. It defines spirituality for that believer.

The three Jewish models that I would like to describe in this preliminary way are respectively the behavioral, the pietistic, and the intellectual. Each has its roots in classical formulations of Judaism, in the Bible and rabbinic literature. But each emerges again at different points in Jewish history in response to different tempers and different conditions, to this very day. Each becomes institutionalized and implies a curriculum for the education of the believer. Each determines what should take place within the synagogue, the home, and the academy, or on the street. The fact that there is a plurality of models inevitably leads to conflict within the community, and many of the major controversies in Jewish history can be understood as clashes between different models of spirituality embraced by different segments of the community at one time.

The behavioral model is rooted in the biblical notion of covenant. The biblical community understood itself to have been brought into being through God's covenant, established at

Sinai. Every covenant implies concrete behavioral patterns, usually expressed in the form of law, that are tied to the covenant and that define the difference between being covenanted and its alternative. Hence, the prevalence of codes of law in the Bible and, since biblical times, the omnipresent nexus between authentic Jewishness and mitzvot, those actions that the Jew is commanded to observe as a member of the covenanted community. Over and again, the Bible tells us that what God wants from the biblical community above all is for members to walk in God's ways, to observe the commandments, statutes, and laws. Until very recently, all Jews implicitly understood that to be an authentic Jew meant to observe Jewish law. The Rabbis correctly grasped the centrality of this form of expression in biblical religion, and most of rabbinic literature is an elaboration of biblical law to the point where it becomes omnipresent in the life of the Jew. It is no accident that the first formal literary product of rabbinic Judaism is the Mishnah, an elaborate codification of biblical law and its rabbinic interpretation over centuries.

The observance of the mitzvot emerges as a model of spirituality when it becomes the focal point of Jewish energy and the ultimate defining mark of Jewish identity. This observance becomes infused with meticulousness, precision, and an obsession with detail. For example, one finds a Talmudic master counting the number of commandments, positive and negative, that are incumbent on the Jew. On this model of spirituality, the number of commandments that a Jew observes every day becomes crucially important. One more or one less makes a major difference. Someone coming from a different model or a different religion might well ask, who cares whether there are 613 or 614 or 612? From within this model, however, the Jew cares a great deal because each commandment observed, every sin avoided, pleases God.

One of the ways in which it is possible to recognize a model of spirituality is to see it as somewhat of a caricature. The term "caricature" of course, represents the judgment of the outsider. To the person operating within the model it is not at all a caricature but Judaism at its most authentic. This behavioral model, for example, appears as a caricature in the tendency of some students of Talmud to dismiss the narrative portions of Talmudic literature as not worthy of serious study; one should concentrate exclusively on the legal portions. Or take this statement: "It really doesn't make that much difference what you believe. Did you put on *tefillin* this morning? That's what's important"; or the dismissal of Jewish philosophy as "sermons," not worthy of a serious curriculum of Jewish studies. Many of us have heard these or similar statements at various points in our Jewish education.

Here is a vivid example of the behavioral model from a paper on euthanasia by Rabbi J. David Bleich, an authority on Jewish law and ethics. Rabbi Bleich describes his learning that an elderly relative who was comatose and in critical condition was not receiving aggressive medical care. The doctors had determined that the patient was terminal. Rabbi Bleich insisted that "as a matter of halakha" the patient should be given every indicated medication though he realized that the decision "was not an easy one." But then the following occurred:

> Late Shabbat afternoon I returned from *Minchah* and, although the patient had been totally unresponsive for over thirty-six hours, I walked into the hospital room and said "*Gut Shabbos*" in a loud voice. I was greeted in response by the flickering of an eyelid and, in a weak but clear voice, the words "*Gut Shabbos*" returned. At that moment there flashed across my mind the comments of Rab Akiva Eger (*Orach Chayyim* 271:1) who declares that even the simple, standard *Shabbat* greeting expressed by one Jew to another constitutes a fulfillment of the mitzvah: "Remember the Sabbath day to keep it holy." At that moment I realized not only intellectually, but also emotionally, that every moment of life is of inestimable value. Here was a dramatic unfolding of the lesson that every moment of life carries with

it the opportunity for the performance of yet one more *mitzvah.*[1]

Bleich's final verdict on the *halakhot* of euthanasia are irrelevent here. What is of interest, however, is his process of reasoning, the values that he invokes in reaching his decision. These reveal his hierarchy of values and his model of spirituality.

This model invariably places less emphasis on emotion, inwardness, devotion, or the place of the intellect, which are never dismissed in principle; in practice, however, the Jew who operates within this model relegates them to an inferior status. Their absence may be mourned but it is not crucial. What would be calamitous would be to cease behaving in this particular way.

Not surprisingly the most powerful contemporary attack on this model of spirituality can be found in Abraham Joshua Heschel's tirade against what he so felicitously calls "religious behaviorism."

> Through sheer punctiliousness in observing the law one may become oblivious of the living presence and forget that the law is not for its own sake but for the sake of God. Indeed, the essence of observance has, at times, become encrusted with so many customs and conventions that the jewel was lost in the selling. Outward compliance with externalities of the law took the place of the engagement of the whole person to the living God. What is the ultimate objective of observance if not to become sensitive to the spirit of Him, in whose ways the mitsvot are signposts?
>
> Halacha must not be observed for its own sake but for the sake of God. The law must not be idolized. It is a part, not all, of the Torah. We live and die for the sake of God rather than for the sake of the law.[2]

Parenthetically, Heschel's writings show a bewildering plurality of models of spirituality. We will study them below.

The polar opposite of the behavioral model of spirituality is the pietistic. One of the most accurate descriptions of this model can be found, not surprisingly, in Martin Buber's early (1910) paper entitled "Jewish Religiosity." This paper contains a prefiguration of what Buber was later to characterize as the distinction between I-Thou and I-it. In this paper the contrast is between "religiosity" and "religion," where religiosity emerges as the Buberian ideal (later to become I-Thou) and religion as everything that is inauthentic in religious practice (later to be dubbed I-it).

> I say and mean: religiosity. I do not say and do not mean: religion. Religiosity is man's sense of wonder and adoration, an ever anew becoming, an ever anew articulation and formulation of his feeling that, transcending his conditioned being yet bursting from its very core, there is something that is unconditioned. Religiosity is his longing to establish a living communion with the unconditioned, his will to realize the unconditioned through his action, transposing it into the world of man. Religion is the sum total of the customs and teachings articulated and formulated by the religiosity of a certain epoch in a people's life; its prescriptions and dogmas are rigidly determined and handed down as unalterably binding to all future generations, without regard for their newly developed religiosity, which seeks new forms.... Thus religiosity is the creative, religion the organizing, principle. Religiosity starts anew with every young person, shaken to his very core by the mystery; religion wants to force him into a system stabilized for all time. Religiosity means activity—the elemental entering-into-relation with the absolute; religion means passivity—an acceptance of the handed-down command. Religiosity has only one goal; religion several. Religiosity induces sons who want to find their own God, to rebel against their fathers;

155

religion induces fathers to reject their sons, who will not let their fathers' God be forced upon them. Religion means preservation; religiosity, renewal.[3]

On this second, pietistic model, what God wants above all is inner devotion, that elusive term *kavanah*. Those of us who know something about Buber's background will identify this model with Hasidism, but its roots are much earlier. It is reflected in the biblical injunction that above all we must love the Lord our God with all our heart, with all our soul, and with all our might. It is frequently encountered in the Psalms, for example in these verses:

> Like a hind crying for water, my soul cries for You, O God; my soul thirsts for God, the living God; O when will I come to appear before God! (Ps. 42:2–3)

> Where can I escape from Your spirit? Where can I flee from Your presence? If I ascend to heaven, You are there; if I descend to Sheol, You are there too. If I take wing with the dawn to come to rest on the western horizon, even there Your hand will be guiding me, Your right hand will be holding me fast. If I say, "Surely darkness will conceal me, night will provide me with cover," darkness is not dark for You; night is as light as day; darkness and light are the same. (Ps. 139:7–12)[4]

It is eloquently expressed in the *piyyut* "Yedid Nefesh" by the sixteenth-century mystic Eliezer Azikri:

> Soul mate, loving God, compassion's gentle source,
> Take my disposition and shape it to Your will.
> Like a darting deer will I rush to You,
> Before Your glorious Presence humbly will I bow.
> Let Your sweet love delight me with its thrill,
> Because no other dainty will my hunger fill.

How splendid is Your light, illumining the world.
My soul is weary yearning for Your love's delight.
Please, good God, do heal her; reveal to her Your face,
The pleasure of Your Presence, bathed in Your grace.
She will find strength and healing in Your sight;
Forever will she serve You, grateful, with all her might.

What mercy stirs in You since days of old, my God.
Be kind to me, Your own child; my love for You
    requite.
With deep and endless longing I yearned for Your
    embrace.
To see my light in Your light, basking in Your grace.
My heart's desire, find me worthy in Your sight.
Do not delay Your mercy, please hide not Your light.

Reveal Yourself, Beloved, for all the world to see,
And shelter me in peace beneath Your canopy.
Illumine all creation, lighting up the earth,
And we shall celebrate You in choruses of mirth.
The time, my Love, is now; rush, be quick, be bold.
Let Your favor grace me, in the spirit of days of old.[5]

It is present in the rabbinic statement that above all, "God demands the heart" (B. Sanhedrin 106b). Buber sees an expression of this model in early Christianity,[6] and he is undoubtedly correct. It is also at the heart of Paul's claim that justification is through faith and not through works. The dispute between Jews and Christians on the relative primacy of faith over "works" (i.e., behavior), of course, represents a conflict between the behavioral and pietistic models of spirituality. The rabbinic dispute as to whether or not observance of the mitzvot requires *kavanah* (B. B'rachot 13a) is a similar but Jewish version of Paul's struggle between justification by faith or by works. Pietism is also the operative model for all forms of Jewish mysticism.

Again pietism becomes a model of spirituality when it is emphasized as supremely important, leading even to the disregard of other authentic Jewish values. The non-intellectualism that is a central strain in certain forms of Hasidism has long been noted. We are familiar with the Hasidic story in which the rebbe points to the poor, ignorant shepherd who cannot recite the proper words of the prayer in the proper order but who instead plays on his flute or recites the alphabet and pleads that God arrange the letters of the alphabet into suitable prayers. He is the authentic Jew, not the masses who observe the letter of the law. His prayer is authentic, not theirs. We find these stories charming and inspirational, and frequently use or misuse them to mobilize our congregants into feeling a greater sense of inwardness. However, one can see clearly why these stories outraged other Jews operating within different spiritual models. In effect, these stories cast into question not only the entire value of Jewish law but also the authority of the proponent of these alternative structures, the rav, as opposed to the rebbe. The dispute then between *hasidim* and their opponents was at its root a conflict between models of spirituality, between the pietistic model and its behavioral, or intellectualist counterparts. What this dispute clearly highlights is the way in which two models become institutionalized, leading to different visions of leadership, different curricula, and different patterns of religious expression. When these coexist at any one time, conflict, often vicious, is inevitable.

As fervently as Heschel attacked the behavioral model of spirituality, his writings also include a passionate attack on this pietistic model as well, however congenial it is to his Hasidic roots. For all of his openness to Christianity, Heschel understood the Pauline doctrine of justification through faith and its explicit rejection of the behavioral model to be a radical distortion of religion. He attacks it with passion. Here is a representative passage:

> It would be a device of conceit, if not presumption, to insist that purity of the heart is the exclusive test of

piety. Perfect purity is something we rarely know how to obtain or how to retain. No one can claim to have purged all the dross even from his finest desire. The self is finite, but selfishness is infinite.

God asks for the heart, but the heart is oppressed with uncertainty in its own twilight. God asks for faith, and the heart is not sure of its own faith. It is good that there is a dawn of decision for the night of the heart; deeds to objectify faith, definite forms to verify belief.[7]

Heschel pleads for an integration of the behavioral and pietistic models. One of the most eloquent chapters in all of his work is his study of prayer in *Man's Quest for God*, which argues for the indispensability of both *keva* and *kavanah*, structure and spontaneity, behavior and piety in the life of religion and in the experience of worship.[8] Heschel likes to deal with these polarities and to insist that we maintain both in a state of tension.[9] The difficulties inherent in living with this tension are obvious.

The third model, the intellectual, is more elusive. It claims that what God wants above all is knowledge, understanding, the mind. It also is implicit in the Bible, where God's words and covenant are embodied in a book. The book is read to the community as part of the covenant experience. The biblical community is commanded to study the book and teach it diligently to its children. As soon as the book is seen as embodying God's revelation to the community, the study of the book becomes the primary means to discovering God's will. Study becomes a model of spirituality when it is no longer a means to authenticity but rather an end in itself. Understandably, then, this model is shaped once the book is closed. At that moment revelation ceases, the book becomes canonical, and the leader of the community is no longer the bearer of revelation but rather the one that has access to the book: the *sofer* or "man of the book,"[10] rather than the prophet. In Jewish history, these factors coincide at the time of Ezra and Nehemiah in the fifth century BCE. On this basis, we trace the roots of Pharisaic Judaism to Ezra and Nehemiah and discern within Pharisaic Judaism the notion that *talmud Torah*, or the worshipful study of Torah, becomes the central religious act. This view is epitomized in the rabbinic notion that the ignorant can never achieve piety. It is reflected in the rabbinic dispute as to what has supremacy, study or the observance of the mitzvot. In the later tradition, it is reflected in the idealization of the *matmid*, the student who spends his entire day pouring over the Talmud, as a religious hero-type. In other circles, it was the *lamdan*. Study or, as it is characterized in the Yiddish, *lernen*, becomes the religious ideal, and the study of Torah becomes the primary form of religious expression, a model of spirituality. Only in Judaism is it even conceivable to find a dispute as to whether one may or may not interrupt one's study of Torah to engage in worship. We know, of course, that the majority opinion is that one should. But the dispute itself, the very fact that this should be an issue, reflects an intellectualist view of spirituality, one that sees study of the sacred text as the ultimate religious ideal above all else, even possibly above prayer.

The paradigmatic statement of this model can be found in the writings of Maimonides, the most Aristotelian of Jewish medieval philosophers. For Aristotle, the acquisition of metaphysical knowledge is uniquely and supremely redemptive, and Maimonides agrees. The classical expression of that model is in chapter 51 of part 3 of Maimonides' *Guide for the Perplexed*, the parable of the ruler who is in his palace and whose subjects are located at various distances from him.

> Now I shall interpret to you this parable that I have invented. I say then: Those who are outside the city are all human individuals who have no doctrinal belief, neither one based on speculation nor one that accepts the authority of tradition: such individuals as the furthermost Turks found in the remote North, the Negroes found in the remote South, and those who resemble them from among them that are with us in

160

these climes. The status of those is like that of irrational animals. To my mind they do not have the rank of men, but have among the beings a rank lower than the rank of man but higher than the rank of apes. For they have the external shape and lineaments of a man and a faculty of discernment that is superior to that of the apes.

Those who are within the city, but have turned their backs upon the ruler's habitation, are people who have opinions and are engaged in speculation, but who have adopted incorrect opinions either because of some great error that befell them in the course of their speculation or because of their following the traditional authority of one who had fallen into error. Accordingly because of these opinions, the more these people walk, the greater is their distance from the ruler's habitation. And they are far worse than the first. They are those concerning whom necessity at certain times impels killing them and blotting out the traces of their opinions lest they should lead astray the ways of others.

Those who seek to reach the ruler's habitation and to enter it, but never see the ruler's habitation, are the multitude of the adherents of the Law. I refer to the ignoramuses who observe the commandments.

Those who have come up to the habitation and walk around it are the jurists who believe true opinions on the basis of traditional authority and study the law concerning this practice of divine service, but do not engage in speculation concerning the fundamental principles or religion and make no inquiry whatever regarding the rectification of belief.

Those who have plunged into speculation concerning the fundamental principles of religion, have entered the antechambers. People there indubitably have different ranks. He, however, who has achieved demonstration, to the extent that that is possible, or everything that may be demonstrated; and who has ascertained in divine matters, to the extent that that is possible, everything that may be ascertained; and who has come close to certainty in those matters in which one can only come close to it—has come to be with the ruler in the inner part of the habitation.[11]

More recently this model was embodied in the *Wissenschaft* school of Jewish scholarship. An anecdotal formulation of that model is Professor Louis Finkelstein's statement that "when I pray I speak to God; when I study, God speaks to me." It was clear that at The Jewish Theological Seminary during the Finkelstein era, study was the preeminent Jewish virtue. He insisted that no matter what issues might be raging in the Jewish or general community at large, classes at the seminary would never be cancelled. At its best, the contemporary version of this model is exemplified in the attempt of the senior faculty of that school to try to get to the most precise formulation of the *p'shat* or literal meaning of a particular verse of the Bible or passage of the Talmud. Every possible method of inquiry, every piece of evidence, every scholarly tool was used to arrive at the most precise formulation of the literal meaning of the text.

In retrospect, the experience of studying Bible with Professor H. L. Ginsberg provided a paradigm for this approach. Ginsberg's struggle was to get to the clearest formulation of the literal meaning of the text. In our student days, many of us mocked this approach. We too asked, as more recent generations of students have asked: So what if we now understand what Isaiah was trying to say? What difference does it make to me? What difference will it make to my congregants? How do I translate that into an adult education lecture or into a sermon? These questions may be legitimate, but to Professor Ginsberg and his colleagues, the attempt to unearth the precise meaning of the text was far more than an exercise in technical, scholarly activity. It was, I believe, a genuinely modern version of an ancient Jewish spiritual exercise, the study of the text as a way of getting to what it is that God wants of God's community. It was a modern version of the *talmud Torah* model of spirituality, where the ultimate religious goal is to use the mind to discern God's intent. In both the ancient and modern versions of this model, that intellectual effort came to be the end itself. Sure, behavior is important, inwardness is important. But what did you spend day and night doing? What monopolized your best energies, your best efforts? The study—here, the critical study—of the sacred text.

This model, as much as the other two, has its own trade-offs. It creates an aristocracy of the intellect, effectively denigrating those who cannot play according to its rules. It tends to minimize overt expressions of religious feeling. It generally takes a minimalist view of behavioral expression; one performs what is required, not more—and that, often in a routinized way. Maimonides' parable says it all. Those citizens who circle around the ruler's habitation without entering it are "the ignoramuses who observe the commandments." Those who are with the ruler in his inner habitation are those few who have achieved demonstrable metaphysical truth. These prophet-philosophers are Maimonides' ideal.

It is possible that these three models do not exhaust the possibilities. Others may be equally authentic. Two of these should be mentioned here: the ethical model as embodied in classical Reform Judaism, and the ascetic model that reigned in some Jewish circles both in antiquity and in the Middle Ages. My sense, however, is that each of these is a submodel of one of my three; the ethical is clearly a version of the behavioral model, and the ascetic, an extreme formulation of the pietistic. I continue to believe that my three models are irreducible one to the other. Hence I view them as paradigmatic.

Finally, what lends any one of these models religious significance? What makes it precisely a model of spirituality? The fact that it is a response of the believer to the presence of God, to God's command. We should never trivialize that. The believer, within the context of any one model, is convinced that this response alone lends ultimate meaning to his or her life. To do otherwise would be to flout God, and who can do that and live?

Of interest are the varying ways in which different believers within the same community concretize what it is that God commands. What happens at the point of contact between the psyche of the believer and God? How is that experience shaped into a specific form of religious expression? Why one form and not another? These questions remain for a further inquiry.

To turn to our situation today, it is not at all grandiose to suggest that despite the generalized ignorance and casualness of most American Jews toward Jewish religious expression, contemporary Jews are genuinely searching for models of spirituality. After all, the models are just that—models, ideal formulations, only rarely fully embodied and then only among a handful of Jews at any time. Most Jews in most ages who cared at all about their Jewishness were and remained on the road, in search. Whatever model they tried to achieve was in fact embodied only in a fragmentary and transitory way. So is it today. Comparative statistics are irrelevant. As long as there are some Jews out there who care and who inquire, however fragmentary their expressions may be, we must deal with their concerns. And there are such Jews out there.

Second, it is crucial to this inquiry that we encourage the legitimacy of a plurality of models. We simply cannot do otherwise. If our analysis of the classical material is in any way accurate, Judaism has always been rich and vital enough to provide the resources for many such models. Its survival through such a wide variety of historical, cultural, and geographic settings testifies to its ability to speak to the full range of human and cultural tempers. And if our generation is, as we say it is, one that puts a premium on individual expression—if we are all, as we say we are, Jews by choice—then we must flaunt Judaism's ability to speak in many idioms. If we need caring Jews, we should accept and encourage whatever way they want to express that concern.

That plurality of models assumes our more neutral and open definition of Jewish spirituality. The more we turn to a narrow, rigorous definition, the more we view that ideal in its literal sense as postulating the supremacy of the spirit over the body, inwardness and emotion over external behavior, or some other nonmaterial world over this familiar world of social and interpersonal activity, the less we are speaking authentically as Jews.

To be effective, each model of spirituality had to be institutionalized. We do not have available to us a scholarly study of what may be called the sociology of Jewish spirituality, a social history of Jewish life as the embodiment of shifting and competing models of authenticity, nor of how and why these emerged and were displaced only to emerge again in a different setting. But in a preliminary way, it is clear that each model implies first a curriculum for Jewish education; that is, not simply what subjects and texts should be studied, but also a vision of the Jewish ideal, the Jewish hero-type, and of how such a Jew is to be produced. It also implies a portrait of the Jewish authority figure, the ultimate model in Jewish life: the *rav* as legal decision-maker, the Hasidic rebbe, the scholar, and the philosopher-theologian are very different hero-types who function in very different ways for their respective communities. Third, each implies a vision of what the Jew devotes the major portion of time and energy to doing as a Jew. Is it study? vigorous activity? meditation and prayer?

Finally, each implies a conception of what the central institution of Jewish life, the synagogue, should look like, what functions it should serve, and what type of activities should take place within its walls. And if our thesis that Judaism should be open to the widest possibility of models is accurate, it leads to the conclusion that the contemporary synagogue should provide a setting that is as neutral as possible in regard to any one specific mode.

Here is one concrete example. Communal worship is central to every form of authentic Jewish spiritual expression. But communal worship can take many forms. Compare a Rosh Hashanah service in a Hasidic informal worship space and a contemporary suburban Conservative sanctuary synaogue. The liturgy of each of these services would be roughly similar, but almost everything else would be different; an ethnographic profile of the two services would highlight notable dissimilarities.

On the most elementary level, the design of the physical space where worship takes place both reflects and in turn predetermines the model of spirituality that can be embodied in the worship service taking place within that space. Of these two examples, clearly the sanctuary in the suburban Conservative synagogue is the least neutral or the most aggressive in limiting the available options. Rows of seats riveted to the floor occupy the entire sanctuary space; the bimah is an elevated, stagelike structure with two pulpits for the rabbi and cantor, who are located above and facing the congregation. Here, physical design predetermines—or in this case, limits—much of what can transpire within the sanctuary. The congregation is restricted in its ability to move physically and is hence largely passive. It is situated facing a rabbi and a cantor who "lead" the service and who, in contrast to the congregation, are constantly "doing" something or other. The focus is on the pulpit, not on the worshiping community. The model is a theatrical one: a passive audience facing the primary actors, who perform the drama of worship on a stage. A congregant who would be moved to pace as he prays, to fall to his knees during the *Alenu* prayer at the High Holy Days worship service, or to go to the shelves to consult a Bible or a medieval text on a passage of the service as part of the experience of worship would be totally frustrated in that setting. But each of these forms of activity could be easily carried out in the other setting. The physical design thus makes a number of statements about the type of spirituality possible within that first structure. Prayer is something that you watch others do; study takes place not within the sanctuary on the Sabbath or festival but in a classroom elsewhere in the building on some weekday night; rituals of worship are observed being performed by others, not participated in; excessive displays of emotion in prayer (for example, putting one's *talit* over one's head) are discouraged as indecorous.

This is a classic example of the way in which just one dimension of the synagogue, here, the design concept as reflected in the sanctuary, predetermines the options that are available to the worshiper who seeks to express his own spiritual search within the service of worship. The more neutral the design, the more options are available and the more useful the synagogue becomes as a setting for spiritual expression.

Analyses of a similar kind could be carried out on a host of other dimensions of the service. Who is selected to serve as cantor, the professional or the layperson? What place is assigned to music, and what kind of music is employed in the service? What prayer book is selected? What Pentateuch is used to follow the Torah reading? What place do children have within the formal service of worship? Any or all of these issues reflect and in turn mold the forms of spiritual expression available to a member of that particular community. Given our earlier description of the suburban synagogue, is it any wonder that many young Jewish families want to abandon the sanctuary service in favor of a *havurah*-type service that takes place in some much more neutral place such as a library, where there are no fixed seats, where physical movement is possible, where children move in and out freely, where the lay group leads its own service of worship, where teaching and studying are an integral part of the service? The contrast could not be more striking. That too reflects a conflict in models of spirituality.

Every single decision that a congregation reaches in regard to what transpires within the walls of a synagogue and within the parameters of congregational life must be seen as encouraging or discouraging specific models of Jewish expression. It pervades the budgetary process; it influences the work of a search committee that is selecting a rabbi or a cantor for the congregation; as we have seen, it affects the decisions of the architect who is designing the sacred space in which worship takes place. It affects how the space available within the synagogue building is apportioned. Educationally, it influences the choice of a curriculum, of a textbook, and of teachers to serve as models. It permeates the messages that are conveyed by the rabbi as teacher, preacher, and counselor. In short, it is simply omnipresent.

And if it is omnipresent, it should be at the forefront of the consciousness of all who are responsible for the formulation of synagogue policy. Beyond this, the most effective of our contemporary congregations are those that provide, within the framework of the synagogue, the widest possible set of options. For example, the synagogue should provide different kinds of worship experiences within its own walls on a Shabbat morning. The criticism that such a program is destructive of community completely misunderstands the nature of community. There simply is no community unless the individual needs of the worshiper are met. Community never implied a universal sameness of experience; on the contrary, only the individual congregant who feels genuinely at home can begin to relate to the wider body. Beyond this, opportunities for serious and intensive study, for social action, for communal activity, and for experiential learning all must have their place within the parameters of congregational life. If the synagogue does not provide for all of these, the congregant will look for them elsewhere, and justly so.

Finally, a word about the role of the rabbi. The rabbi is, of course, first and foremost a Jew. He or she is entitled to express a subjective spiritual ideal, to embody one form of spirituality, and to present that model as authentic and desirable. However, I am inclined to question, given the conditions of modernity, whether to do so is the most effective use of the rabbinic role.

If our analysis has any merit, the modern rabbi would do well to be perceived not as the embodiment of any one model of spirituality, but rather as a contemporary Jew who is in search, who is wrestling with the multiple claims of both tradition and modernity, who is trying to find that model which best expresses his or her own temperament and that of the age. The rabbi remains the authority figure, indeed the only authority figure most Jews ever encounter. But in this model, authority emerges in a different way, no longer as offering a prepackaged model of authenticity, but rather, as an expert on the process by which a contemporary Jew struggles with an ancient tradition and its plurality of models in the attempt to express one reading of that tradition.

This stance makes a number of demands on the contemporary rabbi: patience; confidence; both in the vitality of the tradition and in the seriousness of the congregation; an ability to encourage religious pluralism, to see it as a plus, not a minus; and, finally, a willingness to expose uncertainties, struggles, maybe even failure. This stance in effect bridges the gap that usually separates rabbi and congregant. It places the rabbi within the congregation, not above and facing it. The rabbi becomes one more contemporary Jew. This stance is also totally modern in its awareness of history, its forthright individualism, and its respect for religious pluralism.

Each of our three models of spirituality is very much alive today and we all know Jews who are functioning within each. That this should be the case under the conditions of contemporary American life is an immense tribute to Judaism and to Jews. Our task is to foster the conditions necessary for these various quests to find their fulfillment. The synagogue is simply indispensable to this process. The energy out there is so powerful that if the synagogue fails, Jews will go elsewhere. But why should it fail?

CHAPTER 12

A CONSERVATIVE THEOLOGY FOR

THE TWENTY-FIRST CENTURY

I have claimed that there was precious little theological inquiry in the classrooms of the Seminary over the past century. There was a good deal of historical theology (What did the Rabbis of the Talmudic period believe about God, mitzvah, Sinai and so forth?), but precious little of what I have called "doing theology," that is, a systematic inquiry into our own theological commitments as Conservative Jews, working in a school devoted to *Wissenschaft* and within the context of the activity of the Committee on Jewish Law and Standards and its decisions over the last half of the twentieth century.[1]

That inquiry was pursued most aggressively in the conventions of the Rabbinical Assembly. I note, for example, the 1948 debate between Ira Eisenstein, William Greenfield, Ted Friedman, and Isaac Klein on the topic *Toward a Philosophy of Conservative Judaism*; or the 1949 convention with papers by Milton Steinberg, Will Herberg, and Eugene Kohn on *Recent Theological Trends: A Survey and Analysis*; or the 1974 discussions with Seymour Siegel, Harlan Wechsler, Richard Rubenstein, Arthur Green, and Elliot Dorff on *Grappling with a Theology for Our Lives*; or Fritz Rothschild and David Blumenthal on revelation in 1977; or Ben Kreitman, David Aronson, Jose Faur, and Bob Hammer on halakhah in 1978; or Alan Miller, Wilfred Shuchat, and Alan Yuter on *The Philosophy of Conservative Judaism* in 1980.

I recall also the groundbreaking lectures by Mordecai Kaplan and Abraham Joshua Heschel, Louis Finkelstein and Simon Greenberg, Jacob Agus and Robert Gordis, Harold Schulweis and David Silverman. And this list is admittedly incomplete.

It is no exaggeration to say that the theological groundwork for the movement was laid precisely at conventions of the Rabbinical Assembly. It is a personal honor to continue that tradition in this book.

We should also take note of the unprecedented outpouring of book-length inquiries in theology that have been published by members of the Rabbinical Assembly in recent years. Apart from my own writings, books have been published by our colleagues David Wolpe, Elliot Dorff, Arthur Green, Harlan Wechsler, David Blumenthal, Edward Feld, Ira Stone, William Kaufman, and Howard Addison. That fact in itself constitutes a remarkable statement about the state of theology in our movement, and it corresponds precisely to my own informal observation that rarely within the past few decades has there been such a thirst for theology among our congregants as I discern today.

OUR THEOLOGICAL ASSUMPTIONS

If I were able to add a subtitle to this chapter, I would use the name of a course I taught at the Seminary: The Inherent Dilemmas of Liberal Jewish Theology.

What makes us heirs to the dilemmas of liberal Jewish theology? There are three assumptions that I believe we share and that set the ground rules for all theological inquiry within our midst. The first is an assumption about God-talk, or theological language; the second, about revelation; the third, about halakhah. Each of these is explicitly recorded in *Emet Ve-Emunah*, the Conservative movement's first statement of principles, published in 1986.

On the status of theological language, I believe we share the assumption that nothing any human being can say about God is literally or objectively true. All of our characterizations of God are either—here the language varies—metaphors (to use the formulation in *Emet Ve-Emunah*), symbols, myths, constructs, or midrash. Whatever term you use, what remains is that no human being has a fix or a photograph of God. That is precisely what makes God, God. To claim anything else is to fall into the sin of idolatry.

This is obviously not an original claim. Maimonides, to take the most significant example, also insists that we cannot capture God's essential nature in human language. If we differ from Maimonides, however, it is in our shared belief that these metaphors were not literally or explicitly revealed by God. Rather, they have evolved within our community as our attempt to characterize our personal and communal experience of God in nature and history. This leads to our second assumption.

We do not believe that the biblical account of what happened at Sinai is literally true. We do not believe that God descended on Sinai at a certain specific moment in our history and spoke to Moses and the children of Israel, and that the Torah is an explicit record of God's words. That theology of revelation, articulated in its most explicit and systematic form by Nachmanides in his introduction to his commentary on the Torah, and repeated later in nineteenth-century Germany by Samson Raphael Hirsch and again in our day by Rabbi Norman Lamm in his contribution to the 1965 *Commentary* symposium, "The Condition of Jewish Belief" (God's will was revealed "in discrete words and letters"), has become the central theological assumption of contemporary popular Jewish traditionalism.

In contrast, to quote the words of *Emet Ve-Emunah*, "We reject fundamentalism and literalism which do not admit a human component in revelation, thus excluding an independent role for human experience and reason in the process."

However we characterize the interplay of the divine and the human in revelation—whether as in Heschel (Torah is a midrash on revelation), or as in Rosenzweig (Torah is a response to revelation), or as in Kaplan (Torah is the human discovery of salvational drives in the world and in us)—the point is we insist that there is such a human contribution to Torah, thus forever and inevitably making the Torah also a cultural document, whatever God's contribution to the revelatory event.

Our third assumption, quoting *Emet Ve-Emunah* on halakhah, is that we believe halakhah is indispensable "because it is what the Jewish community understands God's will to be." Note: not because halakhah is God's will, but rather because it is *our understanding* of God's will, a far different matter. What we have is our understanding of God's will. No human being can claim to have anything more. At the same time, we do not believe that what we have is anything less than our understanding of precisely *God's* will.

Our shared acceptance of these three assumptions casts us inevitably into the liberal camp among modern Jewish theologians. Here, I believe, there are only two possibilities: Either we believe that we can characterize God's activities in literal terms, and therefore we know what God wants. Or, we believe that there is no literal truth about God available to human beings, and therefore no human being knows explicitly what God wants. As Samson Raphael Hirsch accurately claims, between these two positions there lies an abyss. Cross that abyss and it is almost impossible to go back. But once the abyss is crossed, all of the rules of the game are transformed. That is our situation today. That is what makes us liberal Jews. That is the source of all of our dilemmas. My sense is that our theological challenge in the twenty-first century is to confront these dilemmas and their implications courageously and forthrightly.

DO WE INVENT OR DO WE DISCOVER GOD?

The first of these dilemmas is more purely one of religious epistemology. I call it "the invent-discover dilemma." The most persistent question I receive from students who listen to what I have to say on the issue of God-language is this: Rabbi Gillman, if you believe that all our characterizations of God are metaphors, doesn't that mean that we have invented God, that God is a fiction, that there's nothing really "out there"? Or: Rabbi Gillman, how can you pray to a metaphor?

What lies behind the question is the assumption that all metaphors are fictions, that only that which we can characterize literally and objectively has ontological reality, that whatever eludes definitive description has no ultimate reality—and the obverse, that in fact it is in principle impossible for us humans to characterize any reality, let alone a reality as elusive as God, with total objective accuracy.

My answer is that our language and our conceptualizations are replete with metaphors or constructs, and in these cases we do not deny that there is a reality "out there" but rather claim that whatever the reality is, we can only grasp it impressionistically with a measure of subjectivity. Take two examples: Freud's "ego" and the physicists' "quark."

In neither case do we literally "see" egos and quarks. What we do literally see in one case is a pattern of human behavior, and in the other case, a computer printout of what is happening in our superconductor when subatomic particles explode. But when certain structures of meaning (our theories or myths) are in place, we translate our perceptions into a different language and use terms such as "ego" and "quark" to characterize the realities that lie behind our perceptions.

These realities are not entities as apples are entities. They are rather complex activities, patterns in time and nature that are elusive and difficult to capture in precise form. But they are not invented. They are experienced or discovered. We discover the realities and then invent ways of characterizing them so that they

174

enter into our conceptual schemes and our languages. Then we can use them to do what we have to do, which is to explain why things are the way they are.

Also note well: For that matter, we don't literally see apples either. It is our education and our structures of meaning that help us translate what we do see—that is, colors and shapes—into apples. In the case of egos and quarks, the process may be more complicated, but it is, in principle, identical.

And also with God. We discover—that is, see—complex patterns in time and history. The structures of meaning we bring to our experience help us translate these perceptions into the notion of God—personal, transcendent, unique, and so on—all of which form the core of our metaphor.

In fact the chronology is more complex. As any scientist will tell you, there is a back-and-forth process that takes place between our perceptions and our constructs. We begin by seeing something, translate that into a structure and theory, look again, now see more clearly, and then modify our theory by what we see now (which is different because now we are looking for something specific), then look again, and so on. In the same way, our own evolving historical experience enables us to shape, refine, and change our metaphorical system for God so that it may remain congruent with our experience.

If indeed our congregants are now more prepared to enter into discussion with us on the issue of God, we must sharpen our own thinking on the issue. And, I submit, we must be prepared to discuss the issue in terms of our own distinctive theological assumptions, one of which deals with how we understand and use God-language.

THE DILEMMA OF AUTHORITY

As with the first of the dilemmas, the dilemma of authority follows inevitably from our theological assumptions, this time on revelation.

I pose this issue, first, not simply in regard to halakhah (though I will have a good deal to say about that issue shortly), but rather much more broadly in relation to the entire content of Jewish religion. If what we have in Torah is our ancestors' midrashim on God's revelation, we have to assume that from the beginning there were in fact multiple such understandings of Sinai. Who, then, determined which of these multiple hearings of God's revelation were preserved, and which dropped? Which were left on the cutting-room floor? What was the process whereby these decisions were reached? What criteria were used in making these determinations?

For example, in my *Sacred Fragments* I had espoused what I then thought was the radical view that surely the notion of *brit* and of "a" halakhah (in contrast to any notion of "the" halakhah) were unassailable in any formulation of the contents of Judaism, though I wasn't as sure about the unassailability of any other form of Jewish religious expression. That's where the parameters lie, I claimed. But in her *Standing Again at Sinai*, Judith Plaskow claims that all of her female ancestors' metaphors, myths, or hearings of Sinai were excluded from the canon, that had they been included, it is conceivable that halakhah might not have become the central form of religious expression that it did. In the light of Plaskow's statement, isn't my claim of the indispensability of *brit* and of a halakhah a totally subjective decision? Why do I assume that there can be no Judaism without *brit* and a halakhah?

On the issue of authority, then, let us begin by dismissing some possibilities.

First, the ultimate authority is clearly no longer God, simply because we no longer believe that what we have in Torah is God's explicit will. Nor, for that matter, does the authority rest in the text of Torah, for that too is no longer understood as a precise record of God's will.

We must conclude, then, that the ultimate authority has always been, and continues to be, vested in a human community.

In rabbis or in rabbinic authorities? But then, as the late Wolfe Kelman used to ask, "Who is a rabbi?"

It seems to me that it is the concerned community that makes a rabbi, simply by the process of accepting him or her as teacher and authority in matters of Torah. The ultimate authority, then, is the concerned lay community acting in concert with its chosen rabbinic authorities.

That's what Solomon Schechter meant in that classic statement, "Historical Judaism," the introduction to his first series of essays in Judaism (and reprinted in *Tradition and Change*). Schechter is uninterested in revelation, in what happened at Sinai, as a theological issue, because to him it is irrelevant. The issue is not what Scripture records but how it was read by the later generations, that is, by the Oral Torah or, as he calls it, by the synagogue, which, clearly, to Schechter, is a thoroughly human body. In other words, Scripture means whatever the later community says it means. Or, to use Schechter's typically whimsical formulation, "God's choice invariably coincides with the wishes of Israel."

Israel, here, is what Schechter calls "Catholic Israel," that consensus of caring, committed, learning Jews who have a stake in the process. That is our community. There lies the ultimate authority for the shaping of Judaism. They will want to turn to rabbis for guidance in that process, but then it is their decision, not that of the Seminary or of any other authority-making body, whom they turn to for that guidance and on what issues.

But then we must ask: Where is our community? Or, more generally, is there such a community within our movement? Does Catholic Israel exist today? From what my colleagues tell me, we are really talking about roughly 10 percent of the Jews affiliated with our Conservative synagogues. I use admittedly informal criteria: a kosher home, regular Shabbat synagogue attendance, adult education participation, children at Camp Ramah and Solomon Schechter Day School.

I recall David Hartman's claim in a conversation with some of us at the Seminary a few years ago. "You people (the

Conservative movement) could have captured the heart of American religious Jewry. But you failed. You have not created an observant community. You have not created a davening community. You have not created a learning community. You were far too interested in critical editions."

This is the fruit of a century of Jewish education in our movement. That statistic sharpens the issue of authority for all of us here.

THE DILEMMA OF PARAMETERS

The dilemma regarding parameters flows directly from the problem surrounding authority. For if the community, not God or Scripture itself, is truly the authority, then what are the limits within which that community can exercise its authority? If Torah means whatever the community decides it means, then is everything up for grabs, all the time? I believe that the question can only be answered inductively. There are parameters, but no intrinsic parameters. The parameters are set wherever the community wants to set them, that is, set when the community is acting seriously, committedly, in fear and trembling, not casually or capriciously.

Despite *Emet Ve-Emunah*'s claim to the contrary here, my sense is that the Conservative community cannot escape the potential for relativization that is inherent in the process. We fear the slippery slope. But we also fear its obverse, what the late Gerson Cohen used to call the "frumometer" approach. But isn't it clearly the case that both of these impulses implicitly concede that there are no intrinsic parameters, that the parameters are set inductively by each community, depending on its own personal reading of God's will? Note well: We do not for a moment believe that we alone introduce a subjective element into the process. The ultra-Orthodox are equally subjective. There is no more subjective dimension in Jewish decision making than the concept of *daas Torah*, that is, that whatever the supreme rabbinic authority rules is by definition God's word and must not be challenged. They are as subjective as we are. The only difference is that we acknowledge our subjectivity; they don't.

And if we take Deuteronomy 17:8ff and the Akhnai story (Baba Metzia 59b) seriously, it seems to me that there is absolutely no heresy in the claim that God has surrendered God's authority to human authorities. I have suggested as an analogy the "best interest of baseball" clause in the rules of Major League Baseball. The system itself gives the authority the right even to subvert the system's own regulations, if that authority deems it to be in the best interest of the system. The only question is: Who is that authority? And here again, it seems to me that the community chooses its authority and grants him or her the right to act in its best interest.

The problem with our Conservative system is that we have multiple communities, multiple versions of the rules of the game, and multiple views of who is the authority, which makes our situation infinitely more complicated than that of Major League Baseball. We have no alternative, then, but to live with the imminent danger of relativism. There are no absolutes, no blacks and whites, no clear-cut immediate decisions, no divine voices. Rather, we must live with pluralistic responses, prolonged periods of indecision, considerable tension and pain as the process works itself out, and a seemingly perpetual threat of divisiveness and fragmentation.

But how else to characterize a movement that says yes on feminist issues, says no on patrilineality, and is willing to debate homosexuality; that claims that we can marry a *kohen* to a divorcee but insists that oysters are still *treif*? We make these decisions because although we clearly do include the notions of a revealing, commanding God, of *brit*, and at least of a halakhah within the parameters of what we understand Jewish religion to stand for, we do not believe that we know beyond question what God wants. We do believe that God wants what we, in utter seriousness, perceive God as wanting: God's will is to be discerned by consensual decision making based on a host of factors:

halakhic precedents, educational strategies, changing value systems, socioeconomic and demographic forces, our moral intuition, the politics of the movement, and, above all, our own subjective experience of God's command directed to *us* in the here and now—all extrinsic, not intrinsic factors. We also believe that multiple varying decisions on any one issue may all be equally legitimate at the same time. The system is undeniably messy and anxiety making.

Equally subjective are the criteria that go into determining who is an arbiter on halakhic issues. We would agree on learning and piety, for example, but how do we measure these? Even more subjective would be the imposition of some sort of theological test regarding the roots of the halakhic system itself. Here again, we can only stipulate extrinsic criteria, not intrinsic ones.

These dilemmas emerge most sharply on halakhic issues, but our theological commitments are not entirely immune. It is clear to me, for example, that my conversions would not be accepted in some circles, not because I didn't do them the right way, but because the theology that underlies the way I do a conversion is not acceptable. That is, I obey the mitzvot about halakhic conversions but not as commanded explicitly by God. That theology effectively subverts the legitimacy of what I do, rendering it invalid for some. That posture is relatively rare, but it has been advanced in some traditionalist circles.

The issue of halakhic parameters, however, is more critical. I have claimed, as noted earlier, that my theology has led me to affirm the legitimacy of multiple halakhic systems, each defined by parameters established consensually by multiple halakhic systems, ranging from Satmar Hasidism on the right to Reform and UJA-type civic religious groups on the left. So far, so good.

Where I drew the line, however, was at a form of Judaism that denies the legitimacy of some forms of obligated behavior as an expression of one's Jewishness. Thus I affirmed the indispensability of a halakhic system, without prejudging the validity of any one specific halakhic system. I made the same claim in regard to what is called "halakhic process." I took a radically pluralistic view of that enterprise as well, claiming that a halakhic process is whatever process a *posek* uses to reach a halakhic decision. Here, as in the former case, there are no intrinsic parameters for defining what is halakhic process. It is rather to be established inductively by looking at what any one *posek* actually does.

What I failed to see, however, was that in insisting on the indispensability of *a* halakhic system I was simply setting my own subjective parameters, that the decision was as subjective as any other, and that it therefore lacked perscriptive validity. I could retain it, even advocate it, but I could not insist on its totally objective validity or in an a priori way dismiss the validity of other positions.

That claim was shaken when I encountered the writings of other liberal Jewish theologians who questioned even that set of parameters as well. Judith Plaskow, for example, insists that if her female ancestors' hearings of Sinai had been accepted and canonized, it is conceivable that what would have emerged is a Jewish religion that did not place such an emphasis on law as a form of religious expression, but rather espoused much more fluid and relational forms of expression.

In fact, Plaskow raises an even stronger question. She suggests that underlying every legal system is a community's social construction of reality; as that community's taxonomy of reality changes, its legal system becomes ever more discordant. What seems to be a halakhic dilemma, then, is in actuality a totally different construction of reality that the halakhic system can never hope to resolve without being stretched beyond recognition.

Take a relatively simple example. I'm told that a majority of Conservative families who light candles Friday evening do so not before sunset but rather when the family assembles around the table for its Shabbat meal. Now it seems to me that the issue here is not purely halakhic. In fact, I doubt whether it is even conceivable for the halakhah to legitimatize this practice. What is at issue here is the social construction of time. The family whose parent figure is still working at sunset simply does not view that moment as the beginning of Shabbat. For that family, Shabbat begins when everyone assembles around the table, whenever that occurs. In other words, the transition from one day to another, from the common week to the sacred day, is determined not by nature but by sociology. The issue may seem to be a halakhic one, but in reality it is one of how we create structures in reality, here in time.

A similar attack on the notion that we are operating within the boundaries of even *a* halakhah is launched by Eugene Borowitz in his book *Renewing the Covenant* (Philadelphia: Jewish Publication Society, 1991, pp. 237–300). For Borowitz, a decision regarding Jewish obligation must take into consideration three factors: the autonomy of the individual conscience, the sense of what the covenanted community demands, and, finally, the individual's reading of God's will. But with this construction in place, Borowitz claims, what results is no longer in any sense obligated by God's own explicit authority, and therefore no longer represents halakhah in the classical sense of the term. God retains only "figurative" authority; what results is "guidance," not obligation.

For Plaskow and Borowitz, then, we have entered a "post-halakhic" age. And those of us who insist that we are continuing to work "within the halakhah" but use an increasingly subjective and flexible view of what the phrase means are deceiving ourselves. Finally, Borowitz points to the fact that since this flexible view of halakhic process is largely ignored by our community, his conclusions are in fact totally accurate.

I believe the Conservative movement is tempted to dismiss Plaskow's and Borowitz's critiques either as based on ignorance or as beyond the pale of legitimate inquiry into the issue. That would be a mistake. First, we should remember that we ourselves and our own Law Committee are subject to these very same charges from our critics on the Jewish religious right. Second, it is clear to me that these questions are being raised by people within our own constituency. We must, then, not simply dismiss them but rather engage and confront them, openly and courageously.

ARE WE THEN A HALAKHIC MOVEMENT?

I have become increasingly impatient with my students who protest or defend a decision of the Law Committee on the grounds that Conservative Judaism is a halakhic movement, not because we are not a halakhic movement but rather because I simply don't know what the phrase means anymore. What parameters are we using to make that decision?

We clearly believe that all of the decisions of our Law Committee are legitimately within the halakhah as we understand it. In fact, we say even more. Part of our rhetoric for the better part of a century has included the claim that in fact we *alone* are really halakhic Jews: Orthodoxy represents a deviation from the classical norm, whereas we are in the line of Akiba and the rest of the great rabbinic masters, and we are simply doing what they did, possibly with greater historical awareness but with no substantive difference. To support that view, we typically refer to the *Tanur Shel Akhnai* (oven of Aknai) story,[2] to the aggadah about Moses' visit to Akiba's *bet-midrash* (school),[3] to the ways in which the Talmudic Rabbis legislated slavery[4] and capital punishment[5] out of existence, among other justifications. Isn't this a case of using the halakhic system to deal with radically new social constructions of reality? Can't we do the same?

I've become increasingly convinced that our claim to being a halakhic movement is largely only rhetorical because it never has been supported by a serious inquiry into how we distinctively conceive the halakhic process to work. We have been operating largely on the basis of intuition alone; we make decisions as the issues arise: yes on a *kohen*'s marrying a divorcée, no on patrilineality. What is missing is a sustained philosophy of halakhah, a theologically and ideologically rooted conception of legal process, a coherent statement on how our aggadah shapes our halakhah—in short, a phenomenology of halakhic development that will support our halakhic activity. That's why our decisions seem to other serious halakhic scholars to be largely capricious. I'm also not convinced that the Law Committee is the proper forum for conducting that larger inquiry.

And what do we do with the fact that precious few of our congregants out there care about any of these halakhic issues in the first place? How many of our people—even of our core 10 percent "Catholic Israel" Jews—do whatever it is they do in terms of ritual observance out of a sense of halakhic obligation? How many would stop driving on Shabbat if we decided to withdraw that decision of the Law Committee?

IN DEFENSE OF THE TRADITIONAL MODEL

There have been cogent defenses by some of our colleagues, notably Joel Roth and Elliot Dorff, of the claim that we are simply continuing the classical model of halakhic development through the writing of responsa based on precedents while, at the same time, invoking extralegal factors in a carefully balanced, consensual manner.

Dorff acknowledges the seductiveness of the post-halakhic position but argues that it leads to anarchy. In contrast, the traditional approach preserves a guarantee of continuity, authority, and coherence: continuity, because it ties each halakhic decision to the past tradition, a singularly important way to preserve the identity of a people as widely scattered as Jews are; authority, because it stipulates clearly that an entire set of qualifications has to be invoked to determine who can legitimately make halakhic judgments; and coherence, because the system as a whole thus preserves an internal unity that it would lack if everything were up for grabs to the individual at any time.[6]

Note well that Dorff insists he is not advocating a rigidly constructivist approach to halakhic decision making. He insists that we must bring our moral judgments to bear on any decision; that laws can be disregarded or even attacked when they are immoral on the face; and that any qualified judge knows how to select appropriate precedents, how to ignore others, and when and how to stretch them.

Similarly, Joel Roth has devoted an entire volume to a study of halakhah as a fully coherent system of its own, with its own principles that govern how the system works, particularly for the appointment of authority figures and for the incorporation of extralegal data into the workings of the system. But note that Roth also concedes that built into the system lies a provision that grants the authorities the right to subvert the system when this is deemed appropriate.[7]

The Dorff-Roth position represents classical Conservative ideology and rhetoric, but it has had minimal impact outside of our own rabbinic circles. Why? First, the position is subtle and complex, much more so than its Orthodox and Reform alternatives: second, the Seminary never provided its rabbis-to-be with the resources to argue, defend, and vindicate the position, largely out of the fear that it might strengthen the hand of the left wing in the Rabbinical Assembly. Finally, we have never developed the systematic theological groundwork that could support the position.

Most important, our ideology has had little impact beyond the rabbinate because we deliberately kept the lay community out of the process. We insisted that halakhic decision making was the province of the seminary's Talmudists alone. Whatever authority the Rabbinical Assembly took for halakhic decision making, it wrested out of the hands of the Seminary. Much of the activity of the Law Committee was viewed with a distinct sense of suspicion by Seminary Talmudists. But our predecessors in the Conservative rabbinate simply repeated the process by transfering the suspicion to the lay community.

At the same time, the Plaskow-Borowitz post-halakhic position has consistently enjoyed a degree of support among our colleagues. I recall, for example, Edward Feld's 1973 article "Towards an Aggadic Judaism," which raised not a few eyebrows when it was first published.[8] My sense is that this position will be argued more and more vigorously within our circles in the years to come. The issue is indeed a benchmark issue between Conservative Judaism and Reform and Reconstructionism to our left. How that dispute works itself out will be decisive in shaping our movement in the coming decades.

One thing is clear to me. If what I have called the classical Conservative Jewish position is to be affirmed, much work remains to be done. First, we have to engage substantial segments of our laity in the halakhic decision-making process. Second, we have to clarify the theological groundings that support the position. Third, we have to maintain that despite our liberal theological assumptions, we do insist on a distinctive set of specifically Jewish obligations, not because that is what God wants us to do but because that is what *we* want to do, because that is our reading of God's will for us today.

I have spoken and written a great deal about the need to change the culture of our movement from a model of infantilization to one of empowerment. But we cannot empower our laity until we first empower ourselves. This is our greatest challenge.

Chapter 13

A NEW AGGADAH FOR THE CONSERVATIVE MOVEMENT[1]

I. AGGADIC JUDAISM

Thirty years ago, *Conservative Judaism* published a paper by my colleague Edward Feld titled "Towards an Aggadic Judaism."[2] As I recall, that article created somewhat of a storm among certain of my colleagues and with good reason, for Feld's argument, as summarized in his concluding paragraph, was that "Law, as a religious form ... is not necessary in the changed condition of modern Jewish life—that is, in a voluntaristic, pluralistic community. Halakha ... must *objectify* universal standards. We are lucky to have arrived at a point where we can allow *subjective* religious standards—a new aggadic Judaism."

Studying a paper by Ira Stone, a friend and rabbinic colleague, led me to recall Feld's paper, not solely because of the appearance of the word *aggadah* in the two titles. It was also because Stone begins by reviewing the various aggadic statements that have been used to characterize the Conservative movement in the past. Stone lists three such *aggadot*: "tradition and change," "pluralism," and most recently "traditionalist egalitarianism."

Curiously, Stone ignores one more aggadic formula that has persisted throughout the years and that, in contrast to the three he cites, remains very much alive. I refer to the rhetorical formula "We are a halakhic movement," which is flaunted again and again, particularly in our current discussions on how to deal with the gay and lesbian population in our communities. Despite Feld's critique, this formula seems to be as popular today as ever.

I have not attempted to research the history of this formula—when it was first used and who introduced it. I can, however, account for its popularity. If its current use is any indication, it emerges each time we prepare to make some radical departure from a traditional halakhic position, as we may be doing in the near future. We flaunt that rhetoric because we want to reassure ourselves and the rest of the religious community that this departure is not really a departure at all. Our use of this formula is a classic defense mechanism. It is designed to protect ourselves against an attack, a looming critique that we fear might inflict a mortal wound on our corporate identity. The thrust of this chapter is to propose that we abandon that self-definition for reasons that will become clear as we proceed. I should be clear at the outset that my critique is directed not at what we do, but at how we define ourselves.

II. FALSIFICATION

The claim that "we are a halakhic movement" is a brilliant defense mechanism because it is unfalsifiable. A statement becomes unfalsifiable when nothing can be adduced that will prove the statement false. Take the proposition "God loves Israel." Should you, for example, respond that the Holocaust disproves that proposition, the claimant can simply reply that God does love Israel, but God brought Holocausts to punish Israel for its sins, or to prepare the ground for the creation of the State of Israel, or because sometimes God is cruel and capricious, or because God's power is limited, or because God wants to test our faith, and so forth. What results, in the immortal words of the British analytic philosopher Anthony Flew, is that the original claim dies "the death by a thousand qualifications." If the claim is compatible with all the data of experience, with all possible facts, then it has become factually meaningless. It may serve other purposes. It may, for example, be an emotional outburst, a covert way of saying, "I am proud to be a Jew!" and that may be very important for us to do. But then all it does is describe our subjective feelings. It says nothing at all about the reality "out there," in the world beyond ourselves and our feelings. In this case, it says nothing about God or God's feelings about Israel. Analytic philosophers would add that since an unfalsifiable claim can never be disproved, neither can it be proved. It is neither true nor false. It is factually irrelevant.[3]

Back to "We are a halakhic movement." How do we falsify that claim? Our critics would charge, how can you be a halakhic movement if you permit a *kohen* to marry a divorcée, or permit women to serve as witnesses in judicial proceedings, or permit the use of electricity and driving to synagogue on Shabbat, or make significant changes in the core halakhic portions of the liturgy, or even contemplate ordaining gays and lesbians and sanctioning commitment rituals? To these charges, we reply, "Ah, but we mean something else by the term 'halakhah.' We view halakhah as evolving in response to changing historical conditions."

We then adduce how cultural changes demand that we make all of those changes. The status of a *kohen* and a divorcée is different today than it was in antiquity. The feminist revolution is now a hard reality and we have to acknowledge it in our ritual life. Demographic changes demand that we permit driving to synagogue on Shabbat. And our new scientific understanding of sexual orientation suggests that it is genetic and therefore unchangeable. To crown this reply, we add that from the outset, halakhah has always been evolving. See how the Rabbis got rid of the biblical institution of slavery and capital punishment! We fortify this argument with references to the contemporary study of law and narrative. All legal codes are embedded in narratives. As the narrative changes, so must the legal codes that are embedded in these narratives.

We also refer to familiar midrashim to support our claim that our position is not an innovation. "See, even Moshe Rabbenu didn't understand Rabbi Akiba's teaching, testimony to how much the Torah had developed in the intervening centuries. If Rabbi Akiba were alive today, he would be a Conservative Jew!" It is we, then, who represent authentic halakhic Judaism.

But by then, our original claim has died a death by a thousand qualifications. It is compatible with all factual conditions, and therefore it has lost all factual meaning. It is a totally idiosyncratic use of the term, unrecognizable by Jews who take halakhah seriously in their personal lives. It is in effect a subjective, emotional outburst, a covert way of saying, "It's great to be a Conservative Jew," or "I'm proud to be a Conservative Jew," which is totally legitimate, as long as we realize that this is what we are doing. We are simply describing how we feel about ourselves.

Parenthetically, a strikingly prescient anticipation of Feld's argument was formulated by our late teacher Seymour Siegel in his contribution to *Commentary*'s 1966 symposium, "The Condition of Jewish Belief." In his response to a question regarding the contributors' understanding of revelation, Siegel writes, "The mitzvot are ... the demands of God upon the community of Israel, which lives in time, and they are subject to change, growth and (all too frequently) decay.... In a real sense the *halakha* is constantly reevaluated by the *aggada*."[4] I find this to be a striking claim. It says, in effect, that halakhah must respond to changing cultural conditions—aggadah in the broadest sense of the term. When the culture changes, halakhah changes in response. This is precisely what happened in the wake of the feminist revolution in America. When the status and the role of women changed, the halakhic status of women changed in response. My sense is that this is an accurate description of how our movement makes its halakhic decisions. But it raises significant questions regarding the authority for halakhah as we understand it.

III. THE VALUE OF TENSION

What I find most suggestive about Stone's proposal for a new aggadah for Conservative Judaism is his use of the biblical Jacob as his model. Stone reads the biblical account of Jacob's career as highlighting the tensions that pervaded his life. It emerges most clearly in Stone's interpretation of Rashi's comment to the opening verse of *Vayeshev* and his (Stone's) original and striking understanding of *olam hazeh* and *olam haba*. It led me to the insight that Jacob lived his entire life in a state of perpetual tension: tension with his brother, with his father, with his extended family in Haran, with his sons. This quality of Jacob's life experience is distinctively his own; it was certainly not characteristic of Isaac's, nor, apart from the *akedah* episode, of Abraham's.

I have long felt that to think and live as a Conservative Jew is to live in a state of perpetual tension. That this should be the hallmark of our movement is somewhat incongruous because if, as contemporary anthropologists suggest, the whole purpose of religion is to order our experience of the world, to subdue the anarchic dimensions of our human experience, to turn chaos into cosmos, then why is all of our activity designed to counter that basic human need? Why are we deliberately introducing more tension into an already tension-filled life experience? And why should we choose this particular thrust to establish our distinctive identity among contemporary Jewish denominations? Finally, if we flaunt our embrace of tension as the hallmark of our approach to Judaism, we should be prepared to educate our young people to embrace tension as healthy and a sign of vitality. Are we prepared to do this? Do we know how to do this?

But if we seek a formula that flaunts what is distinctive about our identity, why not this one? Its very incongruity may be its attraction. It may well be precisely what we need to say about ourselves at this stage in our history.

Our approach to halakhah is a superb paradigm of living with tension. Why do some laws change and others not change? Why can we drive to worship on Shabbat but not to a museum? Why are all cheeses now kosher but oysters still *treif*? Why can a *kohen* marry a divorcée, but a Jew cannot marry a non-Jew? Why ordain women but not gays? Why change some portions of our liturgy but not others? I concede that these distinctions are real and important, and I and my rabbinic colleagues can defend each of them, but for the layperson who has neither the education nor the time to study and speculate about these matters, the impression we make is one of total confusion. Our message is complicated. "They just don't get it," one of my colleagues remarked recently, referring to our lay community's perception of our movement's stances. Even many of our more sophisticated laypeople don't understand how we reach our decisions. In contrast, the messages of the movements to our right and to our left, their *aggadot*, are relatively clear. Polar positions are always clear. Center positions rarely are.

I have become increasingly convinced that our self-definition as a halakhic movement was created by and on behalf of our rabbinic community. From a historical perspective, this definition was thoroughly appropriate for a movement that was founded by rabbis and professors, in deliberate opposition to American Reform, which was created, and to this day remains directed, by its lay community. How ironic is it, then, that our most significant failure as a movement is that we have not created a significant body of ritually observant (that is, halakhic, even by our definition of halakhah) Conservative laypeople! Forget about the subtleties of some Law Committee decisions. How many of our laypeople observe a twenty-five-hour Shabbat, or kashrut both in and out of the home? A familiar refrain voiced by my colleagues in the congregational rabbinate is that they don't have a lay community that shares their values or their lifestyles, or kosher homes where they can send their children to play. My Orthodox and Reform rabbi friends rarely voice this complaint.

IV. WHY HALAKHAH?

But I suspect that a far more basic question underlies our community's puzzlement about our approach to halakhah. That question is, why halakhah in the first place? From the outset, our ideologues have assumed that halakhah is indispensable to any authentic reading of Judaism, and we, of course, must remain authentic. Parenthetically, no one to my knowledge has unpacked a theory that establishes criteria for authenticity. That we are authentic Jews is the "tradition" pole of the "tradition and change" formula. But precisely because the claim that "we are a halakhic movement" has always been assumed, we have never felt the need to justify it. My sense is that many of our laypeople believe they simply do not have the right to question the indispensability of halakhah in principle. And because it is never questioned, we have never felt the need to address it.

We have worked with a positivist approach to halakhah. The halakhic system is simply a given for us. Its procedural rules are intrinsic to the system, and in reaching our halakhic conclusions, we use these procedures to do so. We work within the system, and the system is closed. A comprehensive defense of this approach is expounded with considerable skill by our colleague Dr. Joel Roth in his book *The Halakhic Process: A Systemic Approach.*[5]

But what Roth does not address is why Judaism invokes a halakhic process in the first place. Why halakhah? Or, more broadly speaking, why is law the distinctively Jewish form of religious expression? This is a multidimensional issue that far exceeds the scope of this chapter. It is, in part, a historical issue. Why is it that from the outset, our foundational document, Torah, is replete with codes of law? Why is it that biblical religion posits that what God expects of Israel is a specific set of behaviors that are formulated as law? And why is it that as biblical religion morphed into the Judaism of the Rabbis, this form of religious expression became more and more central, in time yielding the Mishnah, the Talmud, and the subsequent codifications and responsa literature? In short, why is Judaism the way it is? Why is law the major form of Jewish expression? Why is it so different from the prevailing Christian religious culture that surrounds us and that requires no comparable behavioral expectations from its adherents? Why is this issue never addressed by our ideologues?[6]

But a second dimension of this issue, the theological basis for authority, has been addressed.[7] Here, the issue is who or what makes Torah authoritative? More seriously, why is Torah authoritative in the first place? Much of the scholarly output of my colleagues on the JTS faculty suggests that our Judaism today is the way it is because different groupings of human beings, first in the biblical and later in the Talmudic eras, roughly in the sixth-century BCE and later in the sixth-century CE, respectively, determined that this is what should be included within the scope of Torah. Torah, then, and by implication, Jewish religion, is the way it is because for complex historical, sociological, or cultural reasons, our ancestors determined it should be this way.[8] Judaism, then, is the creation of the Jewish people. This is a thoroughly naturalist—as opposed to supernaturalist—understanding of Jewish religion. Authority for what constitutes the Jewish tradition lies, from the beginning, with a human community.

From a scholarly perspective, this understanding of the origins of Judaism as we know it today is thoroughly convincing. It is what our rabbinical students are being taught by many of my colleagues on the JTS faculty. It is also grounded in a theology that was passionately advocated from within our own ranks by our teacher Mordecai Kaplan. But we should recognize that this approach raises the question of God's role in the creation of Judaism, specifically, about God's role in revelation. More generally, it forces us to talk about God. It forces us to do theology, openly and explicitly, from our pulpits and in our educational settings. Here, once again, we encounter the tensions that characterize our distinctive approach to Judaism. And as we have long realized, with significant exceptions, there has been precious little theology emanating from our classrooms and our pulpits.

V. ON REVELATION

The obvious pathway into this theological thicket is through the issue of revelation. Our responsibility is to articulate a theology of revelation that would embrace the following claims. I will spell them out in detail here because we rarely do this, particularly within the hearing of our lay community.

We believe the following:

1. In some sense, God did reveal Torah to the Jewish people (though of course that claim depends on what we mean by "God," "revealed," and "Torah").
2. The biblical account of the revelation at Sinai as narrated in Exodus 19 and 20 is not literally true.
3. Nor is the Pentateuchal narrative as a whole historically accurate; it is a much later reworking of distant communal memories in terms of the historical concerns of later generations.
4. Much of the contents of the Pentateuch, both narrative and law, reflects extensive borrowings from the literature of other ancient Near Eastern peoples.
5. However we may understand God's role in revelation, both the substance and the text of Torah as we have it is the creation of our ancestors, who determined what constituted God's will for Israel in matters of belief and practice.
6. The authority of Scripture, then, was established by our ancestors, by a human community.

7. The formulation of the Oral Torah, rabbinic literature, is totally the work of human authorities.
8. Torah is sacred because our ancestors said it was sacred. Israel sanctified the Torah.

We then reject two polar positions. We do not accept the Exodus version of Sinai as literally true. We do not believe God descended on a mountain and spoke to Moses, who wrote God's words in a text that is the Torah we have before us today. We do not believe this account, first, because we do not accept its portrait of God's activity as literal, and second, because we do not accept the text in which this narrative is embedded as history. Since we do not accept the historicity of this text, and since this text includes the account of revelation, to accept this account as itself authoritative is a circular argument; we cannot invoke as authoritative the very text whose authority we are trying to establish. But neither do we believe that this account and the text in which it is embedded are totally fictitious. My use of the term "myth" constitutes my personal attempt to preserve the power, sanctity, and authority of Torah while rejecting a literalist understanding of revelation. Torah represents the canonization of the classic Jewish religious myth.[9]

We must then articulate a theology of revelation that maintains a role for God and yet accords the substantive role to the human community. We are not the first generation to work at this enterprise. Franz Rosenzweig, Mordecai Kaplan, and Abraham Joshua Heschel have provided us with different models of such a theology, which differ only in the respective roles they accord to God and to human beings, and in how they portray God and God's activity.[10] But the bottom line is that they all agree on one crucial fact: the formulation of the contents of Torah as we have it today is the creation of human beings. Torah may contain God's will for Israel, but it is God's will as understood by a human community, and that version of God's will reflects the concerns of the generations that originally recorded it. If we are a halakhic community, then, it is because our ancestors determined that we should be.

That conclusion is inescapable, as are its implications: whatever authority Torah has is, from the beginning, the authority granted to it by a human community. I take this one step further. It is then the right and responsibility of later human communities to revisit the contents of Torah in light of their ability to reflect these later communities' own perception of God's will for them. To reject the original version of God's will is not, then, in principle, to question God's will, but rather to question that original community's perception of God's will, which is not the same as questioning God. And we can do that because their concerns are not necessarily ours, because their aggadah is not necessarily ours. History plays a decisive role, and we must remember that our teachers at the Seminary were all primarily historians. History pervaded the culture of the Seminary from its inception.

None of this is new or original. But we have avoided saying all of this, openly and explicitly, in our preaching and teaching. Instead, we fudge the issue, possibly because of our fear that saying all of this aloud will justify our laypeople's generalized casualness about ritual observance, or that we may become identified with Reform. The real challenge here is educational or pedagogical: how do we teach this position to our laypeople, and particularly to our children?[11]

A striking example of this fudging is this sentence from *Emet Ve-Emunah,* our first and thus far only attempt to articulate a statement of principles for Conservative Judaism. Writing on revelation, the statement claims, "As such, we reject relativism, which denies any objective source of authoritative truth. We also reject fundamentalism and literalism, which do not admit a human component in revelation, thus excluding an independent role for human experience and reason in the process."[12]

It is beyond me how we can both welcome a human component in revelation and reject relativism in formulating the contents of revelation. To acknowledge the human factor in forming the contents of Torah is inevitably to relativize its contents. Notably, this section on revelation is followed immediately in *Emet Ve-Emunah* by a statement on halakhah subtitled "The Indispensability of Halakhah"; early on, it notes that "for many Conservative Jews, halakhah is indispensable first and foremost because it is what the Jewish community understands God's will to be."[13] Note what this statement does not say. It does not say that halakhah is indispensable because "it is God's will," but rather, "because it is what the Jewish community understands God's will to be." The difference between these two formulations is cosmic. What the text says is that it is not God, but rather our ancestors, a human community, who determined God's will for the community. The authority is not God, but rather human beings. Of course, the remainder of that five-page statement on halakhah—by far the longest statement in the entire pamphlet; God gets only half that space—proceeds to qualify that claim out of existence.

The implicit tension here is our wish to retain the sense of obligation that is inherent in the traditionalist view of revelation. We wish to continue to speak the language of mitzvah, even though the identity of who commands has shifted. If God is no longer the *metzaveh*, then can we continue to speak of mitzvah? We can, of course, by acknowledging that the community has become the *metzaveh*. We can even retain God in that role, all the while acknowledging that from the beginning, God's will is transmitted through the community. But what is clear is that if we are to be a halakhic community, it is because *we* want to be one. But then we have to explain what that means, justify why we want to be that and how to achieve it. We have done neither in any consistent or coherent way.

VI. ON GOD

This discussion leads us inevitably to deal with our understanding of God. More precisely, it leads to a consideration of God-talk because before discussing concepts of God, we have to consider how it is possible in principle for human beings to say anything about God, or for the human mind to form a concept of God in the first place. On this issue, we have three options. We can believe that how we think or what we say of God is literally true. We can acknowledge the impossibility of doing either of these and resort to worshipful silence. Or we can think and talk of God and acknowledge that all of our terms are—take your pick—metaphors, symbols, analogies, *meshalim*, and so on.

The first of these options leads to idolatry. Early in the *Mishneh Torah*, Maimonides cautions against literalism and condemns it in the harshest terms.[14] We do not need to invoke Maimonides here. We also reject the notion that God literally has a body, or is male, or dwells in the heavens, or sits on a throne of judgment, or laughs, or feels sad or angry. But then, neither should we believe that God literally listens to our prayers or speaks to a human community. To resort to worshipful silence may be more respectful of God's transcendence, but if our ancestors had followed this method, we would have neither Scripture, nor a liturgy, nor the rabbinic aggadah and folklore, nor even the literature of the mystics.

This leaves us with the third option: God-talk is figurative. We must speak of God, but we are aware, all along, that God is never literally what we think or say God is. That is because God is God and we are human; God transcends human language and understanding. Each of the terms suggested above is in some way problematic. In my own experience, "metaphor" works best with a non-academic audience, but the term is conventionally used to indicate a literary device, a figure of speech. To say that on Yom Kippur, God sits in judgment is much more than using a figure of speech. "Symbol" is Paul Tillich's term, but though it is an effective way of referring to visual or aural symbols (such as the American flag or "Hatikvah"), it is less successful when we refer to terms such as *Avinu Malkeinu* as symbolic references to God.[15] "Analogy" is vapid and has minimal specifically theological relevance, and *mashal* needs to be translated and explained.

All of these terms share the conviction that we cannot grasp God's essence in thought or language. But the defenders of this third option also contend that our God-talk is not totally fictitious. Our references to God did not emerge out of the blue. Maimonides would probably claim that the *meshalim* were revealed by God; we moderns would more likely suggest that they emerge out of our common human experience.[16] The very consensus reflected in the references to God in Scripture and in the postbiblical tradition, the fact that they are shared by diverse religious traditions, and the realization that many of them—though not all—continue to evoke powerful emotional reactions, both positive and negative, throughout the generations and in multiple cultures testifies that they reflect a common human experience.

This does not totally free us from considering the epistemological issues involved in reaching an awareness of God's presence in our lives. A thorough exploration of those issues is beyond the scope of this study, but their very presence reveals, once again, the tension at the heart of our ideology.

VII. INVENT OR DISCOVER

Briefly, again, if the terms we use to refer to God are of our own devising, then how do we know that they capture what God "really" is? We can't step out of our metaphors to compare them to the "real thing" because if we had any notion of it, we wouldn't need the metaphors in the first place. Even more disturbing, how do we know there is a "real thing" in the first place? Are we not caught in a solipsistic trap? To put it another way, when I advance this position, I am invariably challenged: "Since we create the metaphors, and the metaphors are all we have, do we not create God?" Or, more brutally, "The Bible tells us that God created human beings. But you claim that human beings created God!"

My response is "No, we discover God and create the metaphors." But this "discovery" is fraught with subjectivity. We do not see God. All we see is the broadest possible canvas: nature, history, and the human experience all taken together, what physicists would call a unified field theory. But this "seeing" is highly interpretive. It is a seeing of our minds, not only of our senses. We see what we want to see, what we are prepared to see, what we are educated to see. To use a common metaphor, it is a connecting of the dots of our experience, much like, in our childhood, we connected the numbered dots on a page and then saw a tiger. Except now the dots are not numbered and there are different ways of connecting them. We choose the dots that we seek to connect, and then proceed to connect them. Here again, the term "myth" continues to work for me. A myth is the connective tissue, the "in-between-ness" that lends coherence and meaning to our experience of the world.[17]

Atheists and believers, Christians and Jews connect the dots of their experience in different ways. They employ different myths. The subjective element in the choice of a myth is thus unavoidable. And with subjectivity comes tension. But it is clear that there is no thoroughly rational, objectively valid, logically unassailable proof of God's existence; philosophers have been searching for such proofs for centuries without success. The only alternative is to resort to experience and, as we concluded in discussing revelation, to invoke human experience is inevitably to relativize its discoveries.

The pattern, throughout, is clear and consistent. In matters of practice and belief, the hallmarks of our ideology are subjectivity, relativism, uncertainty, and tension. If we extend our discussion to consider two further theological issues, the problem of evil and eschatology, the pattern remains. On the first, we cannot affirm any single, clear theologically coherent justification for the suffering of the righteous. We reject the Torah's explanation that suffering is punishment for sin; in fact, the Book of Job quotes God as rejecting this explanation (42:7–8). The remaining classical theological resolutions—that God's power is limited, that suffering is an expression of God's love, is a mystery, is a test of faith, or is an inevitable concomitant of human freedom—are hardly more satisfactory. On this issue, I have arrived at a theological impasse and, since Judaism is much more than theology, I turn to ritual, liturgy, and our tradition's embrace of community for a measure of solace.[18]

Theodicy leads to eschatology. My formulation of Stone's concluding point is that this world and the world to come are not sequential eras. Rather, they are two dimensions of the world that we inhabit: the first is the world in which we make moral choices, and the second, the world in which the consequences of those choices become manifest. These two worlds are then in tension, a tension that reflects the tension between our good and evil impulses. This is the tension that Jacob encountered, according to Stone's reading of the midrash on the first verse in *Vayeshev*: Jacob sought the tranquility of the world to come in this world. Instead, he had to deal with the sufferings brought upon him by Joseph.

Again, my critique of the claim that we are a halakhic movement is directed not at how we function but at how we identify ourselves. As an identifying mark, the claim is unfalsifiable and disingenuous, it escapes any clear definition, it has failed to engage our laity who either don't understand it or don't view it as relating to their own lives, and it is subverted by the culture of our movement, by its academic center, and by its implicit theology. It is a claim created by and for rabbis, designed primarily to promote our wish to feel authentic.

In its place, I suggested we embrace the tension and ambiguity that has always been at the heart of our reading of Judaism. If we believe all God-talk is metaphorical, if we deny the historicity and the literalness of the Sinai narrative as it appears in Torah, and if we claim the Jewish religion was essentially the creation of the Jewish people, of groupings of Jews at various critical moments in our history, functioning in response to and within specific cultural contexts that we can describe—a notion I am convinced most of the ideologues of our movement share—then we must conclude that authority in matters of belief and practice lies within the hands of the committed Jews of every generation. To say this is to relativize all of our ideological commitments and effectively to consign us to a life of tension—which I suggest we should embrace and which we will find liberating.

VIII. WE ARE NEITHER REFORM NOR RECONSTRUCTIONIST

Finally, I need to deal with two issues that hover around the periphery of my thinking. The first is the fear that such thinking may lead to the loss of our distinctive identity, specifically, that the markers that distinguish us from Reform or Reconstructionism would become blurred or even obliterated. I understand that fear because however tenuous our commitment to halakhah may have become, the rhetorical statement "We are a halakhic movement" has served as a marker that separates the two movements.

I offer two points in response to this charge. The first is that our two movements do in fact share a common theology. We read and we teach the same theologians. Buber and Rosenzweig, Heschel and Kaplan, their students and the postmoderns are our common legacy. Theologically, the reality is that you can't be more or less liberal. Once you deny a literalist understanding of revelation, you are willy-nilly in the liberal camp.

What distinguishes us then? First, we differ in how much of traditional Jewish ritual practice we want to retain, how much we are prepared to abandon or to change, and how we go about changing. In all of these areas, we are more "conservative." That is more of an emotional stance than a theological one, and it is thoroughly legitimate on its own terms. Feelings are important. Second, we differ in our institutional loyalties. Our loyalty to the institutions of our respective movements, primarily to JTS or to HUC–JIR, is genuine and powerful. Finally, we differ strikingly in our liturgy. No one who has davened in a Reform or in a Conservative synagogue could possibly confuse the two. I have frequently suggested that were you to blindfold me and lead me into five Reform and five Conservative synagogues, I would identify the movement in less than a minute. Whatever my personal theology, I prefer to worship from a traditionalist prayer book. None of this is going to change.

I find it fascinating that though we have long been aware that our location as the center among American Jewish religious movements has made us uniquely vulnerable, recent developments in American Reform and Orthodoxy suggest that both of those movements are slowly gravitating back to the center. The pace is understandably glacial, but the direction is clear. In the latter half of the twentieth century American Reform embraced Hebrew, Zionism, significant aspects of traditional synagogue ritual, and, most recently, an appreciation of the value of conversion. Orthodoxy, for its part, began to recognize Jewish women as halakhic authorities in their own right, and even allowed them to assume selected but significant liturgical and ritual roles. These developments should be appreciated as a backhanded tribute to where we have located ourselves all along.

IX. A PARADIGM IN CRISIS

The second issue is much more complex. I have asserted with a measure of confidence that tension is healthy. That issue merits a full-length study of its own, but I suggest that our situation is similar to those studied by Thomas S. Kuhn in his seminal *The Structure of Scientific Revolutions.*[19] Kuhn traces the process by which a scientific paradigm, a basic way of seeing the data—for example, the one embodied in Ptolemaic astronomy—develops anomalies. An anomaly, for Kuhn, is a piece of data for which the paradigm cannot account. It just doesn't fit, but it cannot be ignored. In time, these anomalies accumulate until the scientists who work in the discipline begin to sense that the gaps in the theory have become so overwhelming that the entire paradigm is now in question. The holes in the tapestry are more numerous than the patterns.

Kuhn labels that moment a crisis. When a hypothesis or a paradigm is in crisis, it is no longer sufficient to work at patching up the anomalies. Now the entire structure must be replaced with a new way of looking at the data, a new paradigm that generates a new hypothesis whereby the anomalies now disappear. Thus Copernican astronomy replaced the Ptolemaic. A scientific revolution is at hand.

This hardly does justice to Kuhn's exposition. But note three points. First, paradigms are important; they are at the heart of every scientific endeavor. Think of Freud, or Einstein, or string theory, or John Maynard Keynes. Each embodies a picture, a way of looking at the data, a pattern, a gestalt. Second, paradigms create elaborate institutional structures, organizations, journals, grant proposals, and laboratory equipment and the companies that build and market them. Paradigms are powerful political and financial realities. Third, paradigms go to great lengths to resist being overthrown. They are inherently conservative because careers (think tenure), enormous sums of money, and political power are tied to every paradigm. Their defenders go to great lengths to account for the anomaly. Finally, paradigms are never overthrown until a more effective substitute paradigm is available.

Our movement is not a scientific hypothesis, and I concede that the parallel is not precise. But it is similar enough to generate thoughtful inquiry. The crisis that ensues when the anomalies overwhelm the solutions is familiar to us. We are not doing well; most of us are aware that the movement needs a new vision, a new direction, a new aggadah—in short, a new paradigm.

The claim that we are a halakhic movement is a paradigm in crisis. It has been singularly persistent because it has made us feel authentic and enabled us to fend off attacks from the right. The anxiety that overwhelms theoreticians when their paradigm has begun to collapse can help illuminate what we collectively feel today.

I propose that this welcoming embrace of tension in matters of belief and practice serve as the distinctive hallmark of
Conservative Judaism. I do not know, at this point, how to
translate this notion into a pithy slogan, but that will come in
time. I am fully aware that this view subverts the conventional
understanding of the function of religion, and that may be
enough to disqualify it for some. Others, however—hopefully
the more sophisticated of our laypeople—may agree that tension
is ultimately healthy, that it can serve as a source of vitality,
growth, and creativity. Research in the social sciences should
help to document that claim. We should also learn how to teach
our children that this dimension of our Judaism is a source of its
strength. After all, our model is the biblical Jacob. Jacob wres-
tled with an angel and emerged both wounded and blessed.
Maybe we too need to feel wounded before we can be blessed.
We could do much worse than emulate Jacob.

Chapter 14

RITUALS, MYTHS, AND COMMUNITIES[1]

There is no precise Hebrew equivalent for the world "ritual." When classic Jewish texts refer to the body of observances such as the dietary laws, tefillin, Sabbath and festival practices, immersion in a *mikvah*, or rites of passage such as circumcision, they use phrases such as *mitzvot shebein adam lamakom*, "commands [dealing with the relationship] between human beings and God," as opposed to *mitzvot shebein adam l'havero*, "commands [dealing with the relationship] between one human being and another." Or they use the terms coined by Saadia Gaon in the tenth century: *mitzvot shimiyot*, "revelational" (literally, "heavenly") commands, as opposed to *mitzvot sikhliyot* or "rational" commands,[2] or, finally, the rabbinic interpretation of a biblical distinction between God's *hukkim* and *mishpatim*. The former, according to the rabbinic interpretation of passages such as Leviticus 18:4, are ordinances that idolaters (or the evil impulse) tempt us to flout precisely because they are totally arbitrary divine decrees.[3] The latter, had God not revealed them, would have been decreed by humanity itself, for they are the reasonable axioms of our social order.

These are practices, then, that have no clear interpersonal (read "ethical") impact but deal rather with our relationship to

God; have no rational basis, but are arbitrary and hence more likely to be flouted; and are binding simply because of the weight of divine authority that lies behind them.

These characteristics account for the problems we face in making sense of these practices today. Obedience to arbitrary divine decrees does not come easily. In the scholarly arena, the absence of a precise Hebrew equivalent for "ritual" is often used to justify a vague discomfort with the entire issue. In many circles, the word "ritual" itself carries negative connotations. This entire dimension of religious life does not lend itself to the detached, critical, or scientific approach that has been the hallmark of Jewish scholarship for the past century. With strikingly few exceptions—Gershom Scholem's work on Jewish mysticism being the most noteworthy—Jewish scholars have ignored the range of issues dealing with the phenomenology of religion, that is, the way in which Judaism, specifically as religion, functions in the lives of human beings in their communities. Ritual is central to this inquiry, which must be approached existentially and experientially, not simply objectively or cerebrally. Ritual touches the more primitive layers of our being, that part of us that cultivates fantasy or responds to a mythopoetic reading of our experience. It can have a mysterious yet undeniably powerful impact at critical moments in our personal and communal lives—much more powerful than that of the more intelligible institutions of religious life. And, in fact, it is omnipresent, though often unnoticed precisely because of its omnipresence.

It should be added that "Ritual Studies" is an exciting and growing field of investigation, populated largely by social scientists and scholars in religious studies (largely of primitive religions and Christianity). What follows here is an inquiry into more specifically Jewish understandings of ritual.

In reviewing the more relevant theories on the function of ritual in religion, we need to remember that the distinctions are theoretical or functional, not institutional, and that any believer can fit into any one camp at any one moment. Rituals can serve a variety of functions.

RITUAL AS MAGIC

If performed correctly, ritual, has an immediate, automatically coercive effect on the Force or forces that govern nature and history. Failure to perform the ritual or to perform it in the proper way can lead to disaster. Yehezkel Kaufmann's morphology of pagan ritual stresses its magical character but, as we know, magical residues can be found in the behavior of even the most sophisticated of believers.[4] *Tefillat Haderekh* (the traveler's prayer) for example, can be recited as a magical formula designed to "coerce" God to protect the traveler, as a prayer that God freely intercede, or as a simple acknowledgment of the traveler's vulnerability. The determining factor is more the individual's inner state of mind than the theology (which is rarely explicit). The anxiety that results from not saying the prayer will serve as a reliable indicator of a more magical framework. Unique to this position is the automatic and coercive nature of the cause and effect relationship and the emphasis on the meticulous performance of the ritual itself as decisive. This position can also sometimes serve as the implicit mindset behind the otherwise paradoxical juxtaposition of meticulous adherence to ritual and flagrant violation of the moral law. Jeremiah 7:3–15 records an early manifestation of that position and Jeremiah's appropriately monotheistic response. Finally, some formulations of the problem of theodicy actually signal the breakdown of a magical framework where the fulfillment of the *moral* law (sometimes along with the ritual) is intended to *coerce* the desired reward.

RITUAL AS SACRAMENT

Here, too, ritual effects a substantive change in the nature of things out there. Beyond the believer but in contrast with the magical approach, the sacramentalist insists that the efficacy of the ritual demands the proper state of inwardness, the correct belief structure. The magicalist, in contrast, ascribes inherent power to the performance of the ritual itself. The Roman Catholic understanding of the Eucharist, whereby the bread and wine *become* the flesh and blood of Jesus when the proper formulas are recited by the proper person within the proper belief structure, so that the one who partakes of them, again in the proper belief structure, is thereby saved, is sacramentalism at its purest. Mary Douglas captures that dimension:

> The crux of the doctrine is that a real, invisible transformation has taken place at the priest's saying of the sacred words and that the eating of the consecrated host has saving efficacy for those who take it and for others.... It assumes that humans can take an active part in the work of redemption, both to save themselves and others, through using the sacraments as channels of grace. Sacraments are not only signs, but essentially different from other signs, being instruments. This touches on the belief in *opus operatum,* the efficacious rite.[5]

The more liberal wings of Protestant Christianity transformed the sacrament of the Eucharist into a symbolic pageant or historical reenactment of Jesus' self-sacrifice. In Judaism, the Lurianic view of ritual as effecting a cosmic *tikkun* (repair) when performed with the proper *kavanah* (intent) is sacramentalism in a Jewish vein.[6] Here too, the mitzvot are efficaciously redemptive instruments.

RITUAL AS OBEDIENCE

Ritual does not effect a direct, substantive change in the nature of things but it is explicitly commanded by God. Performing a ritual, then, is nothing more than a concrete way of acknowledging God's authority and obeying God's will. This may result in God's freely bestowed reward, but not automatically, inevitably, or coercively. To ignore the ritual is to flout God; again, this may result in God's freely bestowed punishment. Ethical mitzvot can also serve to acknowledge God's authority, but they can too easily be performed on rational or humanist grounds. Rituals are arbitrary. They serve, then, as the most complete expression of religious submission and therefore of authenticity within the believing community. Norman Lamm, for example, insists that we should perform even the ethical commands as if they were ritual, thereby transforming a "pale humanist act" into a "profound spiritual gesture."[7] Crucial to this position are a literalist understanding of revelation—God has made God's will known unambiguously to God's community—and a concept of God as totally free and non-coercible by any power outside God's own will.

RITUAL AS ANACHRONISM

Ritual was a meaningful form of religious expression in the past, either in the earlier stages of civilization or in premodern times. It is now an anachronism. *Our* preferred forms are ethical behavior and spirituality (inwardness). This position identifies ritual behavior with "ritualism," which can be defined as ritual acts performed in a totally mechanical, routinized way, what Abraham Heschel so felicitously called "religious behaviorism." They have become purely outward forms of behavior, empty of any religious, spiritual or emotional content. Hence they should be abandoned.[8]

SOME PROBLEMS

The problem with the magical position is that it denies the monotheistic God who is, above all, supremely free. It assumes that a human being can coerce natural processes or, in a monotheistic setting, even God. The position may meet deep-seated psychological needs in a human being, but as an explicit theology of Jewish ritual, it is unacceptable.

211

The sacramental position runs into different problems. It can be accommodated to monotheism but, unless one is a Lurianic kabbalist, Jewish ritual simply has not exercised a sacramental function. There is no Jewish parallel to the Roman Catholic understanding of the Eucharist. No Jew, for example, would find himself in the position of the adulterous policeman in Graham Greene's *The Heart of the Matter* who is torn between confessing his adultery and shattering his marriage, or taking the Eucharist in a state of sin, which means eternal damnation. No Jewish ritual carries that kind of power. In fact, there are rabbinic passages that explicitly deny this position. Note, for example, the claim of the third-century master Rav that God does not care if we (ritually) slaughter the animal by the nape or by the neck;[9] or of the first-century rabbi Yohanan ben Zakkai, that "neither does the corpse defile nor does the water [with the ashes of the red heifer] purify, but rather I [God] have issued a set of arbitrary decrees which you are simply not permitted to flout."[10]

More generally, there is not one single Jewish ritual that may not, on occasion, be suspended. Even circumcision, which must be performed on the eighth day—even on the Sabbath *and* the Day of Atonement—may be postponed indefinitely if the infant is ill or if two other children of the same mother died as a result of the ritual.[11] Similar conditions apply to tefillin (for the *onen*—a mourner before the funeral) or Sabbath observance, the Yom Kippur fast, and the dietary laws (for *pikuah nefesh*—safeguarding a life).[12] Neither the magicalist nor the sacramentalist can tolerate the suspension of a central ritual act.

Which brings us to ritual as the paradigmatic act of obedience to God. Here we are on more familiar ground. Obedience to God's will is clearly the central model of spirituality both in the Bible and in rabbinic literature. But the problem with the position is its almost inevitable tendency to elevate ritual behavior to the pinnacle of religious expression. Prophetic literature, for one, insists on a different hierarchy of divine commands, with ethical behavior taking priority. Justice, compassion, righteousness—these are inherently or absolutely divine, for they define

God's relationship with us. Even God is bound by these values, and they then acquire absolute sanctity; that is why they must define our interpersonal relationships as well. But the nonethical commands have a derivative sanctity. God is not bound by them; God does not participate and is not affected by the cult. If God were to choose, Hosea 6:6 tells us, God would want *hesed* over *zevah*, acts of lovingkindness over sacrifice. The first chapter of Isaiah, which we read liturgically prior to the fast of Tisha B'Av (the anniversary of the destruction of the First and Second Temples) has God denouncing Israel's sacrifices and festivals. What God demands of us is that we should cease to do evil, devote ourselves to justice, aid the wronged, uphold the rights of the orphan, and defend the cause of the widow.

What more dramatic repudiation of the priority of ritual can there be than God's decision to destroy the Temple—the very site of the ritual cult in biblical religion—as punishment for Israel's moral shortcomings. God's destruction of the Temple would be inconceivable to the magicalist or the sacramentalist. It *could* be viewed as supporting the view of ritual as anachronistic, but Ezekiel does prophesy about the rebuilding of the Temple; what Isaiah 1, Jeremiah 7, and Amos 5:21ff. denounce is "your" ritual cult, that is, the one being practiced now, not the cult in general; and the exiles did in fact rebuild the Temple with God's clear approval (Haggai 1:2ff.). The destruction of the Temple does, however, challenge the claim that ritual has any kind of priority.

Finally, this position also assumes that all of the mitzvot are explicitly, that is, literally or verbally, revealed by God, a position that raises theological problems all its own.[13] If we prefer an alternative theology of revelation, we have to redefine what we mean by mitzvah in general and the ritual mitzvot in particular.

The reductionist dismissal of religious ritual as anachronistic cannot be evaluated from within any of the customary theological assumptions. Here, the inquiries of the social sciences and our common human experience take on heightened significance. From these sources, we learn this cardinal principle: the issue is never ritual or no ritual but rather *which* ritual—for significant portions of our lives are inherently ritualized.

RITUAL AS LANGUAGE

A tennis club will prescribe certain rules of behavior that must be obeyed by all members. Some of these are perfectly reasonable: tennis shoes must be worn for traction and to preserve the playing surface. Others are completely arbitrary. Just try to appear on the court wearing a navy blue shirt and yellow bathing suit! A detailed code governs every moment of a meal in an expensive restaurant: the placement and use of cutlery, plates, and goblets; the selection and presentation of wine and food; the correlation of wines and dishes; the juxtaposition of foods and even the choice of ingredients—all are subject to stringent and detailed regulation. Elaborate codes of behavior govern an appearance of or before the queen of England; or the president of the United States; or, for that matter, the way in which a baseball team celebrates a home run; or the hierarchy of seating around the table in the boardroom of a large corporation. A violation of any of these regulations would have much the same effect as bringing a slice of bacon into the kitchen of a traditional Jew.

There is a tight nexus between ritual and community. Ritual is a language that, like other languages, creates community. Verbal language is a highly precise form of communication. There are other messages, however, that do not lend themselves to verbal communication. "Words fail me," we say, when we want to express powerful emotions. We hug our children and recognize that it would take many words to express what is in the hug. Or we resort to visual and aural symbols such as showing the flag and singing a national anthem, which communicate powerfully and directly the full weight of our national pride.

Language creates community. It unites those who share the language but it also excludes those who do not. By definition, communities also include and exclude; some people are in and others are out. Languages and communities are inherently separatist. It is no accident that Leviticus 11, which details the foods that the biblical community could or could not eat, concludes with the repeated injunction that this community was to be *kadosh*. We normally translate *kadosh* as "sacred" or "holy," but a more technical definition would be "separated out" or "distinguished" (in the nonvaluative sense of the word). The Sabbath day that is *kadosh* begins with *Kiddush* and ends with *Havdalah*, which are synonyms. The Sabbath is distinguished from the other days of the week as the Israelites are distinguished from other communities, the land of Israel from other lands, or the Hebrew language from other languages.

To say that the issue is never ritual or no ritual, but rather which ritual, is the same as saying that the issue is never community or no community but which community. One invariably belongs to a community and speaks its idiosyncratic languages.

FROM LANGUAGE TO THEATER

How do languages create community? I suggest we broaden the metaphor and see ritual as a form of theater—a miniature, liturgical drama. Theater, too, creates community. The proscenium collapses, and players and audience are united in a shared experience. Take the Jewish rites of passage—circumcision, marriage, burial, and mourning. At each of these, all of Israel is present, symbolically, in the form of a minyan, the quorum of ten Jews necessary for public worship. Each celebrates a private moment in the life of an individual, yet each is also an event in the life of the community—so the community belongs. A script is read—the liturgy. There are the main actors: *mohel* (one who performs the ritual of circumcision) and infant; bride and groom; mourner; and supporting actors: the *sandek* (who holds the infant during circumcision), witnesses, comforters. There arc even offstage fantasy characters: Abraham, Phineas, and Elijah at the circumcision; Adam, Eve, and Jeremiah at the wedding; Job at the graveside. Elijah's throne, the huppah, and the low chairs in the *shiva* house serve as sets. Stage directions are provided: the cutting of the foreskin, the ring on the right forefinger, the tearing of the garment. The characters wear costumes: the groom, a white *kittel*; the mourner, a torn garment. The Passover seder is the pageant at its most elaborate, where word, body language, set, script, stage directions, and even costumes all come together to teach the founding story of a community to its next generation.

Rituals accomplish two purposes superbly well. First they define identity. They shape the social experiences of everyday life—eating, dressing, leisure—and the transitions in nature and life—from day to night, from season to season, from life stage to life stage—and garb them in the distinctive values of a particular community. In the process, this community takes on a distinctive identity. It becomes separated out from other communities.

Second, rituals are powerful pedagogic devices. They transmit identity from generation to generation. Effective education is always theatrical, particularly when it goes beyond the cognitive, when it is tinged with affect, when it speaks to the senses as much as to the mind, when it addresses the whole person. At the Passover seder, the table is both stage and classroom; the haggadah, both script and textbook. The rituals of reclining, eating and drinking, lifting and lowering, covering and uncovering are both stage directions and experiential learning. They are theatrical, also, because they depart from what is usually done "every other night of the year." It is this "why is this night different" quality that transforms a meal into a ritual experience. We don't usually dip our fingers into the wine or eat horseradish root. It is the unfamiliarity of the choreography that makes them educationally unforgettable experiences. But precisely because the choreography is unfamiliar, it is also threatening. Hence we are tempted to substitute a familiar choreography for the unfamiliar. The visit to the house of mourning becomes a social call; the tuxedo replaces the *kittel*; the black ribbon replaces the torn garment. The anachronist claims that we have done away with ritual. In fact we have substituted one set, costume, script, and stage direction for another. There is no escaping ritual.

The trade-off for beginning our inquiry with our common human experience is that ritual behavior becomes generic. We flatten the differences between the rituals of religion and those of everyday life. In the short run, we may gain pedagogically. But eventually we must deal with the distinctive qualities of the rituals of religion.

RITUALS AND MYTH

The rituals of religion are dramatizations of religious myths. As discussed in earlier chapters, no term in contemporary religious scholarship is more misunderstood than "myth." A brief digression, then, is in order to indicate how we understand the term.[14]

In popular parlance, a myth is understood to be either a fiction (the myth of the invincibility of the New York Yankees) or a legendary tale (the myth of Oedipus). Technically, it is neither of these, but rather a structure of meaning through which we make sense of our experience. Experience does not come to us as brute fact laden with objective meaning. The very determination of what constitutes a fact in the first place, let alone how facts assume specific patterns that convey meaning, requires a complex transaction between the "out there" and the way we choose to "read" it. Myths are created by "reading communities," individuals joined in efforts to shape, order, and make sense of what seems to be blooming confusion. Gradually, as the myth works to explain why things are as they are, it is refined, shared, and transmitted from generation to generation. It becomes embodied in official, canonical texts. In its final form, the myth becomes authoritative, even coercive, and quasi-invisible—so much has it become part of our intuitive stance toward the world.

Myths explain, account for, answer questions such as "why." In general, they explain overt data by referring to an invisible or elusive world "behind" the data. This accounts for

217

the imaginative or apparently fictional character of many myths—even, it should be noted, the myths of science. Psychoanalytic theory, quantum mechanics, and astronomy are notable examples of scientific myths; they too explain the overt data of observation by referring to a hidden world "behind" experience.[15]

Myths are intrinsic to communities. A living community acquires its identity through its myth. It explains how that community came to be, what distinguishes it from other communities, how it views its distinctive destiny, what constitutes its value scheme. From its myth, a community derives its raison d'être; when the myth dies, the community's death is not far behind.

Religious myths function in much the same way. They too explain, account for, confer identity, promote loyalty, and motivate behavior on behalf of a religious community. They too reveal unsuspected or elusive depths that lie behind experience. But they differ from other mythic structures in their content. First, they convey the community's distinctive answers to the ultimate questions posed by human existence: Why am I here? What am I to accomplish? How should I live? Why do I suffer? Why must I die? How do I deal with my guilt? How do I achieve authenticity? fulfillment? salvation? In short, they convey a community's answers to the intuitive search for meaning. Second, many religious myths do all of this by viewing the panorama of nature and history as the work of a transcendent God.

To say that God is within the mythic structure is to say that all characterizations of God and God's activity are colored by the fact of our humanness. This is not at all to say that God is a fiction. Our ancestors no more "invented" God than Freud "invented" the psyche or a physicist, the quark. They experienced God's presence in nature and history; that was the original, experiential source for the myth.[16] They simply could not account for their communal experience in any other way. The myth and the original experience fueled and continued to fuel each other. The (mythic) characterization of God shapes the experience. But at the same time, the ongoing experience of

God's presence has verified the myth over countless generations. Otherwise, it would have died long before our time.

Religious myths are canonized in Scriptures, sacred books that record the authoritative version of the myth and become textbooks for communicating it from generation to generation. Though the sacred books are sealed, the myth itself remains plastic enough so that succeeding generations can expand, contract, refine, or revise the mythic structure in terms of their personal experience; we Jews call that process midrash. Religious myths also generate liturgies or dramatic recitations of the myths that celebrate significant moments in the life experience of the community or its members. Often, the sheer recounting of the narrative portion of the myth is itself an act of worship, a way of praising God who is the supreme actor in the story.[17] Finally, religious myths also generate rituals, equally dramatic renderings of the myth, this time in the language of the body.[18]

Ritual draws its power from the myth. A living myth has enormous power to generate emotion, loyalty, and activity. People die for their myths. Ritual draws on that power. In fact, it is precisely through the ritual that the power inherent in the myth is channeled to a community.

Take the ritual of circumcision. Covenant is the linchpin of the Torah myth, and the circumcision is the ritual expression of covenantedness, the visual, dramatic *ot*, or symbol, of the covenant (see Gen. 17:10). The indelibility of the act captures the indelibility of the covenant itself. And the fantasy characters that are invoked—Abraham, Phineas, and Elijah—are all models of undeviating loyalty to the covenant through the most severe of tests. Note also the interplay between the two languages, the verbal and the behavioral, the liturgy and the ritual. Each does what it does best. The ritual lends drama and affect; it creates the almost palpable sense of awe that pervades the room. The liturgy lends specificity. It brings the event into the explicit framework of the myth and locates it within the broader vision of the community. Together they form a complex pageant that celebrates another link in the chain of covenantedness.[19]

Conversely, the absence of a distinctive liturgy and ritual is invariably an indication that the myth has nothing distinctive to say, as yet, about the event or experience at hand. We are keenly aware of the lack of either liturgy or ritual to memorialize the Holocaust, or to celebrate the founding of the State of Israel or, until recently, the birth of a daughter. The flood of new proposals for the last of these is the clearest indication that the impulse for the creation of new liturgical and ritual forms emerges out of a deeply felt human and communal need. We may not teach our children to recite the *Sh'ma* at bedtime, but most children will then produce dramatic and equally coercive bedtime liturgies and rituals of their own.

RITUAL AND RITUALISM

The position advocated here suggests that Jewish ritual be understood as a complex symbolic system. The term "symbol" as used in this context has two implications. First, a symbol "stands for," "represents," "reflects," or "captures" some other, more ultimate reality, usually elusive or hidden, in highly dramatic form. It possesses no inherent meaning or power of its own but draws on the reality it represents. That is what separates ritual-as-symbol from ritual-as-sacrament. On the other hand, a symbol is more than a "sign." A sign is a mere convention, easily established and just as easily abandoned. The red traffic light is a sign; a national flag is a symbol. Spitting on the flag is a very different matter than ignoring a red light. That's what separates rituals from "ritualism."[20]

A symbol can "die," that is, lose its power to represent or capture the reality for which it stands. It then becomes a sign, outward behavior alone, empty of any genuine content. We have then fallen prey to ritualism. But that condition is neither inevitable nor permanent. "The Star Spangled Banner" played before a hockey game at Madison Square Garden is ritualism; the crowd feels free to cheer throughout. But this did not destroy the hymn's power as an authentic national ritual when it was played at the funeral of John F. Kennedy. Sometimes we worship ritualistically; at other times, we can recite the same liturgy as an authentic ritual of prayer.

The danger of degenerating into ritualism applies less to the grand set pieces of Jewish ritual life than to those rituals such as the dietary laws that are part of the furniture of everyday life. What distinguishes the latter is their omnipresence as a structure imposed on the most ordinary aspects of living. These are so far from being theatrical that they become quasi-invisible. To take these common experiences and to classify, organize, and structure them in a distinctive way is intrinsic to community building.

This entire discussion of the interrelationship of myth, ritual, and community converges in the notion of the significance of distinctions. To have an identity is to be different from someone else. By definition, one community is distinct from another community. The community's myth lends content to that distinction and its rituals concretize and dramatize that content in the life experience of its members. This is the point of departure for the anthropological inquiry into the notions of sacred space and sacred time in religion.[21] Thus Leviticus 19:1–20:27, the Torah portion that not incidentally "was recited before the entire assembled community because most of the pillars of Torah are based on its contents,"[22] pursues the making of distinctions of all kinds in meticulous detail. That is how a community becomes *kadosh*, that is, distinguished or sacred.

The confusion of ritual and ritualism is part of a more general contemporary tendency to disparage ritual. For Mary Douglas, this "contempt of external ritual forms" is followed by two successive stages, first "the private internalizing of religious experience" and then "the move to humanist philanthropy," that is, to ethics as substitute for ritual.[23] The process is hauntingly familiar to students of recent Jewish religious history. In effect, to disparage ritual is to disparage distinctions. But what really takes place is the substitution of one set of distinctions for another, one community and its ritual forms for another. There is no escaping community and ritual. The only question is: which community, and which ritual system?

221

OBEDIENCE TO GOD OR SYMBOLIC BEHAVIOR

In the last analysis, my sense is that our choice lies between seeing ritual as obedience to God's will or as symbolic behavior. The two positions are not mutually exclusive, at least in theory. God *can* command us to act in symbolic ways. But in practice, the two positions will lead to widely divergent outcomes. The issues involved in making this choice are both theological and programmatic. The first position assumes explicit literal or verbal revelation of God's will. The second assumes an active human and communal role in the formulation of the content of revelation. Where we stand on that issue will be decisive.

Programmatically, the symbolist position assumes that any ritual can die and that new rituals can be generated by the community. The first, obedience, cannot abide that possibility. It also cannot accept the possibility that a ritual can become morally offensive to segments of the community; the symbolists will have much less difficulty with that eventuality. Having said this, we should be enormously cautious about abandoning any one ritual. We never know when it can be reinfused with meaning, and it is painfully clear that the process of creating new rituals is long and arduous. There is, then, one further difference between the two positions. The symbolist will be much more tolerant of pluralistic ritual patterns and extended periods of indecision as the process of eliminating, revising, retaining or creating works itself out. We are squarely in one of those periods today in regard to prayer rituals for Jewish women. *Kippah*, *talit*, and *tefillin* are being worn or not worn in every possible combination. The process is exciting and not a little anxiety filled.

However, this period also affords us an opportunity to study the process of ritualization, the development of new ritual forms. In regard to the Holocaust, for example, David Roskies's *Night Words*, a liturgical service for Holocaust Remembrance Day, is a particularly creative proposal that unites verbal and body language in a highly theatrical way and is gradually winning communal acceptance as a Holocaust Memorial Day ritual.[24] Presumably the Passover seder began this way as well.

Beyond this, much work remains to be done on sharpening the distinctions between convention, custom, ceremony, and ritual. There are few universally accepted definitions as yet. Even more important is the attempt to catch in a more rigorous way what each of these symbolic forms in fact represents. Finally, still totally obscure is the relationship of Jewish ritual to our view of the human body, which is the instrument for ritual behavior. We are still at the very beginning of the inquiry.

For the present, however, our problem is that we belong to multiple communities with multiple myths and ritual systems. To put the matter in another way, we accept the need and value of distinctions, but we are confused as to which ones we want to retain and which we want to abandon. Some of us have abandoned the distinction in gender roles in the synagogue, but we all maintain the distinction between meat and milk. Sometimes, our multiple communities and languages cohere; we can have a kosher wedding at the Plaza Hotel, even a kosher nouvelle-cuisine wedding. Sometimes they don't cohere; we can't serve shrimp cocktail at a kosher wedding, even at the Plaza. We are then forced to choose. The ambiguities of those choices is one of the most difficult trade-offs of the symbolist position.[25] This is probably what impels some of our contemporaries to the obedience position.

Finally, it should be absolutely clear that the symbolist position in no way advocates a contraction in ritual behavior. If this is an age of communal fragmentation, of growing anomie and isolation, of rootlessness and anxiety, of emotional aridity, then it is an age that demands more ritual, more theatrically performed than ever before. We may or may not be prepared to believe that God explicitly commands us to act in these ways, but we might more easily believe that our very humanness and our communal identity does—and that we should harken as obediently to these demands as our ancestors did to God's.

CHAPTER 15

COPING WITH CHAOS

Jewish Theological and Ritual Resources

In the four decades in which I have been engaged in teaching and writing on Jewish theology, the challenge to faith posed by apparently unjustifiable and irremediable human suffering has become increasingly central to my work. The issue was always present in my course syllabi and in my personal wrestling with God, but it is no longer simply one of a series of issues assigned more or less equal standing. It has become the core issue, the issue that threatens to upset the entire system.

I have tried, without significant success, to account for this change. After all, I did begin to teach in the wake of the Holocaust. I have long been aware that innocent children die from disease. And I know that, each year, thousands of equally innocent human beings perish in a variety of natural disasters. None of that is new. What is decidedly new is the weight I have come to assign to these realities in reaching some considered judgment on the role that the God whom I worship daily plays in history, nature, and the human experience. What is also new, I confess at the outset, is my increasing despair at the very possibility of dealing with this issue in purely theological terms.

In retrospect, on some level, I had begun to be aware of that gradual shift in my theological agenda even prior to the events of September 11, 2001. But the events of that day served to bring it into much sharper focus. I recall standing among a group of students and colleagues, watching transfixed before the television screen as the towers crumbled, when a student turned to me and remarked, "So what does our professor of theology have to say about this?" Totally intuitively, I responded, "Right now, your professor of theology feels that we should declare a moratorium on doing theology for at least a full year." "So," he responded, "our professor of theology's theology works for sunny days only!" I could not summon up an answer, hence the subtitle of this chapter.

Theology is only one of the resources an ancient and respected religious tradition can bring to bear on coping with human experience. Religion is much more than theology. Religion also involves a sense of community, liturgy, ritual, and a wide range of institutions. What role these other resources can play in helping us cope with life, and their relationship to the more cerebral role that is played by theology, are the issues I would like to address. I need not add that I can only work from within my own religious tradition, which is Judaism.

THE FUNCTION OF RELIGION:
COSMOS AND CHAOS

I begin then with a definition of religion that I have found to be useful in all of my work. As noted earlier, the anthropologist Clifford Geertz, in his seminal paper, "Religion as a Cultural System," proposes this definition.[1] I should add that I came across Geertz's paper relatively late in my career but it served to help me concretize a significant transformation in my personal theological approach. I was then in the process of moving toward the theological naturalism of Paul Tillich and of my late teacher, Mordecai Kaplan, which is doubtless why the social science study of religion and the work of an anthropologist such as Geertz proved to be so useful at that stage of my thinking.

"A religion is," Geertz suggests, "a system of symbols which acts to establish powerful, pervasive, and long-lasting moods and motivations in men by formulating conceptions of a general order of existence and clothing these conceptions with such an aura of factuality that the moods and motivations seem uniquely realistic."[2]

The nub of Geertz's definition is the notion of order. Religion is an ordering device. This sense of an ordered world is conveyed through "a system of symbols." As discussed earlier, my own preferred term for this symbolic system is "myth," understood, not in its popular sense as synonymous with "fiction" and contrasted with "the facts," but rather in its academic sense as an imaginative pattern of meaning imposed upon a complex set of data. In the course of this chapter, I will use both "myth" and "symbol" interchangeably, for I understand a myth to be a set of symbols extended and interconnected.[3]

In this definition, we encounter Geertz, the "outsider," the observer, speaking. For the "insider," the believer functioning within the system, this sense of an ordered world and the moods and motivations that it inspires are not at all symbolic but rather utterly factual, as the closing phrase of the definition indicates. For Geertz, the outsider, the sense of order conveyed by the symbolic system conveys not "factuality" pure and simple but rather an "aura of factuality." To use the terminology of Paul Tillich, the myth is both "broken" and "living."

If Geertz is correct, then, the core issue with which any religion must cope is the tension between order and chaos. In this, he acknowledges his debt to Susanne Langer and to Salvador de Madariaga, who reduce the definition to "the relatively modest dogma that God is not mad."[4]

THE MULTIPLE CHALLENGES OF CHAOS

The bulk of Geertz's essay proceeds to unpack his definition, phrase by phrase. For our purposes here, the most significant section of Geertz's analysis deals with the challenge posed to any religion when chaos, which he defines as "a tumult of events which lack not just interpretations but *interpretability*," erupts into our experience.[5] This challenge, Geertz suggests, is three-fold, testing the limits of our analytic capacities, our powers of endurance, and our moral insight. "Bafflement, suffering and a sense of intractable ethical paradox," he writes, "are all ... radical challenges to the proposition that life is comprehensible and that we can ... orient ourselves effectively within it—challenges with which any religion, however 'primitive,' which hopes to persist must attempt somehow to cope."[6]

My own formulation of these three challenges is to define them as, respectively, an intellectual challenge, an emotional challenge, and a moral challenge. The first stretches our intuitive need simply to account for the eruption of the chaotic, to explain how it fits into our developed sense of how the world works or is supposed to work. The second stretches our equally intuitive need to believe that we should be able to cope with, to endure whatever it is that our experience delivers. The third stretches our again equally intuitive sense that the world and human life are or should be fundamentally fair, that our conceptions of right and wrong make sense, and that they cohere with our experience. This last challenge is the impetus for the part of theology that we call theodicy, literally, vindicating or justifying God's judgment.

THE CLASSIC JEWISH EXPLANATION:
SUFFERING AS DIVINE PUNISHMENT

One example of how these three challenges were met in Judaism is the biblical understanding of human suffering as God's punishment for Israel's sin. According to this doctrine—articulated, for example, in Deuteronomy 11:13–21, recited twice daily by the worshiping Jew, or, in a more detailed form, in the sixty-eight verses of Deuteronomy 28—which permeates all of prophetic historiography, obedience to God's command as embodied in the covenant will bring all manner of blessing; and disobedience, all manner of suffering, including pestilence, famine, drought, exile, military defeat, and exile.

This doctrine can be shown to meet all three of Geertz's challenges. It explains why the suffering has come upon the community—because despite God's admonitions, Israel disobeyed God's command. It gives the community a liturgical and ritual vocabulary for coping with the suffering that ensued—a vocabulary that centers on repentance, ritual sacrifice (in biblical times), confession of sin, return to God, and renewed obedience to the covenant. Finally, it vindicates God's justice—sin is punished and obedience is rewarded. In prophetic historiography, this doctrine is invoked, first to predict, and then to justify the destruction of the First Temple in 586 BCE, and in rabbinic historiography, to justify the destruction of the Second Temple in 70 CE. It has in fact enjoyed a singular tenacity: to this day, in certain Orthodox Jewish circles, it is invoked as a response to the Holocaust. God punished European Jewry for its "sins," including the "sins" of Zionism, emancipation, Enlightenment, assimilation, and the rest.[7]

That doctrine works as long as one accepts all of its theological underpinnings, which require, first, that the believer recognize God's hand in history and understand the Torah, God's covenant and the system of Jewish law to have been explicitly revealed by God. Equally important, the doctrine must be perceived to cohere with the community's perception of its historical experience.

BUT WHAT ABOUT JOB?

The Bible itself, however, provides at least one instance where the doctrine is repudiated, precisely because it seemed to be contradicted by experience. The Book of Job portrays a totally righteous man who suffers terribly as a result of God's wager with the Satan. The bulk of the book has Job's consolers articulating classical biblical theodicy: Job has suffered because he must have sinned. Throughout, in Job's responses to his consolers, he disagrees; he has not sinned, or sinned sufficiently to merit his suffering. At the very end of the book (chapters 38–41), in God's communication out of the whirlwind, God challenges Job's attempts to account for his suffering. Finally, in the concluding chapter of the book (42), God repudiates the consolers and vindicates Job's own judgment that—at least in this instance, if not in principle—suffering was not the result of Job's putative sin and had nothing to do with divine punishment. The author of Job, then, perceived the weakness at the heart of the traditional doctrine; sometimes, it simply is not true to the facts. More subversively, in this book that idea was accepted into the canon, for the book has God explicitly repudiating traditional theodicies.

To put all this in more modern terms, the data of experience are never perceived in a totally objective way; we see what we want to see, what we are prepared to see, what we have been educated to see, what we already believe we are going to see. Job's consolers wanted or needed to uphold the traditional doctrine so they "saw" Job's sinfulness as a necessary cause for his suffering. But the author of the book perceived no such need. He saw a different Job, and when he pitted his picture against the doctrine, not only did the doctrine yield, but God did as well. Job himself, in 42:5–6, seems to find a measure of closure: "I had heard You with my ears, but now I see You with my eyes. Therefore, I recant and relent, being but dust and ashes."[8]

He seems to have achieved a deeper understanding of God's complex and not altogether humanly understandable dealings with humanity.

Job may have found a measure of closure, but can we? After denying the traditional doctrine, all that the author can offer as an alternative is the message of God's concluding speeches, which affirm human suffering to be an inescapably mysterious dimension of God's complex dealings with creation. I, for one, am left in a state of bewilderment. What has happened to Geertz's three challenges? In the world according to Job, chaos now triumphs over cosmos, anarchy over order. All that God can offer Job is the assurance that the world is incredibly complex, that God is in control, that there is order beyond the apparent anarchy, but that Job, as a mere human, cannot hope to understand it.

The problem with this conclusion is that it is precisely we humans who need to understand it, who must have a way of coping with the chaos—not God. We also need to find answers that will satisfy us today, in the wake of the Holocaust and the events of September 11. In terms of Geertz's definition of religion, therefore, the Book of Job is the most antireligious book in the Bible, for it leaves the task of bringing order out of the chaos completely up to Job. Indeed, some traditional Jewish commentators argue that Job was a Gentile, as if to say his religion is not *Jewish* religion. That may be why citations from this book appear almost nowhere in the later liturgy of rabbinic Judaism, which is the way we measure the impact of biblical texts on the postbiblical Jewish consciousness.

The most prominent exception is the oft-quoted verse in Job 1:21, "the Lord has given, and the Lord has taken away; blessed be the name of the Lord," which appears in the Jewish burial service, but is perhaps more a cry of human impotence than any form of explanation.

IN THE WAKE OF JOB

From a strictly theological perspective, where then does the Book of Job leave us? It leaves us, I believe, with four options. First is the notion that suffering is the ultimate mystery. That response is echoed most frequently in the face of a premature or particularly horrifying death—the death, for example, of a young person from a dreaded disease. This is the conventional interpretation of God's response to Job at the end of the book and it is omnipresent in our eulogies. God's message to Job seems to be, "You are a mere human being and I am God; you cannot hope to understand my complex dealings with creation. You must simply accept the fact that I am here, that I am in control of creation, and that I continue to be in a relationship with you."

But note that the one thing God does not tell Job is the real reason why he suffered, namely, that God wagered with the Satan that Job would retain his faith, even in the face of his suffering. What would Job have made of this revelation? What can we? There are no easy answers to these questions.

As a second option, we may believe that certain instances of suffering are the inevitable result of human freedom. God created human beings free. In the exercise of that freedom, we can inflict terrible suffering on other human beings. Indeed, the more power we wield, the greater the suffering we can and often do inflict. God must simply accept that as the inevitable trade-off for the way God created us, as must we. True. But first, this does not justify the kind of suffering caused by nature, which was also created by God but seems to operate randomly. Even for the kind of massive suffering inflicted by human beings on other human beings—the events of 9/11, for example—can we let God off the hook so easily? At the very least, does this image of a God who tolerates historical evil not compromise our readiness to credit God for those moments when human beings manifest astonishing charity to other human beings, for example, in the case of the numerous incidents when people sacrificed themselves to save others as the towers fell on 9/11, or in the fourth plane that day that was crashed in a Pennsylvania field by passengers halting its progress toward sabotage? If the latter is an example of God's intervention in history, as some have maintained, how do we account for those moments when God chooses not to intervene? Or to use an example that is closer to home for the Jewish community, can we praise God for bringing the State of Israel into existence, as some liturgical traditions do, and not condemn God for having tolerated the Holocaust? Can we have it both ways?[9]

A third option that we can elect after Job is the eschatological response. In this world, in this aeon, there simply is no equitable distribution of justice, no accounting for the suffering of the righteous and the flourishing of the evildoer. But if we broaden the frame to include an eschatological age, God's power and justice will assert themselves, the righteous will receive their ultimate reward, and the evildoers, their ultimate punishment.

It is worth noting that in a very large part of the Bible, death is terminal; it marks the total end of a human being's relation to God. God's power over my destiny ends with my death. Only toward the very end of the biblical era does the notion of life after death enter into biblical thinking—most notably in the concluding chapter of the Book of Daniel, in a passage (12:2) composed in the middle of the second century BCE—after which it becomes a centerpiece of rabbinic theology. It may well be that one of the impulses behind the reversal of the biblical notion that death limits God's power over the destiny of the individual human being to life on earth was precisely the impasse left in the wake of Job. Eschatology answers the community's demand for theodicy.

Finally, there is the option that chaos is simply an inherent and persistent dimension of God's creation. There are two versions of this response. One has received a great deal of attention with the popularity of Harold Kushner's *When Bad Things Happen to Good People*, arguably the most widely read book written by a rabbi in centuries.[10] Kushner's book is primarily a pastoral response to human suffering, but there is a theology at its core, a theology that posits a limited God. "Residual chaos, chance, mischance, things happening for no reason will continue to be with us," Kushner writes. "We will simply have to learn to live with it, sustained and comforted by the knowledge that the earthquake and the accident ... are not the will of God, but represent that aspect of reality which stands independent of His will, and which angers and saddens God even as it angers and saddens us."[11]

A significantly different and more scholarly version of this notion is the thesis of Harvard theologian Jon D. Levenson's *Creation and the Persistence of Evil*.[12] Levenson suggests that in contrast to Genesis 1, where God's creation of the world is unopposed, the Bible preserves vestiges of alternative creation myths where God's creation is achieved after a primordial combat against the forces of chaos, and where God's mastery of these chaotic forces remains fragile and perpetually imperiled. Levenson cites passages such as Job 38 in which God is portrayed as barricading the surging waters, setting up bars and doors, ordering the waters to stop and proceed no farther. In Psalm 74, God is portrayed as "driving back" the sea, "smashing" the heads of the monsters of the deep, and "crushing" the head of Leviathan. Here, God's creation is triumphant despite the opposition of natural forces that constantly threaten to erupt once again.

In that same psalm, God's victory over the chaotic forces of nature is contrasted with God's failure to control the equally chaotic forces of history as manifested in the apparent victory of Israel's enemies over God's people. The most vivid portrayal of God's failure is Psalm 44. Here, the psalmist contrasts God's victories in the past with a current, unspecified situation where God seems to have abandoned Israel:

> You let them devour us like sheep,
> You disperse us among the nations.
> You sell Your people for no fortune ...
> You make us a byword among the nations ... a laughing
>   stock among the peoples ...
> Yet none of this can be accounted for as divine pun-
>   ishment for Israel's sin.
> All this has come upon us, yet we have not forgotten
>   You,
> or been false to your covenant. (Ps. 44:12, 13, 15, 18)

Indeed, the very opposite is the case, in one of the most painful passages in the entire Bible:

> It is for Your sake that we are slain all day long,
> that we are regarded as sheep for the slaughter.
>   (Ps. 44:23)

Job could not have said it more clearly. That passage makes this psalm the most appropriate response to the Holocaust. In this Job-like repudiation of the traditional doctrine, the psalmist claims that Israel is suffering precisely *because* of its loyalty to God.

What is most striking here is that in confronting God's abandonment of Israel, God's apparent absence, God's impotence in the face of historical chaos, the psalmist does not abandon the covenant. Rather, he turns his despair, indeed his rage, into a challenge to God from within the covenant. In the concluding verses of the psalm, he exclaims:

> Rouse yourself, why do you sleep O Lord?
> Awaken! Do not cast us off forever! (Ps. 44:24)

In contrast to Kushner, the psalmist is not suggesting that the prevalence of chaos in history testifies to a limited God. The very opposite is the case. God's power is not limited. It is assumed. That is precisely why the psalmist despairs, why he cries out for God to manifest God's power once again, as in the past. The point is that chaos seems to be an intrinsic dimension of God's creation, an echo of Isaiah 45:7's claim that God has created both light and darkness, both *shalom* (cosmos, harmony, order) and *ra* (the bad, or chaos). Consider the sixteenth-century kabbalistic myth of Isaac Luria, where the notion that the chaotic forces in nature and history are the result of some primordial fault inherent in God's creation, what Luria called "the breaking of the vessels."[13] This response projects God's ultimate conquest of chaos into the eschatological future. In historical time, we can only wait and hope, and live with the tension.

All of this is speaking theologically, to which I add one final note on this aspect of our inquiry.[14] In a peculiar way, the image of God in Job 1, however disturbing it may be, is also liberating. In fact the classical texts of Judaism are populated by a plethora of images of God, many positive, nurturing, and comforting, but others quite disturbing. The very richness of the imagery reminds us that no human being has a fix on God, simply because God is God and we are humans. That those responsible for editing the canon felt free to include all of these images permits us, their heirs, to select those images that speak to our own experience at any point in our lives. The failure of any one of these images to address our own needs does not, then, preclude the success of others, even the God of Job and of Psalm 44.

In a more extended sense, the unraveling of one corner of the Jewish religious myth does not forecast the undoing of the myth as a whole. Another way of making that claim is to say that myths enjoy a degree of plasticity. They too evolve in time; portions die and disappear; others continue to live; still others are reformulated. This element of plasticity accounts for the singular tenacity that ancient religious myths exhibit. To this believing Jew, then, the substance of the classic Jewish religious myth, however broken, remains palpably alive, despite the death of the doctrine of suffering as punishment, and maybe even because of Job.

BEYOND THEOLOGY

As we noted at the outset, religion is much more than theology. The theological impasse opens the way for other religious resources to assert themselves. Of Geertz's three challenges—the intellectual, the emotional, and the moral—theology deals with the first and the third. The second remains, and it is here that these other resources may be of help.

This is what Geertz has to say about ritual:

> It is in ritual—that is to say consecrated behavior—that this conviction that religious conceptions are veridical and that religious directives are sound is somehow

> generated. It is in some sort of ceremonial form ... — the recitation of a myth, the consultation of an oracle, or the decoration of a grave—that the moods and motivations which sacred symbols induce in men and the general conceptions of the order of existence which they formulate ... meet and reinforce one another. In a ritual, the world as lived and the world as imagined, fused under the agency of a single set of symbolic forms, turn out to be the same world.[15]

Our religious symbols, our myths, are frequently implicit, buried in our unconscious. The dramatic effect of ritual is to make us aware, to bring the myth into the forefront of our consciousness. The late Barbara Myerhoff, in her remarkable *Number Our Days*, tells us how ritual accomplishes these tasks:

> Ritual may be likened to a vessel into which anything may be poured: an order-endowing device, it gives shape to its contents. This ordering function is furthered by the morphological characteristics of a ritual—precision, accuracy, predictability, formality, and repetition. Thus the characteristics of ritual as a medium suggest that its contents ... are enduring and orderly. By virtue of these traits, ritual always delivers a message about continuity.[16]

Similarly, the second of Geertz's three challenges that is posed by the eruption of chaos into our ordered world—what we named the emotional challenge, the challenge to our ability to suffer and to cope—to the extent that it is effective, is anchored in a religion that provides "symbolic resources for expressing emotions—moods, sentiments, passions affections, feelings." Geertz concludes, "For those able to embrace them, and for so long as they are able to embrace them, religious symbols provide a cosmic guarantee not only for their ability to comprehend the world, but also, comprehending it, to give a precision to their feeling, a definition to their emotions which enables them, morosely or joyfully, grimly or cavalierly, to endure it."[17] These symbols are all a central component of ritual.

Ritual thus defines our feelings; it lends precision to our emotions. It helps us identify what we feel. It gives us a vocabulary, both verbal and behavioral, to articulate our feelings by placing human suffering "in a meaningful context, providing a mode of action through which it can be expressed, being expressed understood, and being understood endured."[18] That progression—from expression to understanding to enduring—strikes me as a remarkably insightful formulation of what we might call the therapeutic effect of ritual behavior. If, on this issue of human suffering, Judaism leaves us at a theological impasse, it more than compensates by encircling the experience of mourning with a ritual pageantry that does everything that Geertz and Myerhoff attribute to great ritual.

JEWISH MOURNING RITUALS

My illustrations are taken from Jewish mourning rituals because for most of us, the death of a member of the immediate family constitutes our most familiar encounter with chaos. Judaism structures the act of mourning from the moment of death to burial, from burial through the initial seven days (*shiva*) of mourning, to the thirty days (*shloshim*) of less intensive mourning, to the eleven months and a day (for the death of a parent, thirty days for the death of a spouse, child, or sibling) during which the mourner recites the mourner's *Kaddish*. Then there is the annual observance of the anniversary of the death (*yahrzeit*), and the five occasions during the year when the memorial prayers (*Yizkor*) are recited. Judaism provides the mourner with a vocabulary of words and behaviors that lend precision to feelings, and formality and predictability to behavior. And all of this fuses Judaism's myth with the life experience of the believer so that they become one. The net effect of the entire experience is that the sense of the chaotic, now at its most acute, is immersed in the sense of an ordered world.

An exhaustive illustration of this claim would require a full-fledged description of the Jewish laws of mourning;[19] I will restrict myself to a few.

Those present at the moment of death are commanded to recite the blessing "*Barukh dayyan emet.*"[20] I have long struggled to find an accurate English translation of these three Hebrew words. The conventional translation is "Blessed is the true Judge." More accurate may be, " ... the Judge whose judgment is true."

Is this theodicy? Not at all, for it justifies nothing, least of all God. It is not a vindication of God's judgment. It is, rather, pure ritual, a verbal throwing up of the hands in despair, an affirmation of God's justice, a case of "doing things with words." If anything, it is the repudiation of the very possibility of theodicy.

The blessing is recited again at the funeral or burial, and this time it is accompanied by the ritual of the tearing of a garment; on the left side above the heart for the death of a parent, and on the right for the death of a spouse, child, or sibling. That ritual gesture is a choreographed scream. Job tears his garment after hearing of the death of his children (1:20), as does Jacob when he is informed of Joseph's death (Genesis 37:34). The tear symbolizes the tear in the mourner's life, in the family, in the community. It is pure feeling, an externalization of what is inside. It lends precision to the mourner's feelings. Again, none of this has anything to do with theology.

Then there is the mourner's *Kaddish*, literally the prayer of "sanctification" of God's name. It is conventional to claim that these words say nothing whatsoever about death, which is correct. In fact, in its origins, it was a prayer recited after the study of Torah, and since it was customary to study Torah in memory of the departed, it subsequently became a mourner's prayer even when not preceded by study.

The liturgical content of the prayer sanctifies God and God's name, asks God to establish God's dominion on earth, and asks that as God established *shalom*—literally order, harmony, cosmos—in heaven, so may God establish *shalom* on earth.[21] Again, there is a minimum of theology here. But anyone who has recited the *Kaddish* for the prescribed period is well aware that after a few weeks of doing this one, two, or three times daily, the words become irrelevant. Here, it is primarily the medium that conveys the message. The very fact that one joins a community of Jews—for one needs a minyan, a quorum of ten Jews, to say the *Kaddish*—and recites an ancient and sanctified text in a formalized, totally predictable manner, is the entire story. I recall that when I was reciting *Kaddish* following the death of my parents, I lay in bed early in the morning and planned my day around the two moments in the morning and the evening when I would have to find a minyan in order to fulfill my obligation. The *Kaddish* is an act of ordering. It lends structure to the day, to the week, to the year, and—on the anniversary of the death—to one's entire lifetime. It is pure ritual.

There is one occasion when the *Kaddish* also includes formidable theological content. That is in the form of the *Kaddish* recited at the graveside, immediately following the burial. At that moment, the following text is added:

> May God's name be sanctified and exalted in the world which will be renewed, where God will resurrect the dead and raise them to eternal life, and rebuild the city of Jerusalem, and establish the Temple in its midst, and uproot alien worship from the earth and establish the worship of heaven in its place, and when the Holy Blessed One will reign in sovereignty and splendor, in your lifetimes, in your days, and in the lifetime of all of Israel.[22]

This complex theological statement is in effect a one-paragraph summary of classic Jewish eschatology.

RITUAL AND THEOLOGY

It may be useful, in this context, to note that the distinction between ritual and theology may not be as sharp as I have suggested. Clearly, ritual always nurses from the myth and, at least in Judaism, liturgy carries a formidable theological content. But theology addresses our intellectual need, while ritual addresses our emotional needs.

One further point: the entire pageantry of mourning demands community. The Jew is forbidden to mourn alone. From the moment of death, the entire funeral process is arranged by a *hevrah kadishah*, literally, a "sacred society," a burial society. The mourner does not go to the synagogue during the week of *shiva*—the community comes to him or her, to worship with the mourner and the family in their home. The door of the house of mourning is never locked; the assumption is that the community will come in and out, and the mourner should not have to open or close the door. Upon leaving the mourner, one recites a formal, liturgical formula: "May God console you, among the other mourners of Zion and Jerusalem." There is a community of perpetual mourners in the Jewish community.

Great rituals are rarely created by committee. They evolve, in time, as a community searches for ways to express feelings, to recall transforming events, and even more complicated, to determine what the event means, how it fits into the community's way of ordering the world, how it affects the community's classic myth.

In regard to the events of 9/11, that process has already begun, as we witnessed in the year following the catastrophe: the visit to Ground Zero, the recitation of the names of the deceased, the tolling of bells, the singing of "God Bless America," the moment of silence, the erection of mini-shrines throughout the city, the assemblage of photographs of the deceased, the recitation of Lincoln's Gettysburg address—these are all ritual expressions. Some will survive, some will pass, and new ones will be forged. It will probably take a generation.

I have a strikingly informal test for judging the power of a ritual. I call it the "goose bump effect." A ritual that leaves me with goose bumps on my flesh is one that has genuinely moved me; that effect testifies to great ritual. I recall reexperiencing the drama of President John F. Kennedy's funeral on the fortieth anniversary of his assassination. Like most of my generation, I have vivid memories of the four-day period from his death to his burial. For that entire period, I sat transfixed and could barely leave my spot in front of the television screen. To my amazement, watching the video of his military funeral—the drumbeat, the riderless horse, the folding of the flag, the music—the formality, the precision, and the drama of the entire pageant produced the same goose bumps they did some forty years ago. My sense is that forty years from now, we will watch a video of the events of 9/11 and of the rituals of remembrance that will have evolved just as transfixed as we were that day.

But recall that it took centuries for the Passover seder—arguably, the single most impressive ritual pageant in the life of the Jewish community—to assume the shape that it has for Jews today, and that even after more than half a century, the Jewish community has yet to create vivid new rituals to commemorate the two transforming Jewish events of the past century: the Holocaust and Israel Independence Day. My sense is that this failure to create new rituals for these events reflects our continuing struggle to integrate them into our classic religious myth. We are still not clear, in our minds, what the events mean, and therefore, we have not as yet achieved a consensus regarding what the rituals should say. The more immediate challenge, then, is to achieve a similar consensus on the meaning of the events of September 11, 2001. Once we have achieved that consensus, the rituals will follow by themselves.

CHAPTER 16

IN PRAISE OF *BIRKAT KOHANIM*

There are invariably three points in the course of my public lectures where my audience begins to squirm. The first is when I question the historicity of the biblical account of Sinai. (However casual their practice may be, their expectation is that I, at least—a rabbi, theologian, and observant Jew—should present a literalist view of revelation. Otherwise, "Why be Jewish!") The second is when I affirm the doctrine of bodily resurrection as a mythic, not a biological claim, and as profoundly true. ("Rabbi, isn't that a Christian belief?") The third is when I plead for non-traditionalist congregations to restore the *Birkat Kohanim*, the blessing of the congregation by its members who are *kohanim*, descendents of the biblical priestly family.

I have written extensively on the first two of these issues. This is my first attempt to support the third.

I was raised in a small all-purpose synagogue where the *nusah hatefillah*, the liturgy (though very few of the congregants), was traditionalist and *Birkat Kohanim* was recited every festival. The year prior to my bar mitzvah, my father suggested that I join him in the ritual. I continued to do so throughout my high school and college years.

242

When I came to The Jewish Theological Seminary in 1954 (and until 1984), there was only one worship service that, apart from the lack of a formal *mehitzah* (separating curtain), was staunchly traditionalist. One of my earliest Seminary memories is of Chancellor Louis Finkelstein, a *levi* (descendent of the biblical Levites), pouring water over my hands before *Birkat Kohanim*—a practice that continued until his death in 1991. That ritual became one of the many bonds that linked us. In his last years, he would write to me before a festival, formally inviting me to "bless him" in the upcoming holiday. Later there would be a second letter, thanking me "for your blessing."

I realized, early on, that the ritual was controversial. Some members of our congregation back home, themselves hardly role models for Jewish behavior, would walk out in protest: "What business does such-and-such a crook have to bless me!" I felt that there was something incongruous about selectively imposing a moral test for this role, but not for serving as congregational president or *gabbai* (synagogue "sexton"). And of course, it is not the *kohen* who blesses, but rather God. But those arguments proved singularly ineffective.

Then came my religious maturation, my emergence as a "liberal" on theological issues, and at least to some, on halakhic issues as well, and my growing sympathy with the feminist-egalitarian cause.

ARE ALL JEWS NOT CREATED EQUAL?

The other perquisites of my status cause little conflict. I officiate at a *pidyon haben* (redemption of the firstborn male child). The *gabbai'im* in the Seminary's egalitarian minyan where I now daven frequently offer me the first *aliyah*, even if it is identified as *rishon* (first) and not as *kohen*, though I will accept whatever *aliyah* is assigned to me. Since I am not a congregational rabbi, I am not faced with the problem of officiating at funerals (traditional practice forbids members of the priestly clan from contact with the dead). I have attended four funerals in my entire life-time, my parents' and those of two aunts who had no survivors and with whom I felt particularly close. Otherwise, my general practice is to stand outside the funeral home.

But *Birkat Kohanim* remains a problem. My friends, col-leagues, and students challenge me. How can I, a Jew who advo-cates a fully egalitarian approach to Jewish ritual practice, who davens regularly in a minyan with women who wear *talit* and *tefillin*, who claims that Sinai is a metaphor!—how can I cling to this ritual?

The problem is that I find it an extraordinarily powerful religious experience, predictably the single most striking experi-ence I have. I remove my shoes and see myself creating sacred space. My hands are laved by the Levites—and I reflect on the range of activities I carry out with my hands. I put the *talit* over my head—for a moment, shutting out the world and enabling me to focus on my own feelings. I raise my hands and shape my fingers to form the letter *shin* for the Hebrew word *Shaddai*, one of God's names, and my blessing assumes a distinct focus. I pro-nounce the benediction commanding me to bless my commu-nity *be'ahavah*, lovingly—something I sorely need to be reminded to do.

And there is the text of the liturgy itself: that God should bless you; that God's face should be turned *toward* you, in favor—not hidden from you, in anger; and that God grant you *shalom*—not simply peace, of course, but wholeness, integrity, a life freed of inner discord.

There are also the *kavanot* (brief prayers that serve to focus attention) before and after the ritual, and the haunting melody that I insist on chanting, slowly and deliberately, even with the humming that comes before the final word of each benediction, giving the congregation an opportunity to recite the longer meditations (even though most prayer books no longer include the full text).

When defending my advocacy of the ritual, I usually begin by pointing out that our synagogue service is so lacking in drama, so overwhelmingly verbal. Here is an opportunity to introduce a choreography: people leave their seats, hands are washed, slippers are worn, *talitot* cover heads. And our service is so nonparticipatory, so much in the hands of the professionals. Here is an opportunity for laypeople to participate actively in liturgical roles. And there are priceless educational opportunities: to teach the institution of the biblical priesthood, the ritual, the biblical and liturgical texts, and the music.

One of the problems is that this is a ritual that is selectively designed for only one portion of the congregation. Does our impulse toward egalitarianism mean that *everything* has to be leveled? Might it not dictate that we discover other equally selective rituals for other distinct groups within the congregation? Do we have to abolish this one practice just because we haven't as yet discovered other meaningful rituals for these other groups?

I argue that there is a substantive difference in the application of the egalitarian impulse to male and female roles and to *kohen*, *levi*, and *yisrael* roles. The former embodies a genuine ethical issue; the latter does not. To be different does not have to mean to be better. I am painfully aware that the antifeminists among us apply that argument to the male versus female issue as well, but on that issue my sense is that they are arguing disingenuously. Is it necessary to engage in a massive flattening of *all* distinctions in order to refute that position? The difference between the two issues may be subtle, but it is real.

I also acknowledge that in its origins, the *kehunna* constituted a hierarchical statement, but it is clear that this dimension of the problem has long been irrelevant. There is precious little increased standing or status accruing to me today because I am a *kohen*.

I would be more impressed with the counterargument if I really believed that the ritual was dropped out of an impulse for egalitarianism. My speculation is that it was dropped either because it just felt or sounded primitive and "out of sync" with the impulse to create a modern American feel to the service, or because our predecessors in the nontraditionalist rabbinate simply did not believe that they could aggressively advocate any maximalist standard of observance from their congregants. If they didn't push Sabbath observance and the dietary laws, why should they push *Birkat Kohanim?* And if their *kohanim* congregants were not observing kashrut and Shabbat, how could they expect them to observe this far more arcane ritual?

Another operative factor was the sense that all liturgical material reflecting the Temple cult had become anachronistic and had to be dropped or reformulated. This led, for example, to transforming the prayer for the restoration of sacrifices into a historical memory. What was not understood was that this material could be presented as liturgical reenactment (on the model of the Passover seder) and in this way could serve as a resource for education on the nature of liturgy and ritual. In general, our predecessors did not know how to teach religious ritual. The result is that we have inherited a community of basically nonobservant Jews.

When all else fails, I concede that my wish to preserve this ritual may be anomalous, but I insist on the value of anomaly in religious life. I find this a healthy corrective to my intuitive impulse to have my theology, my ideology, and my practice form one coherent and integrated pattern. *Birkat Kohanim* messes up my pattern. But life is also messy. Now, since I have two daughters and no sons, my task is to find a congregation that will help me redefine the status of the daughters of *kohanim* so that my daughters and I can do *Birkat Kohanim* together. How's that for an anomaly!

NOTES

Chapter 2

1. To be precise, physicists cannot see "a" quark because quarks appear only in combinations that form larger particles. But my point would apply equally to these larger particles as well.

2. John Wisdom, "Gods," in *Religious Language and the Problem of Religious Knowledge,* ed. Ronald E. Santoni (Bloomington: Indiana University Press, 1968), 295–314.

3. Thomas S. Kuhn, *The Structure of Scientific Revolutions* (Chicago: University of Chicago Press, 1970).

Chapter 3

1. See the first volume of the two-volume biography of Heschel's life, *Abraham Joshua Heschel: Prophetic Witness,* by Edward K. Kaplan and Samuel H. Dresner (New Haven: Yale University Press, 1998). This first volume takes Heschel from his birth to his arrival in America in 1940. The second volume, *Spiritual Radical: Abraham Joshua Heschel in America (1940–1972)* (New Haven: Yale University Press, 2007) is authored by Kaplan alone—Dr. Dresner passed away in 2000.

2. A "selected" bibliography of Heschel's writings can be found in Kaplan and Dresner (1998), 364ff.

3. All of my page references to *The Prophets* (Heschel, 1962) come from the original hardcover edition published by the Jewish Publication Society of America in 1962. The pertinent chapters are 12–18. The appendix is on pp. 498ff. Readers should note that the

paper edition of the book is in two volumes and in this edition both chapter numbers and the pagination differ.

4. Heschel, *The Prophets*, 223–24.
5. Ibid., 223.
6. Ibid., 234.
7. Ibid., 258–59.
8. Ibid., 257.
9. Ibid., 283.
10. Ibid., 284.
11. The plain sense of Genesis 1 seems to suggest that according to this version of creation, God's creation was more a matter of bringing order out of a preexisting anarchy, than creating something out of nothing.
12. For a masterful overview of the teachings of Isaac Luria, see Gershom Scholem, *Major Trends in Jewish Mysticism*, seventh lecture (New York: Schocken Books, 1941).
13. Heschel's Hasidic roots are traced in Kaplan and Dresner (1998), xi–xiii and 2ff.
14. An anthology of Heschel's writings on social and political issues can be found in his *The Insecurity of Freedom: Essays on Human Existence* (New York: Farrar, Straus, and Giroux, 1966).
15. Abraham Joshua Heschel, *God in Search of Man* (New York: Farrar, Straus and Giroux, 1955), 138.
16. Heschel's most extensive discussion of religious experience is in his *God in Search of Man*.
17. The term appears in *The Prophets*, 260, and in *God in Search of Man*, 114ff.
18. The clearest statement of these claims is in *God in Search of Man* (1955), 114ff. See in particular, 120–22.
19. Ibid. For a more extended discussion of this issue, see my article "Epistemological Tensions in Heschel's Thought," *Conservative Judism Journal* 50, nos. 2–3 (1998): 77–83.

Chapter 4

1. An index of the psalms that appear in their entirety in the liturgy is in Joseph H. Hertz, *The Authorized Daily Prayer Book*, rev. ed. (New York: Bloch Publishing, 1948), 1120.
2. For this understanding of worship as a form of human activity, I am indebted to Lawrence A. Hoffman, *Beyond the Text: A Holistic Approach to Liturgy* (Bloomington: Indiana University Press, 1987), 6ff.
3. In Clifford Geertz, *The Interpretation of Cultures: Selected Essays* (New York: Basic Books, 1973): 87–125.
4. Ibid., 90. Geertz's paper is a systematic unpacking of that definition.
5. There is no end to the literature on the nature and definition of myth and on the relation of myth and symbol. My own preferred

studies are Paul Tillich, *Dynamics of Faith* (New York: Harper and Row, 1957), part 3; and Ian G. Barbour, *Myths, Models, and Paradigms: A Comparative Study in Science and Religion* (Harper: San Francisco, 1974), chap. 2. On the role of myth in Judaism, see the collection of papers in *The Seductiveness of Jewish Myth: Challenge or Response?* ed. S. Daniel Breslauer (Albany: State University of New York Press, 1997).

6. Rollo May, *The Cry for Myth* (New York: W. W. Norton, 1991), 6.

7. Geertz, *Interpretation of Cultures*, 112ff. Whether a ritual preceded the myth or developed out of the myth remains an open question that does not bear upon this discussion. See Barbour, *Myths, Models, and Paradigms*, 22.

8. *Ketubot* 8a.

9. The seven benedictions are recited both at the wedding ceremony itself and in conjunction with the blessings following the wedding meal (and again whenever the bride and groom partake of a festive meal with friends and family during the seven days of celebration following the wedding). In the latter recitations, the blessing over wine that is the first in the series at the wedding becomes the last.

10. For a partial bibliographical listing, see Joseph Tabory, "Jewish Prayer and the Yearly Cycle: A List of Articles," *Kirjat Sepher* (Jerusalem: Jewish National and University Library), supplement to vol. 64 (1992–93): 130–31.

11. See the note on this text in Yitzchak Baer, *Seder Avodat Yisrael* (Tel Aviv, 1957), 563.

12. David Flusser and Shmuel Safrai, "*Betzelem D'mut Tavnito*," in *Sefer Yitzchak Arye Zeligman*, eds. Yair Zakowitz and Alexander Rofe (Jerusalem: Elchanan Rubenstein, 1983), 1:461.

13. The postbiblical understanding of these two terms reflects a Platonic influence. In the Bible, they signify simply "a living person" as in Exodus 1:5 and Psalm 150:6. The two terms appear in the Genesis 2:7 account of the creation of the human being: God formed man from the dust of the earth and blew into his nostrils the "breath of life" (*nishmat hayyim*), and man became "a living being" (*nefesh hayyah*). God created man by vivifying a clod of earth, not by implanting within the body a preexisting entity of any kind. See the extended discussion of these terms in biblical and postbiblical tradition in my *The Death of Death: Resurrection and Immortality in Jewish Thought* (Woodstock, Vt.: Jewish Lights Publishing, 1997), 75ff. and 106ff.

14. See, for example, Maimonides, *Guide of the Perplexed*, 1.1.

15. *Ketubot* 8a.

16. See the paraphrase of the rabbinic traditions on Adam and Eve's wedding in Louis Ginzberg's *The Legends of the Jews* (Philadelphia: Jewish Publication Society of America, 1968), 1:68, and the listing of his sources, 5:90, n. 48.

17. M. *Sanhedrin* 4:5. In the Mishnah, this is part of the judges' admonition to witnesses regarding their responsibilities in a capital case.
18. This conventional interpretation uses Psalm 137:5–6 as the basis for recalling the destruction of Jerusalem at our happiest moments.
19. I find a parallel "return to history" in the custom of opening the door while Elijah is present in our homes at the climax of the Passover seder. Elijah's presence is a totally appropriate (for the climax of the festival of redemption) eschatological symbol, following Malachi 3:23.
20. The formal, communal (as distinct from the personal) morning worship service is centered about the recitation of the *Sh'ma*, composed of three biblical portions (Deuteronomy 6:4–9 and 11:13–21, and Numbers 15:37–41). This is preceded by two liturgical units or extended benedictions and followed by one. The two opening benedictions are, first, the *Yotzer* that praises God for creation, and then the *Birkat HaTorah*, which praises God for revealing the Torah. The benediction following the *Sh'ma* is the *Ge'ulah*, which praises God's redemptive work. The service as a whole may be found in any traditional prayerbook, for example, *The Complete ArtScroll Siddur: Weekday, Sabbath, Festival* (Brooklyn, N.Y.: Mesorah Publications, 1986), 85–96.
21. Isaiah 45:7 is conventionally understood as a rejection of Persian dualism. But see the qualifying comment in *Second Isaiah*, trans. John L. McKenzie, vol. 20 of *The Anchor Bible* (Garden City, N.Y.: Doubleday, 1968), 77.
22. On the controversy regarding *creatio ex nihilo* in medieval Jewish philosophy, see, for example, Colette Sirat, *A History of Jewish Philosophy in the Middle Ages* (Cambridge: Cambridge University Press, 1985), 22–24 (on Saadia), 188–92 (on Maimonides), 304–308 (on Gersonides), and 305 (on Abrabanel).
23. On the place of the angelology in the liturgy, see the extended discussion in Ismar Elbogen, *Jewish Liturgy: A Comprehensive History* (Philadelphia: Jewish Publication Society, 1993), 59–62.
24. See the full text in *ArtScroll Siddur*, 256–59.
25. On the controversy surrounding the use of this passage, see Elbogen, *Jewish Liturgy*, 18–19; and, more extensively, Lawrence A. Hoffman, *The Canonization of the Synagogue Service* (Notre Dame, Ind.: University of Notre Dame Press, 1979), 24–30.
26. In the translation and abridgement of Kaufmann's work by Moshe Greenberg, *The Religion of Israel: From Its Beginnings to the Babylonian Exile* (Chicago: University of Chicago Press, 1960), 22.
27. The classic summary of Lurianic thought is in Gershom G. Scholem, *Major Trends in Jewish Mysticism* (New York: Schocken Books, 1941), seventh lecture. On the exile of the *Shekhinah*, see 232 and 275.

28. I am indebted to my colleague Rabbi Lawrence Troster for this point.
29. See note 5 above.
30. In Tillich, *Dynamics of Faith*, 50–54.
31. On the liturgical changes introduced by the early Reform movement, see Jacob J. Petuchowski, *Prayerbook Reform in Europe: The Liturgy of European Liberal and Reform Judaism* (New York: World Union for Progressive Judaism, 1968).

Chapter 5

1. This chapter, in its original form, was first presented as an address delivered at Columbia University under the auspices of the Center for the Study of Science and Religion on November 17, 2004. The author acknowledges the editorial assistance of his student Daniel Ain in preparing the text for publication.
2. Clifford Geertz, "Religion as a Cultural System," in *The Interpretation of Cultures* (New York: Basic Books, 1973), 90. Geertz also quotes Susan Langer, American philosopher of art, who writes that "[Man] can adapt himself somehow to anything his imagination can cope with; but he cannot deal with Chaos. Because his characteristic function and highest asset is conception, his greatest fright is to meet with what he cannot construe—the 'uncanny,' as it is popularly called. It need not be a new object; we do meet new things, and 'understand' them promptly, if tentatively, by nearest analogy, when our minds are functioning freely; but under mental stress even perfectly familiar things may become suddenly disorganized and give us the horrors. Therefore our most important assets are always the symbols of our general *orientation* in nature, on the earth, in society, and in what we are doing" (ibid., 99).
3. Intergovernmental Panel on Climate Change, *Climate Change 2007: The Physical Science Basis*, 2007, 5. "Warming of the climate system is unequivocal, as is now evident from observations of increases in global average air and ocean temperatures, widespread melting of snow and ice, and rising global average sea level." A summary of the report can be found online at www.ipcc.ch.
4. John Polkinghorne, *The God of Hope and the End of the World* (New Haven, Conn.: Yale University Press, 2002), 139–40.

Chapter 6

1. For a detailed documentation of this process, see my book *The Death of Death: Resurrection and Immortality in Jewish Thought* (Woodstock, Vt.: Jewish Lights, 1997), ch. 8.
2. See, for example, the Reconstructionist *Sabbath Prayer Book* (New York: Jewish Reconstructionist Foundation, 1945), xxvii–xxviii. Although this introduction is signed "the Editors," it was probably written by Kaplan himself, and it surely reflects his thinking.

3. See, for example, Robert Gordis, *A Faith for Moderns* (New York: 1960), 250–52. Gordis was a noted rabbi, theologian, and ideologue of the Conservative movement.

4. For an overview, see Gillman, *Death of Death*, ch. 9.

5. Will Herberg, *Judaism and Modern Man* (New York: Farrar, Straus and Young, 1951, rpt. 1997). The citations that follow are taken from chs. 15 and 16; see especially 229ff.

6. See Arthur A. Cohen, "Resurrection of the Dead," in *Contemporary Jewish Religious Thought: Original Essays on Critical Concepts, Movements and Beliefs*, eds. Arthur A. Cohen and Paul Mendes-Flohr (New York: Charles Scribner's Sons, 1987), 807–13.

7. Probably a reference to the vision of the dry bones in Ezekiel 37:1–14.

8. Richard N. Levy, "Upon Arising: An Affirmation of *Techiyat Hametim*," *Journal of Reform Judaism* 29, no. 4 (Fall 1982), 12–20.

9. Steven Schwarzschild, "On Jewish Eschatology," in *The Pursuit of the Ideal: Jewish Writings of Steven Schwarzschild*, ed. Menachem Kellner (Albany: SUNY Press, 1990), 209–28.

10. Hershel Matt, "An Outline of Jewish Eschatology," *Judaism* 17, no. 2 (Spring 1968), 186–96.

11. Michael Wyschogrod, "Resurrection," *Pro Ecclesia* 1, no. 1 (Fall 1992), 104–12.

12. A useful comparison of the Pittsburgh and Columbus Platforms and the Centenary Platform is found in the supplement to Eugene Borowitz's *Reform Judaism Today* (New York: Behrman House, 1983).

13. Ibid., Book 2, 42–49.

14. Eugene Borowitz, *Liberal Judaism* (New York: UAHC Press, 1984), 222.

15. *Emet Ve-Emunah: Statement of Principles of Conservative Judaism* (New York: United Synagogue Book Service, 1988), 29–30.

16. See Rifat Sonsino and Daniel B. Syme (eds.), *What Happens after I Die? Jewish Views of Life after Death* (New York: UAHC Press, 1990).

17. See Simcha Paull Raphael, *Jewish Views of the Afterlife* (Northvale, N.J.: Jason Aronson, 1994).

18. For a more detailed version of these three arguments, see Gillman, *Death of Death*, ch. 10.

19. For the complete text of the Pittsburgh Platform, see, for example, Borowitz, *Reform Judaism Today* (supplement). For an illuminating discussion of the historical context of the platform, together with the proceedings of the 1885 conference, see Walter Jacobs (ed.), *The Changing World of Reform Judaism: The Pittsburgh Platform in Retrospect* (Pittsburgh: Rodeph Shalom Congregation, 1985).

20. Editorial note, *Reform Judaism* 27, no. 2 (Winter 1998). The cover of the issue featured a photograph of a bearded Rabbi Levy garbed in a traditional long, black-and-white-striped *talit*, with *tzitzit* pressed to his lips.

21. A new Reform prayerbook, *Mishkan T'filah: A Reform Siddur* (New York: URJ Press, 2007), includes the traditional formula for the *Gevurot* benediction in parenthesis (see, for example, p. 78) as an option to the more familiar version in the Reform prayerbook commonly in use since 1975, *Gates of Prayer: The New Union Prayerbook* (New York: CCAR, 1975). The traditional formula is retained in the eighth of ten versions of the Sabbath evening service found in here (255), as well as in the *minhah* service for Yom Kippur in *Gates of Repentance: The New Union Prayerbook for the Days of Awe* (New York: CCAR, 1978), 399.

22. *Kavanah* is the inward dimension of the life of religion; *keva* is its more external or structured dimension.

23. On the dynamics of the *Wissenschaft* school, see Ismar Schorsch, *From Text to Context: The Turn to History in Modern Judaism* (Waltham, Mass.: Brandeis University Press, 1994).

24. On the emergence of *Wissenschaft* methods in America, see Moshe Davis, *The Emergence of Conservative Judaism: The Historical School in Nineteenth Century America* (Philadelphia: Jewish Publication Society, 1963).

25. To the best of my recollection, among my teachers at The Jewish Theological Seminary, only Mordecai Kaplan and Robert Gordis served as congregational rabbis during their teaching years, although Louis Finkelstein and Moshe Zucker did serve in this role before joining the faculty. Max Arzt and Simon Greenberg also served as rabbis for many years before joining the faculty. However, their positions at the seminary were more closely tied to administration, their teaching being limited to "practical" courses such as homiletics and education. One priceless anecdote illustrates Finkelstein's priorities with regard to the school he headed. He once told me that I had no idea how much money he could have raised if only Mordecai Kaplan had not served on the JTS faculty. (Originally appointed by Solomon Schechter in 1909, Kaplan retired in 1962.) When I asked why he had not fired Kaplan, he explained that he had spent his entire career ensuring the Seminary's reputation in American academic circles. All he had to do was fire one member of the faculty because he disagreed with what was being taught, and he would have destroyed everything he had created. Finkelstein was prepared to allow Kaplan to teach what he (Finkelstein) clearly regarded as a heretical theology to hundreds of future rabbis in order to preserve the Seminary's academic reputation.

26. For an extensive study of this model of rabbinic education as embodied in rabbinical studies at The Jewish Theological Seminary,

see "On the Religious Education of American Rabbis," pp. 114–135, in this book. There is abundant anecdotal evidence on the way the model was reflected in classroom instruction. My most vivid recollection was the comment of an eminent Talmud professor to a student who was struggling to interpret a Talmudic passage: "That was a great sermon. Now what does the text really mean?" His denigration of the congregational rabbi's main format for teaching his congregants was obvious. In retrospect, it is clear that the Seminary expected the brightest students in the school to pursue a scholarly career; the rest of the students could become congregational rabbis. To be fair, however, certain teachers had a profound religious impact on us: Abraham Heschel, Mordecai Kaplan, and Shalom Spiegel managed to free themselves from the model of instruction that dominated the school.

27. Tillich's classical and seminal definition of these terms is found in his *Dynamics of Faith* (New York: Harper Torachbooks, 1957), 41ff.

28. On "second naïveté," see Paul Ricoeur, *The Symbolism of Evil* (Boston: Beacon Press, 1967), 351.

29. Quoted in ibid., 15.

Chapter 7

1. *Mishneh Torah, Hilkhot Yesodei Hatorah*, 1:1.

2. *Tanhuma Genesis* (ed. S. Buber), par. 11.

3. *The Guide of the Perplexed*, trans. Shlomo Pines (Chicago: University of Chicago Press, 1963), 5–6.

4. Saadia Gaon, *The Book of Beliefs and Opinions*, trans. Samuel Rosenblatt (New Haven, Conn.: Yale University Press, 1948), Introductory Treatise, 3–37. See in particular pp. 26–33, where Saadia defends his rational approach as mandatory in his day.

5. Abraham Joshua Heschel, *God in Search of Man* (Philadelphia: Jewish Publicalion Society of America, 1956), 185ff and 260ff.

6. London: Soncino Press, vol. 1, 1962; vol. 2, 1965. Now available as *Heavenly Torah as Refracted through the Generations*, eds. and trans. Gordon Tucker with Leonard Levin (New York: Continuum, 2005.]

7. The seminal statement suggesting that the language of religion should be understood as myth is Paul Tillich's *Dynamics of Faith* (New York: Harper and Row, 1957). See also an imaginative extension of Tillich's argument in John Herman Randall Jr., *The Role of Knowledge in Religion* (Boston: Starr King Press, 1968), 103–34.

8. Harold Kushner, *When Bad Things Happen to Good People* (New York: Schocken, 1981).

Chapter 8

1. *The Condition of Jewish Belief: A Symposium by the Editors of* Commentary *Magazine* (London: Macmillan, 1966; Northvale, N.J.: Jason Aronson, 2005), 124–126.
2. Abraham Joshua Heschel, *God in Search of Man* (Philadelphia: Jewish Publication Society, 1956), 185.
3. Ibid., 265.
4. Ibid., 274.
5. Ibid.
6. Franz Rosenzweig, *On Jewish Learning*, ed. Nahum N. Glatzer (New York: Schocken Books, 1955), 118.
7. Ibid., 113–14.
8. This particular formulation is Ira Eisenstein's in *The Condition of Jewish Belief*, 46. Kaplan would surely have agreed.
9. Solomon Schechter, "Historical Judaism," ed., in *Tradition and Change: The Development of Conservative Judaism* Mordecai Waxman (New York: Burning Bush Press, 1958), 94–95.
10. *Baba Metzia* 59b.
11. Eliezer Berkovits, *Not in Heaven: The Nature and Function of Halakha* (New York: Ktav, 1983), 73.
12. Ibid., 51.
13. Joel Roth, *The Halakhic Process: A Systemic Analysis* (New York: Jewish Theological Seminary of America, 1986), 126.
14. Ibid. 199.
15. Ibid. 144–46.
16. Ibid. 151.
17. Ibid. 151.
18. Significantly, Norman Lamm's discussion of the traditionalist position makes no reference whatsoever to the Oral Torah.
19. The proof text invoked is Deuteronomy 17:11.
20. *Proceedings of the Rabbinical Assembly*, vol. 18, 1954, 55ff.
21. This policy regarding gays and lesbians was abandoned in 2007.
22. A case has been made that however misleading this practice may be, it remains halakhically sound as long as the groom's saying and doing precedes the bride's recitation and ritual. In such a view, everything that follows is halakhically irrelevant. Authorities who forbid this practice are concerned about giving the impression that the bride's formula may have halakhic validity.
23. I insist that "civil religion" Jews do form a halakhic community because they feel obligated to perform a series of mitzvot—essentially those related to the health and well-being of the Jewish people—even though they may ignore ritual mitzvot. They set their parameters as other halakhic communities set theirs.

Chapter 9

1. The issues under discussion in this chapter have been on my agenda for nearly a decade. It would be impossible even to begin to list the people who have helped clarify my thinking, but they would surely include my colleagues on the faculty of The Jewish Theological Seminary—particularly Chancellor Ismar Schorsch; Chancellor Emeritus Gerson D. Cohen; Professors Raymond D. Scheindlin and Gordon Tucker, and generations of rabbinical students who have participated in endless discussions of these questions both in the classroom and out. My gratitude to all of these in no way diminishes my personal responsibility for the conclusions of this contribution to the inquiry.

2. This is my own reformulation of Clifford Geertz's definition of religion in his seminal "Religion as a Cultural System," in *The Interpretation of Cultures* (New York: Basic Books, 1973), 90.

3. In the 1988–89 curriculum of the Seminary's rabbinical school, for example, students were required to register for five required years of study (or be exempt from on the basis of prior, parallel course work elsewhere) that included fifty-four semester courses both textual or academic in nature, and ten semester courses in "Professional Skills." Also required were an additional four semesters of "Synthesis" courses—interdisciplinary, theme-oriented courses that synthesized available bodies of knowledge on a particular issue and attempted to apply them to specific problems that confront the congregational rabbi. These were, in fact, experimental versions of the kind of course work I consider indispensable to rabbinical education. It should be added that beginning in the academic year 1989–90, the curriculum was phased out in favor of an entirely new structure that is informed throughout by an attempt to deal with the issues raised in this chapter. For a somewhat dated but still groundbreaking study of rabbinic education in the United States, see Charles Liebman, "The Training of American Rabbis," *American Jewish Year Book*, 1968, vol. 69, eds. Morris Fine and Milton Himmelfarb (New York: American Jewish Committee; Philadelphia: Jewish Publication Society of America, 1968), 3–112. On the rabbinate as an institution, its evolution, and its role in contemporary America, see the collection of papers in *Understanding American Judaism*, vol. 1, *The Rabbi and the Synagogue*, ed. Jacob Neusner (New York: Ktav, 1975), in particular the contribution by Wolfe Kelman, "The American Synagogue," 69–89.

4. A useful anthology of writings representing the *Wissenschaft* school is collected in part 5 of *The Jew in the Modern World*, eds. Paul R. Mendes-Flohr and Jehuda Reinharz (New York: Oxford University Press, 1980), 182–213. See, in particular, the contributions by Leopold Zunz (1794–1886) and Moritz Steinschneider

(1816–1907), both founding fathers of the school. For an elaboration of the implications of that approach for Jewish law, see Ismar Schorsch, "Zacharias Frankel and the European Origins of Conservative Judaism," *Judaism* 31, no. 2 (Summer 1981): 344–54. Frankel (1794–1875) was the founder of the European movement that, in its American incarnation, became Conservative Judaism.

5. On Reform Judaism's Pittsburgh Platform, see *The Pittsburgh Platform in Retrospect*, ed. Walter Jacob (Pittsburgh: Rodef Shalom Congregation, 1985). The intricate story of the emergence of a "conservative" reaction to nineteenth-century American Reform Judaism and the founding of the Seminary is traced in Moshe Davis, *The Emergence of Conservative Judaism: The Historical School in Nineteenth-Century America* (Philadelphia: Jewish Publication Society of America, 1963). It should be noted that in our own day, Reform Judaism has gone a fair distance in modifying the ideological perspective of the Pittsburgh Platform, including its views on the ritual law. See Eugene B. Borowitz, *Reform Judaism Today* (New York: Behrman House, 1983), particularly book three.

6. On the "founding myth" of the Seminary and its varied "mixed messages," see my "Mordecai Kaplan and the Ideology of Conservative Judaism," *Proceedings of the Rabbinical Assembly*, vol. 46 (1984): 57–68.

7. Solomon Schechter, *Aspects of Rabbinic Theology* (New York: Schocken Books, 1961). Schechter's statements on the Seminary and Conservative Judaism are collected in his *Seminary Addresses and Other Papers* (New York: Burning Bush Press, 1959). An excellent anthology of papers, scholarly and otherwise, by the founding fathers of the school and representatives of its faculty can be found in *Tradition and Change: The Development of Conservative Judaism* (New York: Burning Bush Press, 1958). The absence in all of this material of any attempt to do theology in the modern vein is striking.

8. Mordecai Kaplan's first and most systematic exposition of his thought is in his monumental *Judaism as a Civilization*, enl. ed. (New York: Reconstructionist Press, 1957). An excellent appreciation of Kaplan's impact is the anthology *Mordecai Kaplan: An Evaluation*, eds. Ira Eisenstein and Eugene Kohn (New York: Reconstructionist Press, 1952). See also note 6 above.

9. Eventually the purely theological issues were addressed in a more traditional style than in Kaplan's writings by, among others, Abraham Joshua Heschel, who taught at the Seminary from 1946 until his death in 1972, and his students, the late Seymour Siegel, who taught theology (and Talmud) at the Seminary until his death in 1988, and Fritz Rothschild. Part of Heschel's *God in Search of Man* (Philadelphia: Jewish Publication Society of America, 1956) is a masterful inquiry into the issue of revelation that avoids the

extremes of traditionalist literalism and Kaplanian naturalism. My own "Toward a Theology for Conservative Judaism," *Conservative Judaism* 37 no. 1 (Fall 1983): 4–22, is a survey of possible options on the issue and their legal and programmatic implications.

10. To be fair, they were addressed on the rhetorical level. Seminary mythology includes an exchange that took place when Solomon Schechter (president of the Seminary 1902–15) interviewed Louis Finkelstein (president and then chancellor of the Seminary 1939–72) when the latter applied for admission to the rabbinical school. To Schechter's question, "Why do you want to come to the Seminary?" Finkelstein answered, "To study the great books of the Jewish tradition." To this, Schechter is said to have responded. "To study great books, all you need is a library. The only reason to come to the Seminary is to associate with great men." There is no question, in my mind, that Finkelstein believed that association with great role models can provide an experience in religious education, and it probably does, but that aphorism hardly constitutes a conceptualization for a curriculum.

11. Of this century's giants of Jewish scholarship, the late Gershom Scholem, who almost single-handedly created the field of Jewish mysticism, was the only figure who incorporated the emerging discipline of religious studies into his scholarly work. See, for example, his earliest and most accessible work, *Major Trends in Jewish Mysticism* (New York: Schocken Books, 1941). More recently the scholarly work of Jacob Neusner and his students, particularly on Jewish religion in the Talmudic era, has brought this entire agenda to the forefront of Jewish scholarship.

12. See "Judaism and the Search for Spirituality," pp. 149–169, in this book. The content of this chapter was first delivered at a conference on the Future of the American Synagogue, funded by the Lilly Endowment, with the generous encouragement of its senior vice president, Dr. Robert Lynn.

13. To be precise, all of the Hebrew Scriptures except the Pentateuch were taught critically from the outset. From what I have been able to glean through a perusal of seminary registers, it was not until 1959 that the Pentateuch itself was taught in this manner as well. The issue is somewhat obscure, but my sense is that there was a generalized reluctance to apply critical scholarship to the Pentateuchal text, first, presumably because of its heightened sanctity (why is not clear since no one was willing to address the issue of revelation), and second, because the entire enterprise of higher biblical criticism was thought to reflect an implicit anti-Jewish bias. (It should not be forgotten that it was not until the middle of this century that Jewish scholars joined the enterprise.) In 1903, for example, one year after assuming the presidency of the Seminary, Solomon Schechter delivered an address entitled "Higher

Criticism—Higher Anti-Semitism," published in his *Seminary Addresses and Other Papers*, 35–40. Until 1959, either mastery of the Pentateuch was an entrance requirement, or the text was taught with the traditional, medieval exegetes. The turnabout, when it came—again, this is a matter of speculation—was due, possibly, to a growing sense of the incongruity of distinguishing between the Pentateuch and the rest of Hebrew Scripture, and also to the gradual dissemination of the work of the Israeli Bible scholar Yehezkel Kaufmann, whose multivolume *Toledot Ha-Emunah Ha-Yisraelit* (Tel Aviv: Bialik Institute-Dvir, 1937–56), translated and abridged by Moshe Greenberg as *The Religion of Israel* (Chicago: University of Chicago Press, 1960), used all of the higher-critical apparatus without its presumed anti-Jewish bias. Kaufmann quickly became required reading in all Seminary Bible classes.

14. This is the thrust of the groundbreaking Talmudic scholarship of David Weiss Halivni in his *Meqorot U'Mesorot* (*Sources and Traditions*), 4 vols. (Tel Aviv: Dvir, 1968, 1975, 1982). Halivni's most recent and most thorough English exposition of his method is in *Midrash, Mishnah, and Gemara: The Jewish Predilection for Justified Law* (Cambridge, Mass.: Harvard University Press, 1986). Chapter 2 of this book was published as "The Early Period of Halakhic Midrash," *Tradition* 22 no. 1 (Spring 1986): 37–58. Some sense of the discomfort Halivni's method engenders for the traditionalist can be gleaned from Emanuel Feldman's "The Halakhic Midrash: A Rejoinder," *Tradition* 22 no. 4 (Winter 1987): 65–74.

15. This is the thesis of Louis Finkelstein, *The Pharisees: The Sociological Background of Their Faith*, 3rd ed. with suppl. (Philadelphia: Jewish Publication Society of America, 1962).

16. See Saul Lieberman's "Rabbinic Interpretation of Scripture" in *Hellenism and Jewish Palestine* (New York: Jewish Theological Seminary of America, 1950), 47–67. Lieberman was the dean of Seminary Talmudists from 1940 until his death in 1983 and was generally acknowledged to be the outstanding Talmudic scholar of his generation. For a broader application of the thesis that Talmudic Judaism was shaped by its Hellenistic setting, see Elias Bickerman, *From Ezra to the Last of the Maccabees* (New York: Schocken, 1962). An extension of Bickerman's thesis through the rest of Jewish history is elaborated in Gerson D. Cohen, *The Blessing of Assimilation in Jewish History* (Boston: Boston Hebrew Teacher's College, 1966), anthologized in *Jewish History and Jewish Destiny* (New York: Jewish Theological Seminary of America, 1997).

17. I expand on this claim in "Judaism and the Search for Spirituality," pp. 149–169.

18. William Bean Kennedy's "Toward an Ideological Critique of Theological Education in North America," submitted to a Consultation on Doing Theology in Diverse Contexts, sponsored

by the Programme on Theological Education of the World
Council of Churches, Prague, June 21–25, 1988, and later
published as "Toward an Ideological Analysis of Theological
Education in North America," in *Doing Theology in Different
Contexts* (Geneva: World Council of Churches, 1989), 96–109, is
a stunning dissection of the power structure of much of current
theological education. I am grateful to Professor Kennedy for
having shared his paper with me.

19. I elaborate on this thesis in my contribution to the symposium
    "Entering the Second Century: From Scholarship to the
    Rabbinate," *Proceedings of the Rabbinical Assembly* (1986): 41–46.
    Of course, we should not be deceived about the rabbi's vaunted
    authority, for the congregation retains the authority to hire and
    dismiss its rabbi.

20. For other attempts to address this issue, see the contributions of my
    colleagues Barry W. Holtz, Joseph Lukinsky, and Ivan G. Marcus to
    *The Seminary at 100: Reflections on The Jewish Theological Seminary
    and the Conservative Movement,* eds. Nina Beth Cardin and David
    Wolf Silverman (New York: Rabbinical Assembly and Jewish
    Theological Seminary of America, 1987), 195–204, 205–14, and
    215–22 respectively; and Lawrence A. Hoffman, "Jewish
    Knowledge: Redrawing the Map," *Conservative Judaism* 38, no. 2
    (Winter 1985–86): 36–43.

21. Clifford Geertz, *The Interpretation of Cultures* (New York: Basic
    Books, 1977).

22. Paul Tillich, *The Dynamics of Faith* (New York: Haper Torchbooks,
    1957).

23. James Fowler, *Stages of Faith* (San Francisco: Harper & Row, 1981).

24. For Fowler's discussion of stage 5 and Ricoeur's "second" or "willed
    naïvéte" see *Stages of Faith,* 184–98.

25. *Exodus Rabbah* 5:9.

26. Quoted by Scholem, *On the Kabbalah and Its Symbolism* (New York:
    Schocken Books, 1965), 65.

27. Ibid., 30. The first two chapters of this volume constitute an extended
    discussion of the authority of Torah in Jewish mystical circles.

28. I am grateful to my colleague Professor Edward Greenstein for this
    insight into the layout of the published text of this edition of
    Hebrew Scriptures.

29. I am echoing here a striking rabbinic homily on Ecclesiastes 12:11,
    in the Babylonian Talmud *Hagigah* 3a–3b.

30. My expansion of Tillich's discussion of the functions of symbols in
    religion in *Dynamics of Faith,* 42–43.

31. A more extended discussion of all of these issues is in my "Authority
    and Authenticity in Jewish Philosophy," *Judaism* 35, no. 2 (Spring
    1986): 223–32.

Chapter 10

1. Paul Tillich, *Dynamics of Faith* (New York: Harper and Row, 1957).
2. An exposition of Sam Lauechli's theory and method may be found in his "The Expulsion from the Garden and the Hermeneutics of Play," in *Body and Bible: Interpreting and Experiencing Biblical Narratives*, ed. Bjorn Krondorfet (Philadelphia: Trinity Press, 1992).
3. On the *akedah* narrative itself, particularly on the tradition that Abraham did in fact slaughter his son, see Shalom Spiegel's monumental *The Last Trial* (Woodstock, Vt.: Jewish Lights, 1993); and Jon D. Levenson's *The Death and Resurrection of the Beloved Son* (New Haven, Conn.: Yale University Press, 1993).
4. On the epistemological issues involved in experiencing God's presence, alluded to above, see my article "On Knowing God," *Conservative Judaism* 51, no. 2 (Winter 1999).
5. A comprehensive study of Jewish approaches to talking about God is in my book *The Way into Encountering God in Judaism* (Woodstock, Vt.: Jewish Lights, 2000).
6. A more extended discussion of my views on rabbinic education can be found in "On the Religious Education of American Rabbis," in *Caring for the Commonweal: Education for Religious and Public Life*, eds. Parker J. Palmer, Barbara G. Wheder, and James W. Fowler (Macon, Ga.: Mercer University Press, 1990).

Chapter 11

1. J. David Bleich, "Karen Ann Quinlan: A Torah Perspective," in *Contemporary Jewish Ethics*, ed. Menichem Marc Kellner (New York: Sanhedrin Press, 1978), 304–305. An equally striking statement of this model is Rabbi Bleich's presentation of the halakhic strictures governing the emergency use of an automobile on Shabbat to attend to a gravely ill patient, in his *Contemporary Halakhic Problems*, vol. 1 (New York: Ktav and Yeshiva University Press, 1977), 135–40.
2. Abraham Joshua Heschel, *God in Search of Man* (Philadelphia: Jewish Publication Society of America, 1956), 326.
3. Martin Buber, "Jewish Religosity," in *On Judaism*, ed. Nahum N. Glatzer (New York: Schocken Books, 1972), 80–81.
4. Translation from *Tanakh* (Philadelphia: Jewish Publication Society, 1982).
5. Adapted from the translation by Rabbi Zalman Shachter-Shlomi, *Siddur Sim Shalom: Prayerbook for Shabbat, Festivals and Weekdays*, ed. Rabbi Jules Harlow, copyright 1985 by the Rabbinical Assembly, 253. Reprinted by permission of the Rabbinical Assembly and the United Synagogue of America.
6. *On Judaism*, 90–91.
7. Heschel, *God in Search of Man*, 297.
8. Abraham Joshua Heschel, *Man's Quest for God* (New York: Charles Scribner's Sons, 1954), 64–66.

9. Heschel, *God in Search of Man*, 341.
10. The translation is the late Morris Adler's in his *The World of the Talmud* (Washington, D.C.: B'nai B'rith Hillel Foundations, 1958), 24.
11. *The Guide of the Perplexed*, trans. Shlomo Pines (Chicago: University of Chicago Press, 1963), 618–19.

Chapter 12

1. The content of this chapter represents a slightly revised version of the paper delivered at the 1993 Convention of the Rabbinical Assembly. In the intervening months, I have benefited from reactions to the original draft by numerous colleagues. Some of these have been incorporated into this published version. I am grateful to all of these colleagues for their interest and concern. With respect to the issues discussed in the last portion of the chapter (on the need for doing the theological and ideological groundwork for our view of halakhic process), I would particularly like to direct the attention of the reader to two papers by my colleague Rabbi Gordon Tucker, both of which represent substantive contributions to that inquiry and neither of which was available to me when the content of this chapter was originally drafted. The first is "A Principled Defense of the Current Structure and Status of the Committee on Jewish Law and Standards," prepared for presentation at the convention meeting of the Committee on Jewish Law and Standards. The second is "The Sayings of the Wise Are Like Goads: An Appreciation of the Works of Robert Cover," published in *Conservative Judaism* 45, no. 3 (Spring 1993), 17–39.
2. B.T., *Baba Metzia* 59b.
3. B.T., *Menchot* 29b.
4. See *Mishneh Torah*, Laws of Slavery (or indentured servants).
5. Mishnah, Malkhot 1:10; see also B.T. *Sanhedrin* chapter 4 and J.T. Sanhedrin 41a.
6. Elliot N. Dorff, *For the Love of God and People: A Philosophy of Jewish Law* (Philadelphia: Jewish Publication Society, 2007), 45-86.
7. Joel Roth, *The Halakhic Process: A Systematic Analysis* (New York: Jewish Theological Seminary of America, 1986).
8. "Towards an Aggadic Judaism," in *Conservative Judaism* 29:3 (Spring 1975), 79–84.

Chapter 13

1. The content of this chapter is an expanded and revised version of an address delivered at the 2005 convention of the United Synagogue of Conservative Judaism in Boston. The author wishes to thank Dr. Abigail Gillman and Dr. Michael Prince, together with colleagues and students who read and commented on earlier drafts of the work, most notably Rabbis Robert Abramson, Martin Cohen, Elliot Dorff,

Paul Drazen, and Ira Stone, and Daniel Ain, Nicole Guzik, Benjamin Spratt, Abigail Treu, and Eitan Yeshua.

2. *Conservative Judaism* 29, no. 3 (Spring 1975), 79–84. Emphasis in the original.

3. On the falsifiability of religious claims, see the discussion in *Religious Language and the Problem of Religious Knowledge*, ed. Ronald E. Santoni (Bloomington: University of Indiana Press, 1968), part 4, ch. 19. Flew's contribution is on pp. 315–18, and his judgment that a claim may die "the death by a thousand qualifications" is on p. 316. The debate that was based on John Wisdom's seminal paper, "Gods" (ch. 18 in the anthology) has been widely anthologized.

4. The symposium was reprinted in 1995 by Jason Aronson (Northvale, N.J., 1995). Siegel's comment is on pp. 224–25.

5. New York: Jewish Theological Seminary of America, 1986.

6. These questions are addressed by our colleague Rabbi Elliot Dorff. See in particular his *Mitzvah Means Commandment* (New York: United Synagogue of America, 1989), chs. 1–5, and *To Do the Right and the Good: A Jewish Approach to Modern Social Ethics* (Philadelphia: Jewish Publication of Society, 2002), 270–82. Dorff's approach throughout is more philosophical than historical.

7. For a recently published and remarkably thorough overview of Conservative views on this issue, see Elliot Dorff, *The Unfolding Tradition: Jewish Law after Sinai* (New York: Aviv Press, 2005).

8. For a comprehensive overview of recent scholarship on the origins of the religion of the Bible, see Stephen A. Geller, "The Religion of the Bible," in *The Jewish Study Bible*, eds. Adele Berlin and Marc Zvi Brettler (New York: Oxford University Press, 2004), 2021–40. For a parallel study of the religion of the Rabbis, see Seth Schwartz, *Imperialism and Jewish Society, 200 BCE–640 CE* (Princeton, N.J.: Princeton University Press, 2001). Professors Geller and Schwartz are both full professors on the Seminary faculty.

9. Among my many attempts to spell out how I use the term "myth" in these contexts, see in particular "The Problematics of Myth," *Sh'ma* 32, no. 587 (January 2002).

10. For a review of these and other options, see my *Sacred Fragments: Recovering Theology for the Modern Jew* (Philadelphia: Jewish Publication Society, 1990), chs. 1 and 2.

11. In fact, Dr. Steven M. Brown (dean of the Seminary's Davidson School of Education) and I have been doing precisely this for a number of years. We have been team-teaching a course to rabbinical, cantorial, and education students in which I outline my theology and Dr. Brown provides techniques and curricular skills for teaching this material to students of all ages.

12. Gillman, *Sacred Fragments*, 20.

13. Ibid., 21.

14. "Basic Principles of the Torah," 1:8–12 in *A Maimonides Reader*, ed. Isadore Twersky (Springfield, N.J.: Behrman House, 1972), 44–45.
15. Paul Tillich, *Dynamics of Faith* (New York: Harper and Row, 1957), ch. 3.
16. My sense is that our ancestors imaged God in the light of their own humanness. Theology recapitulates anthropology.
17. For a more extensive study of this issue, see "On Knowing God," pp. 7–15, in this book.
18. See "Coping with Chaos: Jewish Theological and Ritual Resources," pp. 224–241, in this book.
19. Third ed. (Chicago: University of Chicago Press, 1996).

Chapter 14

1. The author acknowledges his debt to his colleagues Dr. Aryeh Davidson, Dr. Elliot Dorff, and Ms. Renee Gutman, and to his students in classes in Jewish philosophy at The Jewish Theological Seminary who read earlier drafts of the content of this chapter and helped clarify many of the issues it raises. Many of their criticisms are reflected in this version, though the author alone is responsible for its content.
2. *Book of Doctrines and Beliefs*, ch. 3.
3. Rashi ad. loc. and on Numbers 19:2, *Yoma* 67b.
4. See, for example, Yehezhel Kaufman's *The Religion of Israel*, trans. Moshe Greenberg (Chicago: University of Chicago Press, 1960), 51–58.
5. *Natural Symbols* (New York: Pantheon Books, 1970), 47–48. Mary Douglas's work on ritual is enormously suggestive, though both my terminology and conceptualizations differ from hers. See, in particular, chapters 1 and 3 in Douglas's volume as well as her provocative "The Abominations of Leviticus" in *Purity and Danger*, (London: Routledge and Kegan Paul, 1966), 41–57. Robert Alter's "A New Theory of Kashrut," *Commentary*, 68, no. 46 (August 1979) 46–52, is an incisive critique of the latter piece.
6. *Major Trends in Jewish Mysticism*, (New York: Schocken Books, 1941), 273–76.
7. See his contribution to *The Condition of Jewish Belief, a Symposium*, compiled by the editors of *Commentary* (Northvale, N.J.: Jason Aronson, 1995), 125–26.
8. A classic expression of this position is in American Reform Judaism's Pittsburgh Platform of 1886 and its European and American antecedents.
9. *Genesis Rabbah* 44:1.
10. *Numbers Rabbah* 19:8.
11. *Shabbat* 19:5; *Yevamot* 64b; *Shulhan Arukh, Yoreh De'ah* 262:2, 263:2.

12. In contrast, we must accept martyrdom rather than commit incest, homicide, or idolatry. *Sanhedrin* 74a; *Mishneh Torah, Yesodei HaTorah*, 5:1–3; and *Shulhan Arukh, Yoreh De'ah* 157:1.

13. Norman Lamm's statement cited above (note 7) is an unapologetic defense of that theology of revelation. See my "Toward a Theology for Conservative Judaism," *Conservative Judaism* 37, no. 1 (Fall 1983), 4–22, for a critique of that position.

14. The literature on the problem of defining myth is abundant. The author continues to find Paul Tillich's *Dynamics of Faith* (New York: Harper and Row, 1957) absolutely indispensable. Also helpful are Lauri Honko, "The Problem of Defining Myth," in *Sacred Narrative: Readings in the Theory of Myth*, ed. Alan Dundes (Los Angeles: University of California Press, 1984), 41–52; Ian G. Barbour, *Myths, Models and Paradigms* (New York: Harper and Row, 1974), chs. 1–2; and Will Herberg's "Some Variant Meanings of the Word 'Myth'" in *Faith Enacted as History* (Philadelphia: Westminster Press, 1976).

15. The three examples noted above share these qualities; they are elaborate, imaginative constructs. On the "mythical" quality of scientific theories, see Ian G. Barbour, *Myths, Models and Paradigms*, chs. 3–5. See also Thomas S. Kuhn, *The Structure of Scientific Revolutions* (Chicago: University of Chicago Press, 1970) for numerous suggestive parallels between the evolution of religious myths and scientific paradigms.

16. An impressive, phenomenological description of that experience is in Henri Frankfort et al., *Before Philosophy* (Baltimore: Penguin Books, 1949), 11–36. This description is helpful for an understanding of religious experience as described in the writings of theologians such as Martin Buber and Abraham Joshua Heschel.

17. Such as Nehemiah 9:6–12 followed by Exodus 14:30–31 in the daily *shaharit* service; also Deuteronomy 26:1–11 and Psalms 105, 106, and 136 as examples of historical narrative in liturgical form.

18. The literature on the relationship of myth and ritual is equally extensive. See, in particular, Theodor H. Gaster's "Myth and Story" in Alan Dundes, *Sacred Narrative*, 110–26; Mircea Eliade's "Methodological Remarks on the Study of Religious Symbolism" in *The History of Religions: Essays in Methodology*, eds. [liade and Joseph M. Kitagawa (Chicago: University of Chicago Press, 1959), 86–107; Edmund R. Leach, "Ritual," *International Encyclopedia of the Social Sciences* (New York: Macmillan Free Press, 1968), vol. 13, 520–26; Victor Turner, "Myth and Symbol," in ibid., vol. 10, 576–82; and Mary Douglas, *Natural Symbols*. In general, the author has found the writings of Eliade, Douglas, and Turner to be most suggestive on this entire complex of issues.

19. There is also, of course, a significant psychological component to the rituals of religion. Specifically in regard to the rites of passage,

see our colleague Amy Eilberg's "Views of Human Development in Jewish Ritual: A Comparison with Eriksonian Theory" in *Smith College Studies in Social Work*, Nov. 1984.

20. On the distinction between "symbol" and "sign," see Paul Tillich, *Dynamics of Faith*, 41–43; also John Herman Randall Jr., *The Role of Knowledge in Western Religion* (Lanham, Md.: University Press of America, 1986) 109–16. The latter, long out of print but now republished, is a masterpiece of scholarship. Tillich and Randall taught all of this material in seminars in philosophy of religion at Columbia University.

21. As in Mircea Eliade, *The Sacred and the Profane* (New York: Harper, 1961), chs. 1–2. Heschel's characterization of Jewish ritual as *"architecture of time"* in *The Sabbath* (New York: Farrar, Straus and Giroux, 1951), 8, is a remarkably felicitous formulation of this position. In general, *The Sabbath* is a phenomenal achievement not only for its poetic, meditative, or pietistic style. Its thesis is that Jewish ritual has to be understood from an anthropological perspective, not only a theological one. In retrospect, that was a radical, groundbreaking proposal. Equally radical in its implications was "Judaism as a System of Symbols" by our teacher, Louis Finkelstein, in Bryson et al., *Symbols and Values: An Initial Study* (New York: Conference on Science, Philosophy and Religion in Their Relation to the Democratic Way of Life, 1954), ch. 5. For a development of Heschel's view of ritual as "sanctification of time," see Arthur Green's "Sabbath as Temple; Some Thoughts on Space and Time in Judaism," in *Go and Study: Essays in Honor of Alfred Jospe*, eds. R. Jospe and S. Z. Fishman (Washington, D.C.: B'nai B'rith Hillel Foundations, 1980), 287–305.

22. Rashi ad. loc.; *Sifra Kedoshim* on Leviticus 19:1. The two sets of structures—the mythic and the ritual—reflect and reinforce each other, one conceptually and the other experientially. The process is captured by Clifford Geertz in his seminal "Religion as a Cultural System" in *The Interpretation of Cultures* (New York: Basic Books, 1973).

23. Douglas, *Natural Symbols*, 7.

24. Published and distributed by B'nai B'rith Hillel Foundations, Washington, D.C. In particular, the ritual of inscribing a number on the arm is a brilliant and classic use of symbolic behavior that has the added advantage of being Holocaust-specific.

25. For example, I have pleaded for the institution of an egalitarian *Birkat Kohanim* (the Ritual Benediction of the Priests) within the framework of an egalitarian synagogue service—an ambiguous position if there ever was one! My sense is that it is mandatory that we restore a heightened sense of drama to the synagogue service, and *Birkat Kohanim* is one way to do that.

Chapter 15

1. Clifford Geertz, *The Interpretation of Cultures* (New York: Basic Books, 1973), ch. 4.
2. Ibid., 90.
3. Paul Tillich, *Dynamics of Faith* (New York: Harper and Row, 1957), ch. 3.
4. Geertz, 99.
5. Ibid., 100ff. (italics in the original).
6. Ibid.
7. For a clear statement of prophetic historiography, see Isaiah 1. The rabbinic model is captured in the liturgical passage "Because of our sins, we were exiled from our land" in the *Musaf Amidah* for festivals. See *The Complete ArtScroll Siddur* (Brooklyn, N.Y.: Mesorah Publications, 1984), 678–81. The contemporary invocation of the doctrine is discussed (and vigorously repudiated) by David Weiss Halivni, "Prayer in the Shoah," *Judaism* 50, no. 3 (Summer 2001), 268–91.
8. This is the conventional translation of these two verses as it appears in the Jewish Publication Society of America's translation of *Tanakh* (Philadelphia, 1985). For a more cynical translation, see Jack Miles, *God: A Biography* (New York: Vintage Books, 1996), pp. 323ff.: "Word of you had reached my ears, but now that my eyes have seen you, I shudder with sorrow for mortal clay." If this translation is correct, Job has hardly achieved closure. The very opposite is the case.
9. See, for example, the version of the *Al HaNissim* ("For the miracles") prayer, commonly recited on the festivals of Hanukkah and Purim, now newly composed for Israel Independence Day, in *Siddur Sim Shalom* (New York: Rabbinical Assembly and United Synagogue of America, 1985), 118–19.
10. New York: Schocken Books, 1981.
11. Ibid., 55.
12. Princeton, N.J.: Princeton University Press, 1988. What follows is my summary of Levenson's thesis in part 1 of his book, "The Mastery of God and the Vulnerability of Order."
13. The classic summary of Lurianic mysticism remains Gershom G. Scholem, *Major Trends in Jewish Mysticism* (New York: Schocken Books, 1941), seventh lecture, 244–86. The "broken vessels" were designed to contain the energy of God's creative power. That they "broke" is understood to be the cause of evil in Creation.
14. These four broad theological options are by no means exclusive. They do, however, seem to this author, at least, to be the most theologically significant ones, the most thoroughly explored in the literature, and the most challenging. Other options refer, for example, to the numerous biblical references to God's momentary

hiding of the divine face, to interpretations of Isaiah's suffering servant, or to the rabbinic notion of human suffering as an expression of divine affection (based on interpretations of Proverbs 3:12, and Psalm 94:12). Understandably, the most interesting explorations of these and other responses deal with the Holocaust. For two notable surveys of these and other options, see Steven T. Katz, *Post-Holocaust Dialogues: Critical Studies in Modern Jewish Thought* (New York: New York University Press, 1983), and Irving Greenberg, "Cloud of Smoke, Pillar of Fire: Judaism, Christianity and Modernity after the Holocaust," in *Auschwitz: Beginning of a New Era? Reflections on the Holocaust*, ed. Eva Fleischner (Ktav, 1977), 7–55.

15. Geertz, 112.
16. New York: Simon and Schuster, 1978, 86.
17. Geertz, 104.
18. Ibid., 105.
19. See "The Laws of Mourning" in Isaac Klein, *A Guide to Jewish Religious Practice* (New York: Jewish Theological Seminary of America, 1979), ch. 19–20.
20. Based on *Mishnah Berakhot* 9:5: "One is bound to bless God for the evil even as he blesses God for the good." More conventionally, both the blessing and the tearing are done before the funeral or the burial.
21. For the full text of the mourner's *Kaddish*, see *ArtScroll Siddur*, 56–57.
22. *ArtScroll Siddur*, 800–801.

GLOSSARY

Aggadah, *aggadot* (pl.): Literally, "narrative." Nonlegal portions of rabbinic literature, including homilies, legends, and theology.

Akiba: A prominent rabbinic teacher (ca. 50–135 CE) whose views are expressed in the Mishnah (70–200 CE).

Aknai: A type of oven that was at the center of a debate between R. Eliezer b. Hyrcanus and R. Joshua b. Hananiah and his colleagues. R. Eliezer declared that the oven could not become ritually impure and used signs from God to prove this. R. Joshua and the others quoted Torah, saying "Torah is not in heaven"—that once God gave the Torah to humanity, it is the sages that have the authority to determine the law.

Aleinu: "It is our duty to praise the Master of all . . ." The concluding prayer of Jewish worship services. Its original setting was in the verses of the Kingship (*malkuyot*) section of the Rosh Hashanah *Musaf* Amidah.

Amidah: Standing prayer. The central prayer of Jewish worship services. The first three and last three blessings remain the same for all services, while the center portion has the sanctification of the day, whether for the weekday or for holidays or Shabbat. It is often described as praise, petition, and thanks.

Avinu Malkeinu: "Our father, our King" is a prayer recited during the Ten Days of Repentance from Rosh Hashanah to Yom Kippur, as well as on some fast days.

Ayin: Literally, "nothing." The inner No-thing of divinity, out of which all being flows; hence the true core of existence. The designation of

269

being as *ayin* reflects the first stage in its journey toward definition. See *Ein Sof.*

Baal Teshuvah: Literally "one who returns"; Jews from a non-Orthodox background who return to (traditional) religious practice.

Bimah: The ritual center stage of the sanctuary; a raised platform from which Jewish worship is conducted.

Daven: To pray.

Ein Sof: Literally, "Endless." The primal undefined Godhead, out of which both the *sefirot* and world emerge.

Enlightenment: A philosophical movement in the seventeenth and eighteenth centuries focusing on rationalism; in Judaism, it sparked the *haskalah.*

Gabbai, gabbaim (pl.): A person who organizes and assists the Torah service; usher.

Ge'ulah: Redemption.

Gevurot: "God's might"; the second blessing of the *Amidah,* focusing on God's power over creation, including the resurrection of the dead. The text of the blessing was changed in early and some modern Reform liturgy to say simply that God has power over all.

Guide of the Perplexed: Maimonides' philosophical magnum opus, written in three parts, to one of his most advanced students. He disparages anthropomorphism (believing that God has a humanlike body) and attempts to integrate Aristotelian philosophy and science with Jewish belief.

Haggadah: Literally, "telling." The book that is used to teach the story of Passover at the Seder, the traditional Passover meal.

Halakhah: Literally, "the path" or "the walking." The system of Jewish religious praxis as codified in sacred law.

Halakhic: Legal, from a Jewish perspective, an acceptable practice.

Halakhot: The specific laws/rules of the Jewish religious praxis.

Hasid: Literally, "a pious one." A strictly observant Jew who strives for *devekut,* communion with God, and often lives among similarly minded Jews.

Hasidism: The movement of the spiritual descendents of the Ba'al Shem Tov (master of the good name, Rabbi Israel Ben Eliezer 1698–1760); a later stage in the evolution of Jewish mysticism, emphasizing our spontaneous relationship to God.

Haskalah: The Jewish Enlightenment movement, opening Judaism and Jews to the outside world, focusing on secular and historical education and release from or leaving the ghetto.

"Hatikvah": Literally, "the hope." The national anthem of Israel written by Naftali Herz Imber, with music arranged by Samuel Cohen. It expresses the hope of the Jewish people for return to the Land of Israel and control over its destiny.

Havdalah: Literally, "separation"; the ritual marking the end of the Sabbath.

Kabbalat Shabbat: The Friday evening prayers welcoming the Sabbath.

Kadosh: Literally, "holy."

Kavanah: Prayer intentionality; the part of prayer that is individual devotion, often in contrast to *keva*, i.e. *keva* and *kavannah*, the fixed and the fluid.

Kehunnah: "The priesthood"; the institution and responsibilities of the Jewish priests, or *kohanim*.

Keva: "Fixed," often in contrast with *kavanah* (see above). *Keva* are the traditional, organized prayers.

Kiddush: "Sanctification." There is a *Kiddush* for Shabbat and holidays, helping to create the holiness of the day.

Kippah, kippot (pl.): A head covering worn either in synagogue or all the time by many Jewish males and some Jewish females.

Kittel: A simple white robe worn by many male Jews at their weddings, and by male and female Jews on the High Holy Days. It also serves as the garment for a corpse, reminding us all that in death, we are all equal.

Kohen, Kohanim (pl.): "Priest." A member of the tribe of Aaron. While in the Temple, the *kohen* had many responsibilities. In modern times, the remnants are the first *aliyah* to the Torah, blessing the community on festivals (or daily in Israel) and redeeming the first born males of Israel.

Lamdan: Hebrew expression for a man who is well informed in rabbinical literature, although not a scholar in the technical sense of the term.

Levi: A descendent of the tribe of Levi. In the Temple, they served as the choir and assisted the *kohanim* (see above). Today, when the *kohanim* bless the community, the Levites wash their hands.

Ma'ariv: Related to the word *erev* (evening), it is the evening prayer service.

Maimonides: Rabbi Moshe ben Maimon (1135–1204), known as Rambam. Born in Spain, escaped an oppressive Muslim regime, fled to Morocco, then to Israel, and finally to Egypt. While medicine was his full-time occupation and he wrote medical treatises, he is celebrated for his code of Jewish law, the Mishneh Torah, and his rationalist philosophical work, *The Guide of the Perplexed.*

Mashal, meshalim (pl.): Hebrew for proverb, parable. It is used in rabbinic literature and in the Bible to explain ideas through examples.

Matmid: Literally, "a diligent one." One who learns Jewish texts full-time. Chaim Nachman Bialik wrote a poem, "*Ha-Matmid*" ("The Diligent One"), dedicated to the students of the Volozhiner yeshiva.

Mechitzah: Barrier separating the women from the men in an Orthodox synagogue.

Metzaveh: Commander; the One who stands as the voice of authority behind the *mitzvot*.

Midrash, midrashim (pl.): Literally, "to examine, interpret holy scripture." Interpretation that expands the meaning of a biblical or rabbinic text.

Midrashim composed between 200 CE and 1200 CE are often divided between those focused on law (halakhic) and narrative (aggadic). Modern midrashim are more often of the narrative variety.

Minyan: Literally, "counting." A quorum required for prayer; or the prayer group itself. It is ten adult Jews in most Reform, Conservative, Renewal, and Reconstructionist settings; ten adult Jewish men in Orthodox settings.

Mishneh Torah: Maimonides' code of Jewish law, composed in Egypt between 1170 and 1180. It teaches Jewish law (without minority opinions) for all aspects of Jewish observance, including laws only applicable in the Temple. While accepted today, it caused great controversy in its day, as it did not include sources and Maimonides intended it to supersede study of Talmud for less educated people.

Mitnagdim: Literally, "opponents." Ashkenazic Jews who virulently opposed Hasidism, most notably, the Vilna Gaon, Rabbi Elijah ben Shlomo Zalman, 1720–1797.

Mitzvah, mitzvot (pl.): Commandment, by extension, good deed.

Mourner's Kaddish: Also known as *kaddish yatom* (orphan's kaddish), the version of the kaddish prayer said by mourners (and those with a *yahrzeit*) at the end of prayer services. Kaddish means sanctification.

Pidyon haben: Redemption of the first born male child.

Piyyut, piyyutim (pl.): A liturgical poem, usually written for singing or chanting during services. They are often alphabetical acrostics, or have other poetic schemes, like *Adon Olam* or *Yigdal*, some of the most common *piyyutim*.

Posek, poskim: From *psak din* or *psak halakhah* (ruling of law), a rabbi and legal scholar who decides Jewish law.

P'shat: Literally, "simple." It is the contextual or straight-forward meaning of biblical texts.

Responsum, Responsa: Written literature of rabbinic decision(s). Responsa collections are filled with the rulings of *poskim* (see above).

Saadia Gaon: Lived in Babylonia (modern-day Iraq) 882–942 CE. He wrote Arabic translations and commentary of most of the Bible, halakhic works, one of the first *siddurim* (prayerbooks), commentaries on the Talmud, the first Hebrew grammar book, and philosophical works including *The Book of Beliefs and Opinions*, where he demonstrated the rationality of Judaism and the legitimacy for a logical Jew to believe Aristolte, Plato, and Torah.

Seder: Literally, "order." The festive Passover evening meal, where the Passover story is told using the haggadah.

Sefirah, sefirot (pl.): According to the kabbalists, the ten stages by which divinity is manifested, as well as the ten rungs to be traversed and unified in the soul's ascent to God.

Shaharit: The daily morning worship service, to be recited at dawn.

Shekhinah: Literally, "indwelling." The tenth *sefirah*; the aspect of divinity most associated with the feminine, receiving and absorbing the qualities of the other *sefirot*. *Shekhinah* is divinity as manifest within this world.

Sheol: Literally, "underworld." The Bible's only mention of an afterlife, much like the Greek Hades, a place where *shades* live pseudo-lives regardless of their conduct in life.

Shiva: From the Hebrew for seven; the seven days, beginning after a funeral, where Jews remain in their homes to mourn for a lost relative. Friends and community members provide food and a minyan, so that the family need not be responsible for leaving their homes.

Sh'ma: "Hear O Israel!" The essential watchword of Jewish faith, found in Deuteronomy 6:4ff. and recited twice daily as the centerpiece of Jewish worship.

Shtiebel: Small neighborhood synagogue.

Talit, talitot (pl.): Jewish prayer shawl worn for *Shaharit*, morning prayers, with fringes at the four corners, based on Numbers 15:37–41, the third paragraph of the *Shema* prayer.

Talmud: A record of rabbinic debates on Jewish law, ethics, customs, and history. While surrounded by medieval commentaries, its main components are the Mishnah, a terse legal collection recorded by 200 CE, and the Gemara, the Israeli or Babylonian commentaries on the Mishnah and related discussions, recorded between 200 and 500 CE. The Gemara is the basis for all codes of Jewish law.

Talmud Torah: Hebrew school.

Tefillin: Phylacteries; holy boxes containing biblical passages, worn by Jews during weekday morning prayers.

Tisha B'Av: The ninth of the Hebrew month of Av; a fast day mourning the destruction of both Temples, the failure of Bar Kohkba's revolt, the razing of Jerusalem, and many other Jewish and general tragedies.

Tohu vavohu: Unformed and void; the condition of the world before creation.

Treif: Literally, "torn"; not kosher. For example, meat from an animal that was not slaughtered according to Jewish law, therefore, not kosher.

Tsimtsum: Voluntary self-constriction. The contraction or concentration of divinity. A key concept in Jewish mystical theories of Creation; the act by which God allowed "room" for the world to exist.

Yeshiva: Jewish parochial school.

Yetzer hara: The evil impulse.

Yotzer: The first benediction preceding the Shema in the morning service.

CREDITS

I would like to extend thanks to the following publishers for granting permission to republish articles that have previously appeared in their publications:

"I Believe." *Sh'ma: A Journal of Jewish Responsibility* (September 1993): 1–3.

"On Knowing God." *Conservative Judaism* 51, no. 2 (Winter 1999): 59–64. New York: Rabbinical Assembly.

"The Dynamics of Prophecy in the Writings of Abraham Joshua Heschel." In *Hearing Visions and Seeing Voices*, part 2, no. 5, edited by Gerrit Glas, Moshe Halevi, Peter J. Verhagen, and Herman M. van Praag. Netherlands: Springer, 2007. Reprinted with kind permission from Springer Science and Business Media.

"Creation in the Bible and in the Liturgy." In *Judaism and Ecology: Created World and Revealed Word*, edited by Hava Tirosh-Samuelson, 133–54. Reprinted with permission of the Center for the Study of World Religions, Harvard Divinity School, Cambridge, Massachusetts. Copyright © 2003 by the President and Fellows of Harvard College.

"How Will It All End? Eschatology in Science and Religion." *CrossCurrents* 57, no. 1 (Spring 2007): 38–50. New York: Association for Religion and Intellectual Life.

"Beyond *Wissenschaft*: The Resurrection of Resurrection in Jewish Thought Since 1950." In *Studies in Contemporary Jewry, Vol. XVII: Who Owns Judaism? Public and Private Faith in America and Israel,* edited by Eli Lederhendler, 88–100. New York: Oxford University Press, 2001. Reprinted by permission of Oxford University Press, Inc.

"The Jewish Philosopher in Search of a Role." *Judaism* 34, no. 4 (Fall 1985): 474–84. New York: American Jewish Congress.

"Authority and Parameters in Jewish Decision-Making." *The Reconstructionist* 59, no. 2 (Fall 1994): 73–79. Wyncote, PA: Reconstructionist Rabbinical Assembly.

"On the Religious Education of American Rabbis." In *Caring for the Commonweal: Education for Religious and Public Life,* edited by Barbara G. Wheeler and James W. Fowler. Macon, GA: Mercer University Press, 1990.

"Teaching the *Akedah*." In *Essays in Education and Judaism in Honor of Joseph S. Lukinsky,* edited by Burton Cohen, 111–22. New York: Jewish Theological Seminary Press, 2002.

"Judaism and the Search for Spirituality." *Conservative Judaism* 38, no. 2 (Winter 1985–86): 5–18. New York: Rabbinical Assembly.

"A Conservative Theology for the Twenty-first Century." *Proceedings of the Rabbinical Assembly* 55 (1993): 9–22. New York: Rabbinical Assembly.

"A New Aggadah for the Conservative Movement." *Conservative Judaism* 58, no. 2 (Winter/Spring 2006): 29–45. New York: Rabbinical Assembly.

"Rituals, Myths and Communities." In *The Seminary at 100: Reflections on the Jewish Theological Seminary and the Conservative Movement,* edited by Nina Beth Cardin and David Wolf Silverman, 327–343. New York: The Rabbinical Assembly and The Jewish Theological Seminary of America, 1987.

"Coping with Chaos: Jewish Theological and Ritual Resources." In *Death, Bereavement, and Mourning,* edited by Samuel Heilman. New Brunswick, N.J.: Transaction Publishers, 2005.

"In Praise of *Birkhat Kohanim*." In *Sh'ma: A Journal of Jewish Responsibility* (September 1992): 122–124.

INDEX

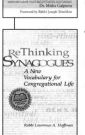

Spirituality

Repentance: The Meaning and Practice of *Teshuvah*
By Dr. Louis E. Newman; Foreword by Rabbi Harold M. Schulweis; Preface by Rabbi Karyn D. Kedar
Examines both the practical and philosophical dimensions of *teshuvah*, Judaism's core religious-moral teaching on repentance, and its value for us—Jews and non-Jews alike—today. 6 x 9, 256 pp, HC, 978-1-58023-426-9 **$24.99**

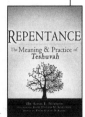

Tanya, the Masterpiece of Hasidic Wisdom
Selections Annotated & Explained
Translation & Annotation by Rabbi Rami Shapiro; Foreword by Rabbi Zalman M. Schachter-Shalomi
Brings the genius of the *Tanya* to anyone seeking to deepen their understanding of the soul and how it relates to and manifests the Divine Source.
5½ x 8½, 240 pp, Quality PB, 978-1-59473-275-1 **$16.99**
(A book from SkyLight Paths, Jewish Lights' sister imprint)

A Book of Life: Embracing Judaism as a Spiritual Practice
By Rabbi Michael Strassfeld 6 x 9, 544 pp, Quality PB, 978-1-58023-247-0 **$19.99**

Meaning and Mitzvah: Daily Practices for Reclaiming Judaism through Prayer, God, Torah, Hebrew, Mitzvot and Peoplehood *By Rabbi Goldie Milgram*
7 x 9, 336 pp, Quality PB, 978-1-58023-256-2 **$19.99**

The Soul of the Story: Meetings with Remarkable People
By Rabbi David Zeller 6 x 9, 288 pp, HC, 978-1-58023-272-2 **$21.99**

Aleph-Bet Yoga: Embodying the Hebrew Letters for Physical and Spiritual Well-Being
By Steven A. Rapp; Foreword by Tamar Frankiel, PhD, and Judy Greenfeld; Preface by Hart Lazer
7 x 10, 128 pp, b/w photos, Quality PB, Layflat binding, 978-1-58023-162-6 **$16.95**

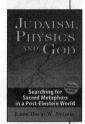

Does the Soul Survive? A Jewish Journey to Belief in Afterlife, Past Lives & Living with Purpose *By Rabbi Elie Kaplan Spitz; Foreword by Brian L. Weiss, MD*
6 x 9, 288 pp, Quality PB, 978-1-58023-165-7 **$16.99**

First Steps to a New Jewish Spirit: Reb Zalman's Guide to Recapturing the Intimacy & Ecstasy in Your Relationship with God *By Rabbi Zalman M. Schachter-Shalomi with Donald Gropman* 6 x 9, 144 pp, Quality PB, 978-1-58023-182-4 **$16.95**

Foundations of Sephardic Spirituality: The Inner Life of Jews of the Ottoman Empire
By Rabbi Marc D. Angel, PhD 6 x 9, 224 pp, Quality PB, 978-1-58023-341-5 **$18.99**

God in Our Relationships: Spirituality between People from the Teachings of Martin Buber *By Rabbi Dennis S. Ross* 5½ x 8½, 160 pp, Quality PB, 978-1-58023-147-3 **$16.95**

Judaism, Physics and God: Searching for Sacred Metaphors in a Post-Einstein World
By Rabbi David W. Nelson 6 x 9, 352 pp, Quality PB, inc. reader's discussion guide,
978-1-58023-306-4 **$18.99**; HC, 352 pp, 978-1-58023-252-4 **$24.99**

The Jewish Lights Spirituality Handbook: A Guide to Understanding, Exploring & Living a Spiritual Life *Edited by Stuart M. Matlins*
What exactly is "Jewish" about spirituality? How do I make it a part of my life? Fifty of today's foremost spiritual leaders share their ideas and experience with us.
6 x 9, 456 pp, Quality PB, 978-1-58023-093-3 **$19.99**

Bringing the Psalms to Life: How to Understand and Use the Book of Psalms
By Rabbi Daniel F. Polish, PhD 6 x 9, 208 pp, Quality PB, 978-1-58023-157-2 **$16.95**

God & the Big Bang: Discovering Harmony between Science & Spirituality
By Dr. Daniel C. Matt 6 x 9, 216 pp, Quality PB, 978-1-879045-89-7 **$16.99**

Minding the Temple of the Soul: Balancing Body, Mind, and Spirit through Traditional Jewish Prayer, Movement, and Meditation *By Tamar Frankiel, PhD, and Judy Greenfeld*
7 x 10, 184 pp, illus., Quality PB, 978-1-879045-64-4 **$16.95**

One God Clapping: The Spiritual Path of a Zen Rabbi *By Alan Lew with Sherril Jaffe*
5½ x 8½, 336 pp, Quality PB, 978-1-58023-115-2 **$16.95**

There Is No Messiah ... and You're It: The Stunning Transformation of Judaism's Most Provocative Idea *By Rabbi Robert N. Levine, DD*
6 x 9, 192 pp, Quality PB, 978-1-58023-255-5 **$16.99**

These Are the Words: A Vocabulary of Jewish Spiritual Life
By Rabbi Arthur Green, PhD 6 x 9, 304 pp, Quality PB, 978-1-58023-107-7 **$18.95**

Theology/Philosophy/The Way Into... Series

The Way Into... series offers an accessible and highly usable "guided tour" of the Jewish faith, people, history and beliefs—in total, an introduction to Judaism that will enable you to understand and interact with the sacred texts of the Jewish tradition. Each volume is written by a leading contemporary scholar and teacher, and explores one key aspect of Judaism. The Way Into... series enables all readers to achieve a real sense of Jewish cultural literacy through guided study.

The Way Into Encountering God in Judaism
By Rabbi Neil Gillman, PhD
For everyone who wants to understand how Jews have encountered God throughout history and today.
6 x 9, 240 pp, Quality PB, 978-1-58023-199-2 **$18.99**; HC, 978-1-58023-025-4 **$21.95**
Also Available: **The Jewish Approach to God:** A Brief Introduction for Christians
By Rabbi Neil Gillman, PhD
5½ x 8¼, 192 pp, Quality PB, 978-1-58023-190-9 **$16.95**

The Way Into Jewish Mystical Tradition
By Rabbi Lawrence Kushner
Allows readers to interact directly with the sacred mystical texts of the Jewish tradition. An accessible introduction to the concepts of Jewish mysticism, their religious and spiritual significance, and how they relate to life today.
6 x 9, 224 pp, Quality PB, 978-1-58023-200-5 **$18.99**; HC, 978-1-58023-029-2 **$21.95**

The Way Into Jewish Prayer
By Rabbi Lawrence A. Hoffman, PhD
Opens the door to 3,000 years of Jewish prayer, making available all anyone needs to feel at home in the Jewish way of communicating with God.
6 x 9, 208 pp, Quality PB, 978-1-58023-201-2 **$18.99**

Also Available: **The Way Into Jewish Prayer Teacher's Guide**
By Rabbi Jennifer Ossakow Goldsmith
8½ x 11, 42 pp, PB, 978-1-58023-345-3 **$8.99**
Download a free copy at www.jewishlights.com.

The Way Into Judaism and the Environment
By Jeremy Benstein, PhD
Explores the ways in which Judaism contributes to contemporary social-environmental issues, the extent to which Judaism is part of the problem and how it can be part of the solution.
6 x 9, 288 pp, Quality PB, 978-1-58023-368-2 **$18.99**; HC, 978-1-58023-268-5 **$24.99**

The Way Into *Tikkun Olam* (Repairing the World)
By Rabbi Elliot N. Dorff, PhD
An accessible introduction to the Jewish concept of the individual's responsibility to care for others and repair the world.
6 x 9, 304 pp, Quality PB, 978-1-58023-328-6 **$18.99**; 320 pp, HC, 978-1-58023-269-2 **$24.99**

The Way Into Torah
By Rabbi Norman J. Cohen, PhD
Helps guide in the exploration of the origins and development of Torah, explains why it should be studied and how to do it.
6 x 9, 176 pp, Quality PB, 978-1-58023-198-5 **$16.99**

The Way Into the Varieties of Jewishness
By Sylvia Barack Fishman, PhD
Explores the religious and historical understanding of what it has meant to be Jewish from ancient times to the present controversy over "Who is a Jew?"
6 x 9, 288 pp, Quality PB, 978-1-58023-367-5 **$18.99**; HC, 978-1-58023-030-8 **$24.99**

Theology/Philosophy

Jewish Theology in Our Time: A New Generation Explores the Foundations and Future of Jewish Belief *Edited by Rabbi Elliot J. Cosgrove, PhD*
A powerful and challenging examination of what Jews can believe—by a new generation's most dynamic and innovative thinkers.
6 x 9, 272 pp, HC, 978-1-58023-413-9 **$24.99**

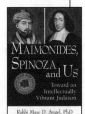

Maimonides, Spinoza and Us: Toward an Intellectually Vibrant Judaism
By Rabbi Marc D. Angel, PhD A challenging look at two great Jewish philosophers, and what their thinking means to our understanding of God, truth, revelation and reason. 6 x 9, 224 pp, HC, 978-1-58023-411-5 **$24.99**

The Death of Death: Resurrection and Immortality in Jewish Thought
By Rabbi Neil Gillman, PhD 6 x 9, 336 pp, Quality PB, 978-1-58023-081-0 **$18.95**

Ethics of the Sages: Pirke Avot—Annotated & Explained
Translation & Annotation by Rabbi Rami Shapiro
5½ x 8¼, 192 pp, Quality PB, 978-1-59473-207-2 **$16.99** *(A book from SkyLight Paths, Jewish Lights' sister imprint)*

Hasidic Tales: Annotated & Explained *Translation & Annotation by Rabbi Rami Shapiro*
5½ x 8¼, 240 pp, Quality PB, 978-1-893361-86-7 **$16.95** *(A book from SkyLight Paths, Jewish Lights' sister imprint)*

A Heart of Many Rooms: Celebrating the Many Voices within Judaism
By Dr. David Hartman 6 x 9, 352 pp, Quality PB, 978-1-58023-156-5 **$19.95**

The Hebrew Prophets: Selections Annotated & Explained
Translation & Annotation by Rabbi Rami Shapiro; Foreword by Rabbi Zalman M. Schachter-Shalomi
5½ x 8¼, 224 pp, Quality PB, 978-1-59473-037-5 **$16.99** *(A book from SkyLight Paths, Jewish Lights' sister imprint)*

A Jewish Understanding of the New Testament
By Rabbi Samuel Sandmel; Preface by Rabbi David Sandmel
5½ x 8¼, 368 pp, Quality PB, 978-1-59473-048-1 **$19.99** *(A book from SkyLight Paths, Jewish Lights' sister imprint)*

Jews and Judaism in the 21st Century: Human Responsibility, the Presence of God and the Future of the Covenant *Edited by Rabbi Edward Feinstein; Foreword by Paula E. Hyman*
6 x 9, 192 pp, Quality PB, 978-1-58023-374-3 **$19.99**; HC, 978-1-58023-315-6 **$24.99**

Keeping Faith with the Psalms: Deepen Your Relationship with God Using the Book of Psalms *By Rabbi Daniel F. Polish, PhD* 6 x 9, 320 pp, Quality PB, 978-1-58023-300-2 **$18.99**

A Living Covenant: The Innovative Spirit in Traditional Judaism
By Dr. David Hartman 6 x 9, 368 pp, Quality PB, 978-1-58023-011-7 **$20.00**

Love and Terror in the God Encounter: The Theological Legacy of Rabbi Joseph B. Soloveitchik *By Dr. David Hartman* 6 x 9, 240 pp, Quality PB, 978-1-58023-176-3 **$19.95**

The Personhood of God: Biblical Theology, Human Faith and the Divine Image
By Dr. Yochanan Muffs; Foreword by Dr. David Hartman
6 x 9, 240 pp, Quality PB, 978-1-58023-338-5 **$18.99**; HC, 978-1-58023-265-4 **$24.99**

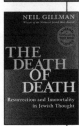

A Touch of the Sacred: A Theologian's Informal Guide to Jewish Belief
By Dr. Eugene B. Borowitz and Frances W. Schwartz
6 x 9, 256 pp, Quality PB, 978-1-58023-416-0 **$16.99**; HC, 978-1-58023-337-8 **$21.99**

Traces of God: Seeing God in Torah, History and Everyday Life *By Rabbi Neil Gillman, PhD*
6 x 9, 240 pp, Quality PB, 978-1-58023-369-9 **$16.99**; HC, 978-1-58023-249-4 **$21.99**

We Jews and Jesus: Exploring Theological Differences for Mutual Understanding
By Rabbi Samuel Sandmel; Preface by Rabbi David Sandmel
6 x 9, 192 pp, Quality PB, 978-1-59473-208-9 **$16.99** *(A book from SkyLight Paths, Jewish Lights' sister imprint)*

Your Word Is Fire: The Hasidic Masters on Contemplative Prayer
Edited and translated by Rabbi Arthur Green, PhD, and Barry W. Holtz
6 x 9, 160 pp, Quality PB, 978-1-879045-25-5 **$15.95**

I Am Jewish

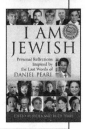

Personal Reflections Inspired by the Last Words of Daniel Pearl
Almost 150 Jews—both famous and not—from all walks of life, from all around the world, write about many aspects of their Judaism.
Edited by Judea and Ruth Pearl 6 x 9, 304 pp, Deluxe PB w/ flaps, 978-1-58023-259-3 **$18.99**
Download a free copy of the *I Am Jewish Teacher's Guide* at www.jewishlights.com.

Hannah Senesh: Her Life and Diary, the First Complete Edition
By Hannah Senesh; Foreword by Marge Piercy; Preface by Eitan Senesh; Afterword by Roberta Grossman
6 x 9, 368 pp, b/w photos, Quality PB, 978-1-58023-342-2 **$19.99**

About Jewish Lights

People of all faiths and backgrounds yearn for books that attract, engage, educate, and spiritually inspire.

Our principal goal is to stimulate thought and help all people learn about who the Jewish People are, where they come from, and what the future can be made to hold. While people of our diverse Jewish heritage are the primary audience, our books speak to people in the Christian world as well and will broaden their understanding of Judaism and the roots of their own faith.

We bring to you authors who are at the forefront of spiritual thought and experience. While each has something different to say, they all say it in a voice that you can hear.

Our books are designed to welcome you and then to engage, stimulate, and inspire. We judge our success not only by whether or not our books are beautiful and commercially successful, but by whether or not they make a difference in your life.

For your information and convenience, at the back of this book we have provided a list of other Jewish Lights books you might find interesting and useful. They cover all the categories of your life:

Stuart M. Matlins, Publisher

Or phone, fax, mail or e-mail to: **JEWISH LIGHTS Publishing**
Sunset Farm Offices, Route 4 • P.O. Box 237 • Woodstock, Vermont 05091
Tel: (802) 457-4000 • Fax: (802) 457-4004 • www.jewishlights.com
Credit card orders: **(800) 962-4544** (8:30AM–5:30PM ET Monday–Friday)
Generous discounts on quantity orders. SATISFACTION GUARANTEED. Prices subject to change.

For more information about each book, visit our website at www.jewishlights.com